IMAGES
of America

EAGLE ISLAND
ADMIRAL PEARY'S HARPSWELL HOME

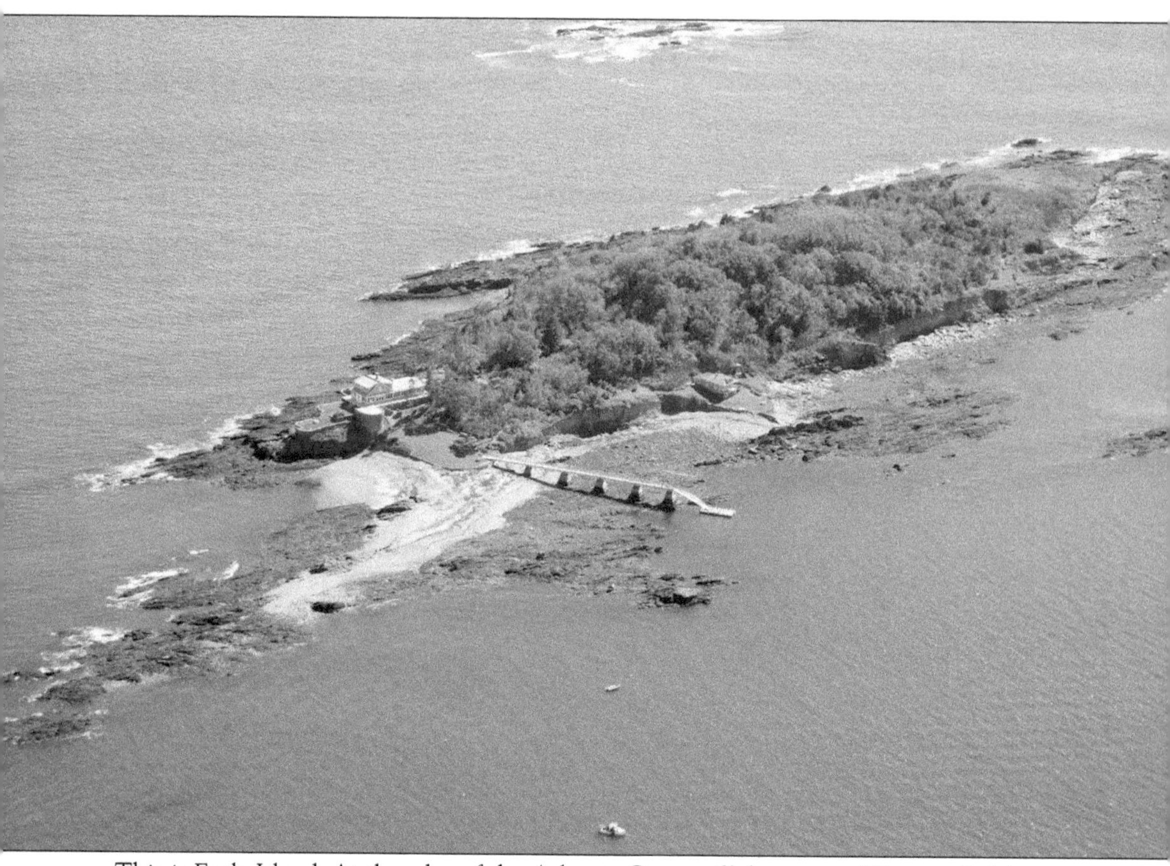

This is Eagle Island. At the edge of the Atlantic Ocean off the coast of Harpswell, Maine, it is the site of the summer home of Adm. Robert E. Peary, America's foremost Arctic explorer and the first to reach the geographic North Pole. As a young man, Peary imagined a home on this island. In 1904, he and his family built and moved into a modest cottage, and here, Peary and his family found their home. (Courtesy of the Bureau of Parks and Lands, State of Maine Department of Agriculture, Conservation and Forestry.)

On the Cover: This photograph, taken in 1911, shows the Peary cottage during its last expansion. The caretaker's cottage sits facing west toward the setting sun. The American flag is flying—signaling that the Pearys are home. Mail, supplies, and news arrived by boat daily, weather permitting. (Courtesy of the Bureau of Parks and Lands, State of Maine Department of Agriculture, Conservation and Forestry.)

IMAGES
of America

Eagle Island
Admiral Peary's Harpswell Home

Elizabeth O'Connell and Stephen Harding
Friends of Peary's Eagle Island

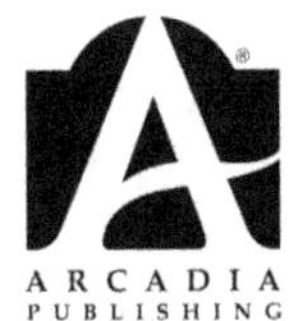

ISBN 978-1-5402-1641-0

Published by Arcadia Publishing
Charleston, South Carolina

Library of Congress Control Number: 2016955474

For all general information, please contact Arcadia Publishing:
Telephone 843-853-2070
Fax 843-853-0044
E-mail sales@arcadiapublishing.com
For customer service and orders:
Toll-Free 1-888-313-2665

Visit us on the Internet at www.arcadiapublishing.com

This collection and story is dedicated to Edward Peary Stafford, Admiral Peary's grandson, whose mission was to share Eagle Island and Peary's legacy with the world.

Contents

ACKNOWLEDGMENTS

Inveniam viam aut facium

—Adm. Robert E. Peary, USN Ret.

The Friends of Peary's Eagle Island would like to thank the following individuals and organizations for their support, research material, photographs, and in-depth knowledge during the research phase of this project: Dr. Susan A. Kaplan, director, and Dr. Genevieve LeMoine, curator/registrar, of the Peary-MacMillan Arctic Museum, Bowdoin College, Brunswick, Maine; the staff of the George J. Mitchell Department of Special Collections & Archives, Bowdoin College, Brunswick, Maine; Cathleen Miller, curator, Catherine Fisher, former assistant, and Laura Taylor, cataloger, of the Women Writers Collection at the University of New England, Portland, Maine; Gary Best, assistant regional manager, southern region of Maine State Parks, Bureau of Parks and Lands, Department of Agriculture, Conservation and Forestry; Zane Wallace, park manager of Eagle Island; the Merriman family from Harpswell, Maine; and Admiral Peary's great-grandson Peary Diebitsch Stafford Jr.

In addition, the Friends of Peary's Eagle Island would like to thank a few specific individuals who gave their valuable time to help put this project together, including Rob O'Connell, who was immensely helpful in getting the scanning process under way; Richard Cunningham and Cameron Cunningham, both of whom helped with support and scanning; Carmen Greenlee, humanities and media librarian at Bowdoin College, who helped two lost souls in the Bowdoin library; Aubrey Armidon of the National Archives; and most importantly, the members of the Friends of Peary's Eagle Island who summer after summer volunteer their time and energy working with the State of Maine to maintain Admiral Peary's Eagle Island and without whose support this project would not have been possible.

Lastly, the Friends of Peary's Eagle Island would like to again acknowledge the example that one of Admiral Peary's grandchildren, Edward P. Stafford, set. He showed us what was special about Eagle Island and his grandfather.

Unless otherwise noted, all images appear courtesy of the Bureau of Parks and Lands, State of Maine Department of Agriculture, Conservation and Forestry.

Other images in this volume appear courtesy of the Peary-MacMillan Arctic Museum, Bowdoin College (PMAMBC); the George J. Mitchell Department of Special Collections & Archives, Bowdoin College (GJMBC); the Josephine Diebitsch Peary papers (JDPUNE) and the Marie Ahnighito Peary papers (MAPUNE), both from the Maine Women Writers Collection at the University of New England, Portland, Maine; the Leon Merriman family (LMF); and the Friends of Peary's Eagle Island (FOPEI).

Introduction

Eagle Island, off the coast of Harpswell, Maine, is far enough into Casco Bay to offer isolation but close enough for its perfect symmetry to be seen from the mainland and capture the imagination of a young man. As a boy, Robert E. Peary could see its mystical shape against the horizon when his family spent summer vacation time in Harpswell. Older, he would row out to explore and found that its northern presentation hid a rocky spine running north to south on which he would sit and watch the open Atlantic swells lose their attack on the rugged cliffs in plumes of brilliant spray. With the first money he could save as a surveyor after graduating from Bowdoin College, Peary bought Eagle Island. As a naval officer and Arctic explorer, he had to forego the luxury of a permanent home until 1904, when 24 years of planning saw fruition in a cottage situated on the northern reach of the central spine.

For the first five years, it was the Peary family's summer retreat—relaxation, recreation, hunting, and fishing. The Peary family—Robert Sr., wife Josephine, daughter Marie, and son Robert Jr.—would arrive early and stay until fall. Peary himself was away on his eighth trip to the Arctic for research, exploration, and another attempt to discover the North Pole, the last geographic frontier left on the planet. So, on September 6, 1909, Josephine, Marie, and Robert Jr. were still at the Eagle Island cottage. Marie, looking out the window of the living room of the cottage, saw a lone, unexpected visitor rowing the last few yards of the two-mile journey from the Harpswell mainland. He hurried up the steep lawn to the cottage with a telegram from Indian Harbor, Labrador. Josephine, opening the telegram, read, "Have made good at last! I have the old Pole." This initiated a transition of Eagle Island as a family retreat to Eagle Island as a family refuge from the celebrity and controversy that followed. Over the next 60 years, as the Peary family expanded through three generations, the cottage was expanded twice in size and comfort. But there was another transition happening simultaneously: As Robert Jr. put it: "We stay in Washington every winter, but we really live on Eagle Island." The Peary family now considered their summer cottage as the family home.

But the most significant transition is the last—from family home to public treasure. In 1967, the Peary descendants, in a magnanimous gesture, donated the island, the buildings, and their contents to the State of Maine under the stipulation that it be maintained and shared with all people, especially the citizens of their adopted state.

Just as it is in *Peary's Promised Land* by Edward P. Stafford (USN Ret.), this is the story of a family's "love affair with an island." But Eagle Island has its own story to tell. Just one of over 400 islands in Casco Bay, it stands proud above the waters, but it is its relationship to humankind that has given it distinction. Admiral Peary called it his "Promised Land"; his family called it "home"; and the State of Maine calls it a "park." What is it about Eagle Island that engenders an emotional motivation to call it "home"? What is it about Eagle Island that engenders a civic commitment to accept the responsibility for the stewardship required of "sharing" a "park" with visitors? What is it about Eagle Island that makes people care? If there were rational answers to these questions, then thinking would reveal them. It does not. So, the mystery persists.

This book stands as testimony that people continue to care, but its images only deepen the mystery of why. Perhaps your visit to Eagle Island will reveal its secrets. Come.

One

The Island and the Admiral

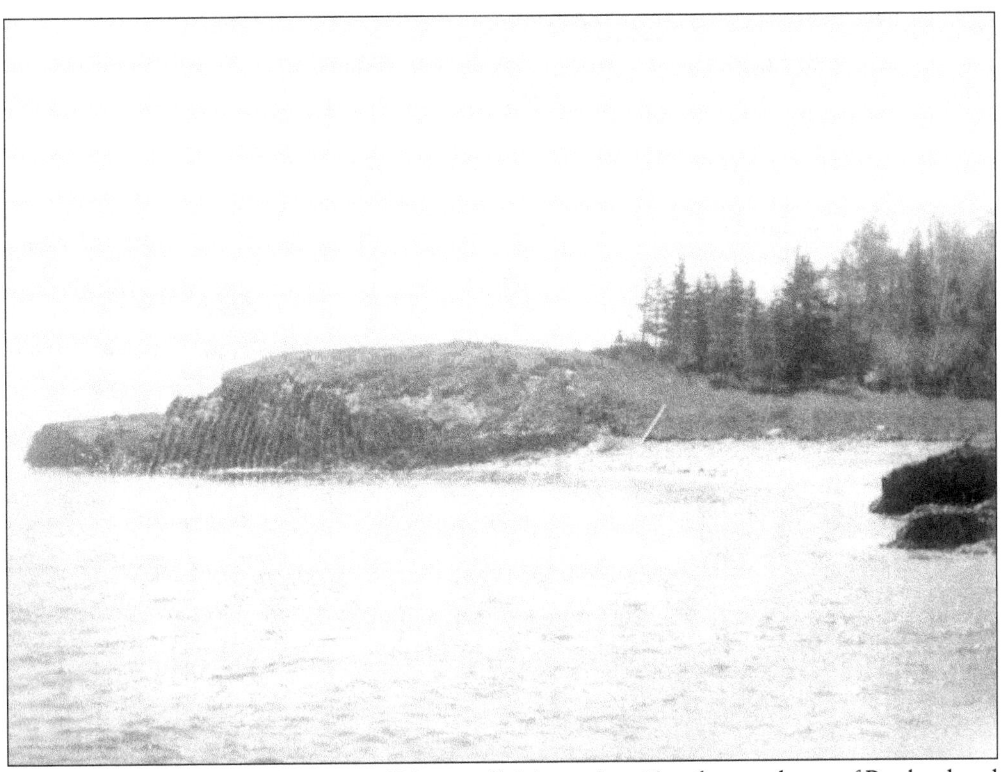

Eagle Island is located in the town of Harpswell, Maine. It is 12 miles northeast of Portland and 15 miles south of Brunswick. This picture from 1903 shows Eagle Island as Peary must have seen it while exploring this area in the 1870s as a student at Portland High School.

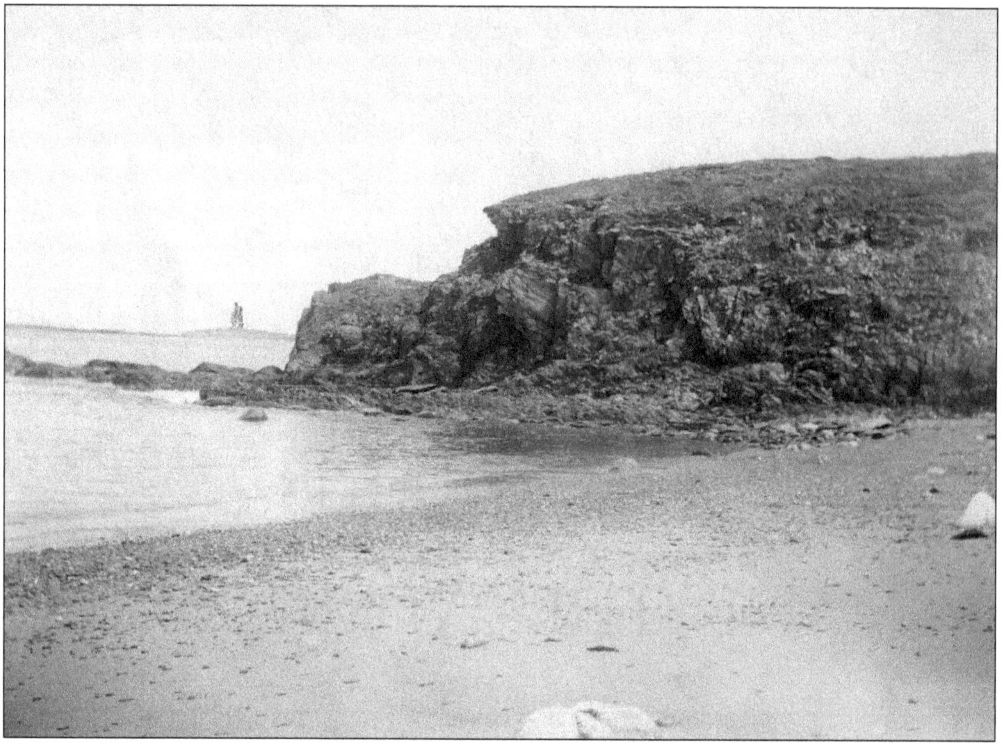

The northeast end of Eagle Island is a rock ledge rising 40 feet above Casco Bay like the prow of a ship. This is where Peary envisioned his house.

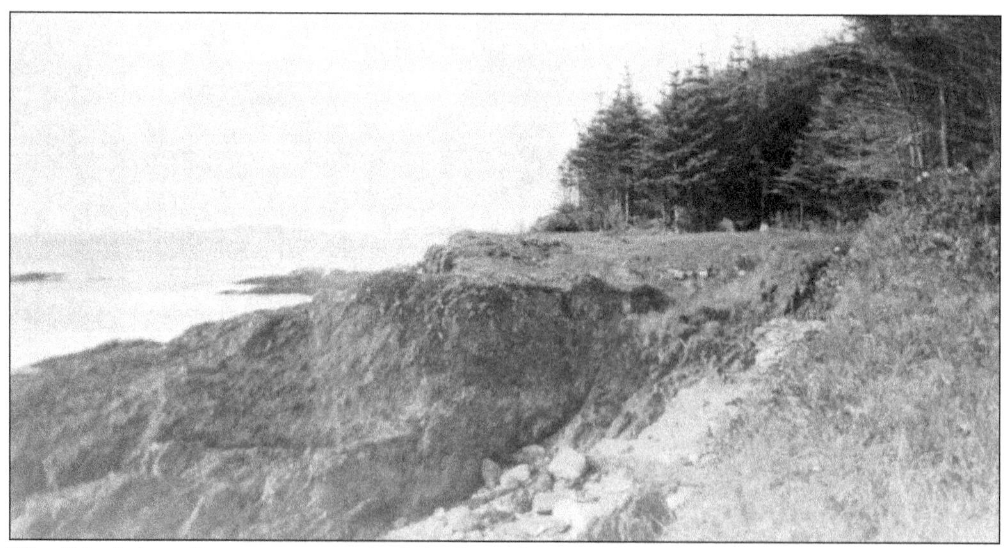

The "black forest" is an area one finds looking due east from the east bastion and was where Admiral Peary could often be found sitting and reading. A heavily forested part of the island, it is where birds often nest. Eagle Island is named for the eagles that once nested there.

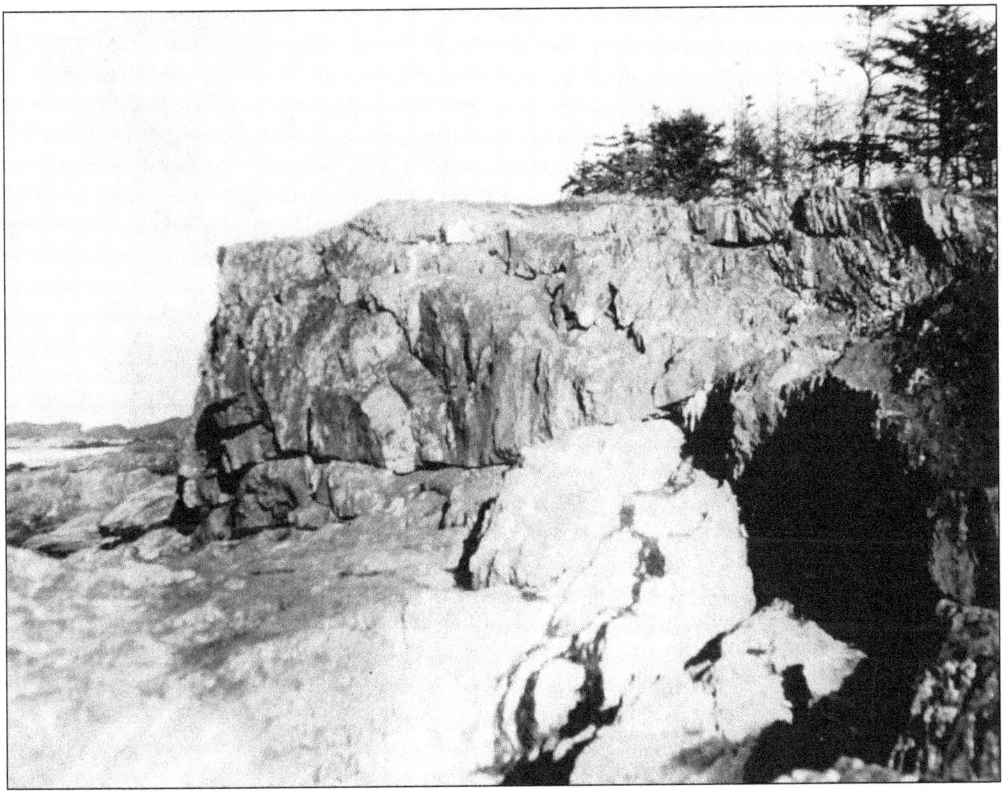

Eagle Island is longer than it is wide, a typical result from the retreating glaciers of 2.5 million years ago. The island lies mainly northeast to southwest. This east side of the island faces the ocean and, in places, rises to almost 60 feet above sea level.

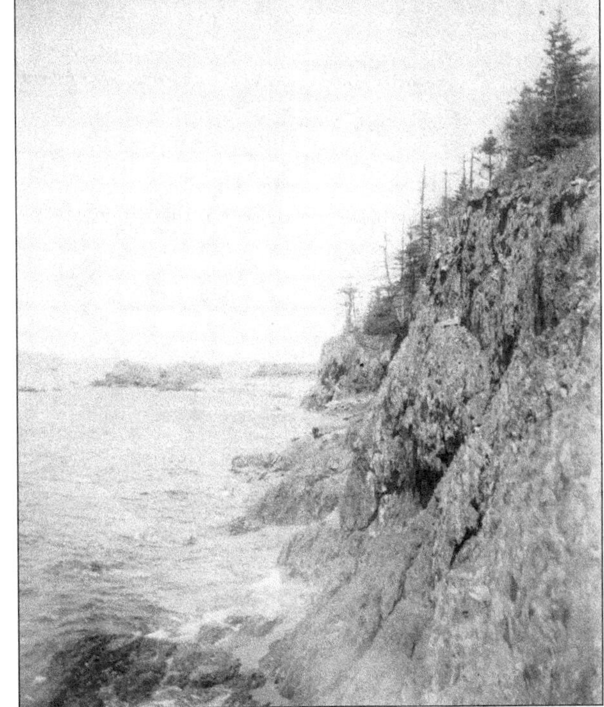

Eagle Island is 17 acres of typical Maine woods, rocks, and beaches, increasing to 21 acres at low tide. Except for Halfway Rock and its lighthouse, there is nothing between the southeast side of the island and the vast Atlantic Ocean.

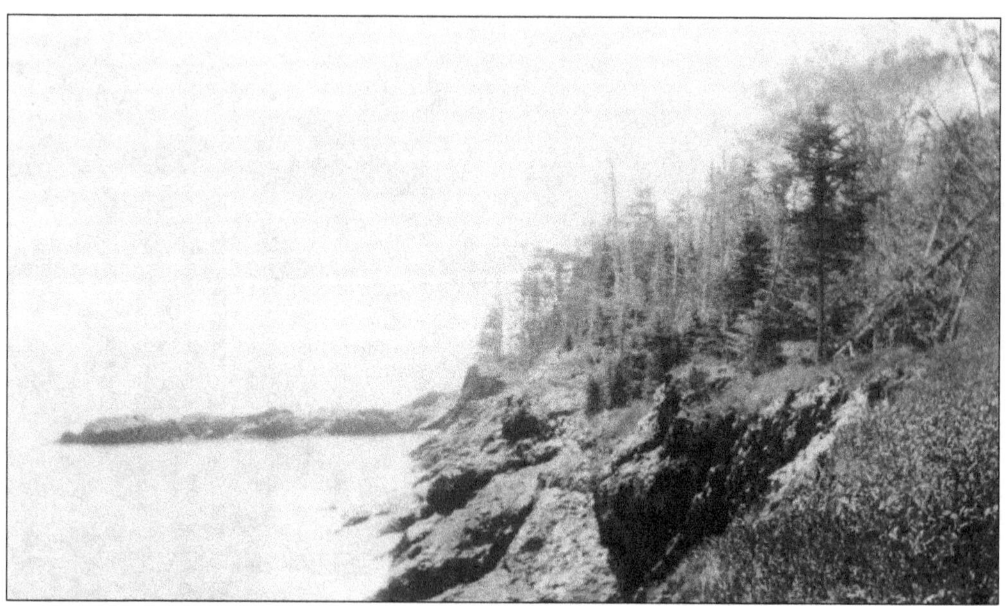

The east side of Eagle Island is covered with a forest of beech, birch, maple, spruce, and fir trees. The integrity of Eagle Island has changed very little since the days when Peary first saw and fell in love with it. This view shows Garden Café and Percy Rock in the background.

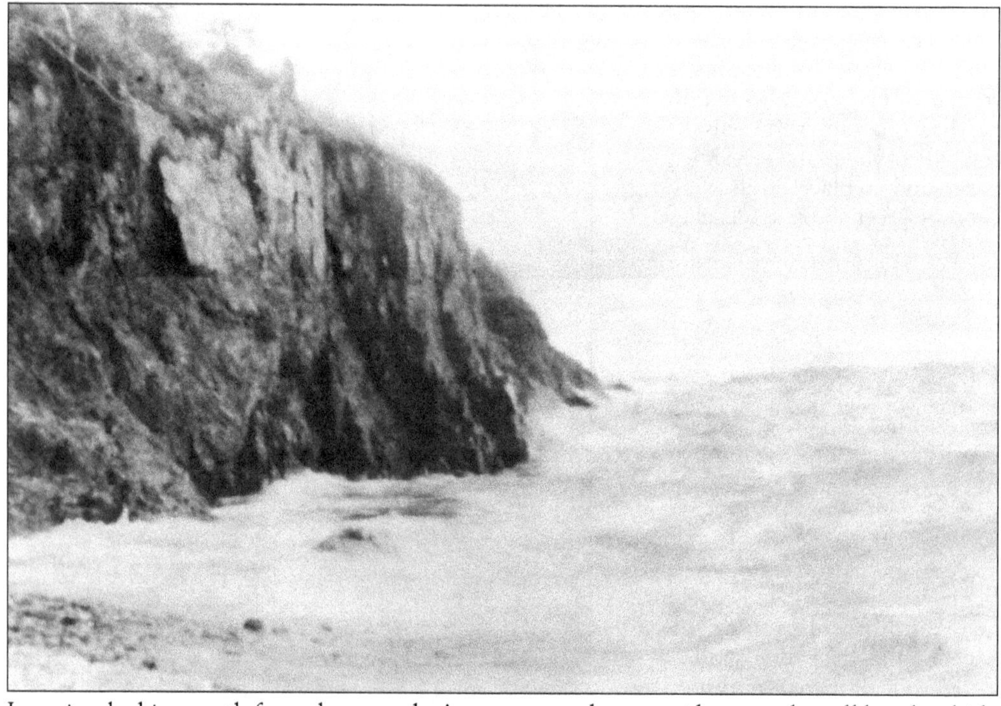

In a view looking south from the caretaker's cottage on the west side, several small beaches hide in the lee of the island and were enjoyed by all members the Peary family.

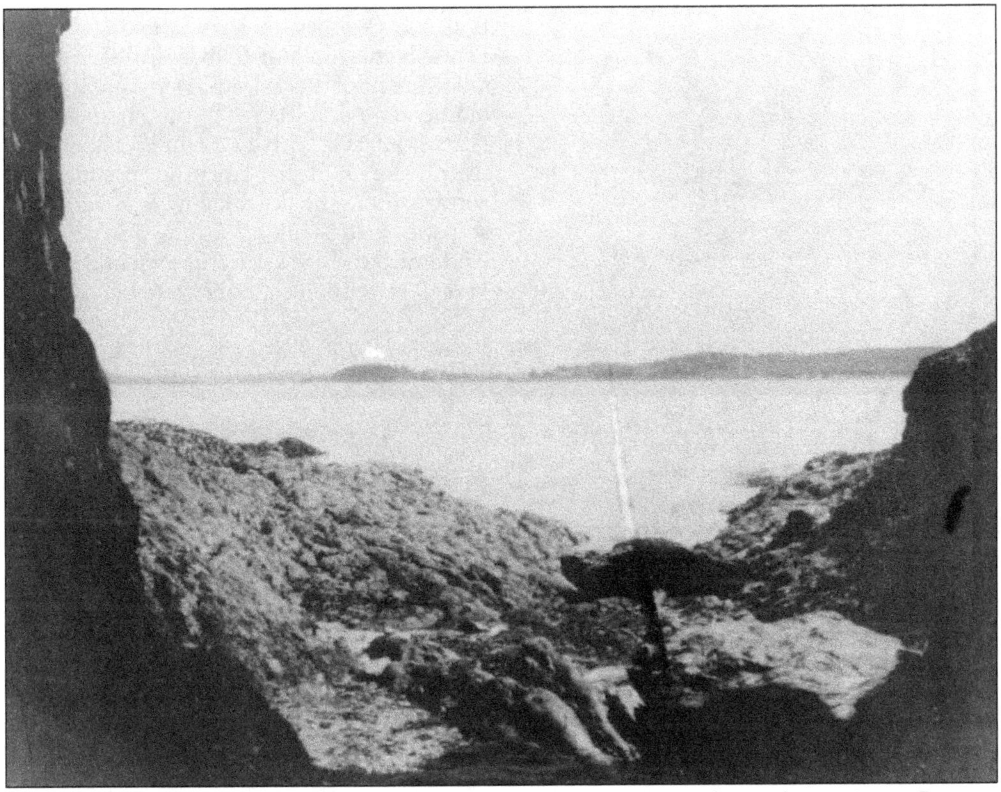

Though the waters off Eagle Island are calm many days, 9- to 11-foot tides in Casco Bay are common. Winter storms can be accompanied by 40- to 50-knot winds, which can and do destroy and then re-create the beaches each year. The photograph below is of the area known as "South Beach," at the southern tip of the island where tides and ice move sizable rocks around like they are pebbles.

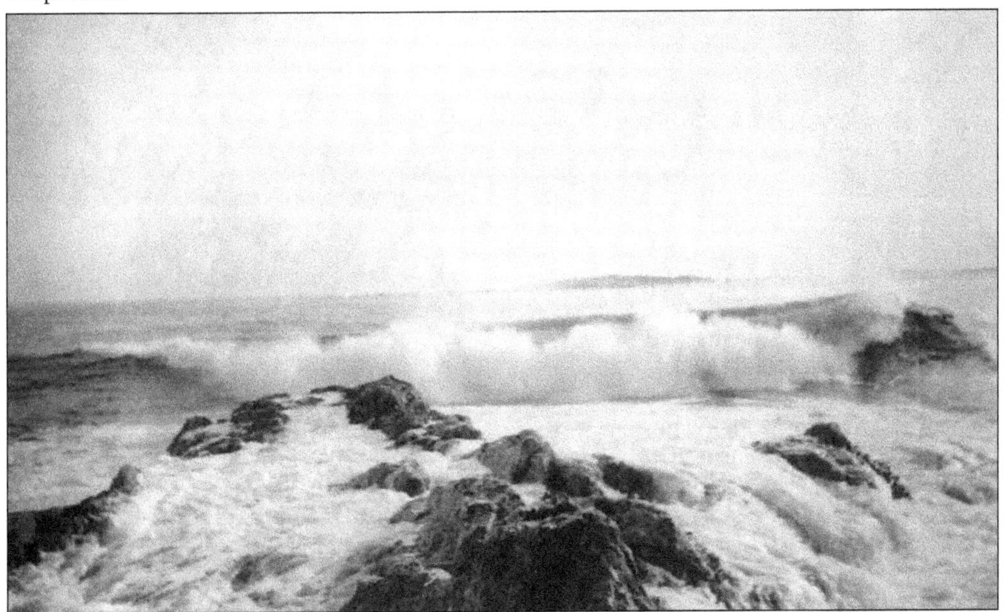

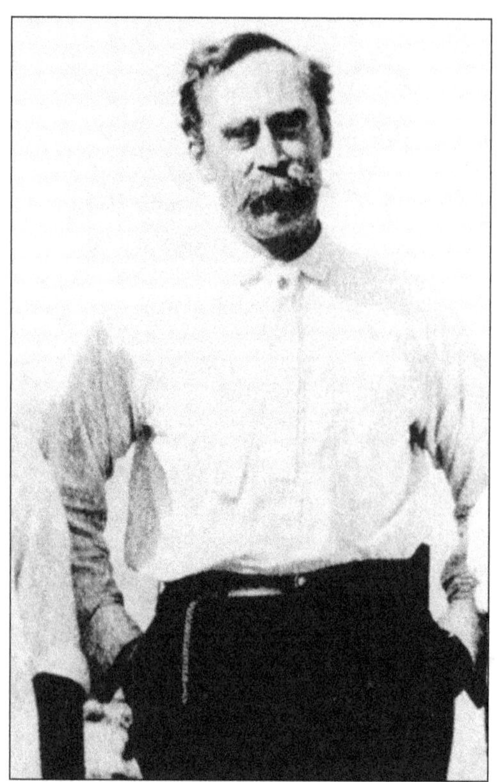

Robert E. Peary was born in Cresson, Pennsylvania, on May 6, 1856. In 1859, following his father's death, Peary and his mother moved to Maine. In this photograph, Peary is relaxed, with a rare smile. Though their house on Eagle Island was a summer cottage where the Peary family enjoyed activities such as hiking, fishing, and swimming, the dress was still somewhat formal. Note the Admiral's white tie.

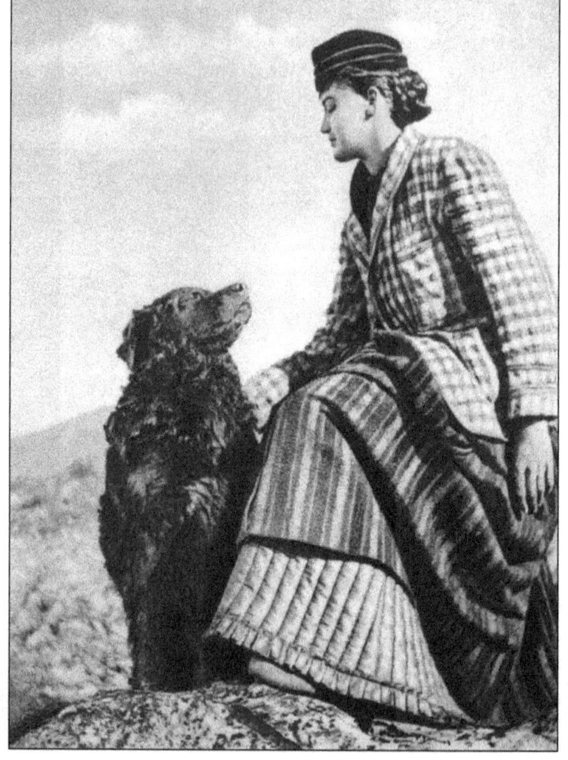

Josephine Cecilia Diebitsch, Peary's wife, was born on May 22, 1863, in Forestville, Maryland; she married Peary on August 11, 1888, and traveled with him to the Arctic twice. Traveling farther north than any other white woman of her time, she earned the distinction of "the First Lady of the Arctic." The National Geographic Society awarded her its highest honor, the Medal of Achievement, for her Arctic accomplishments.

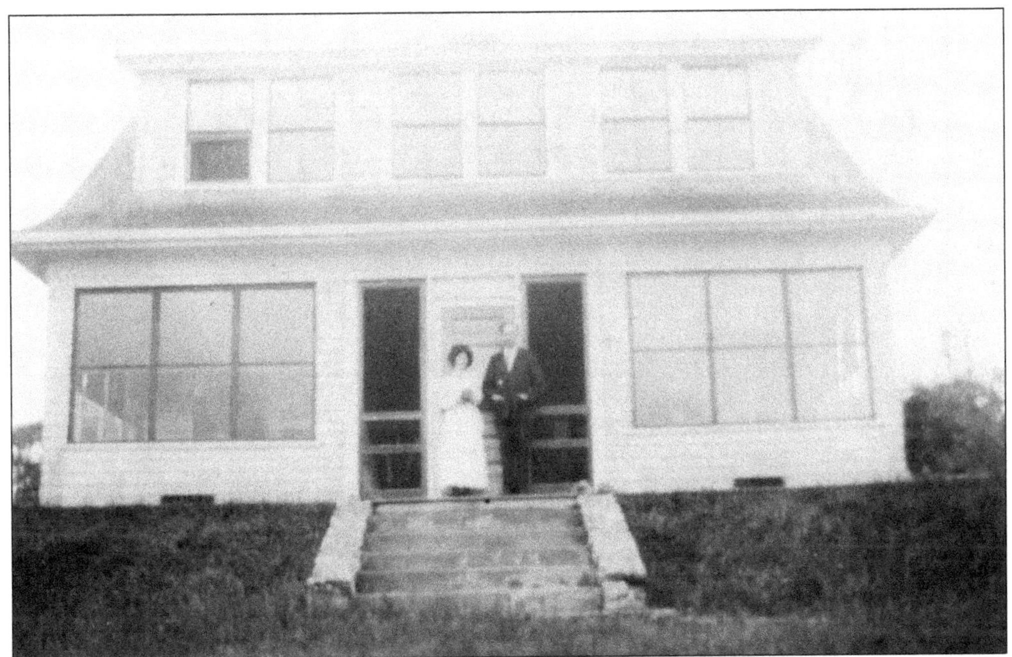

Here, in a photograph from 1907, the Admiral and his wife, Josephine, are standing on the north porch of the original main house, often referred to as their "cottage." By now, the front porch, once wide open, is glassed in. Two screen porch doors lead into the north porch and then into the two first-floor rooms of the house.

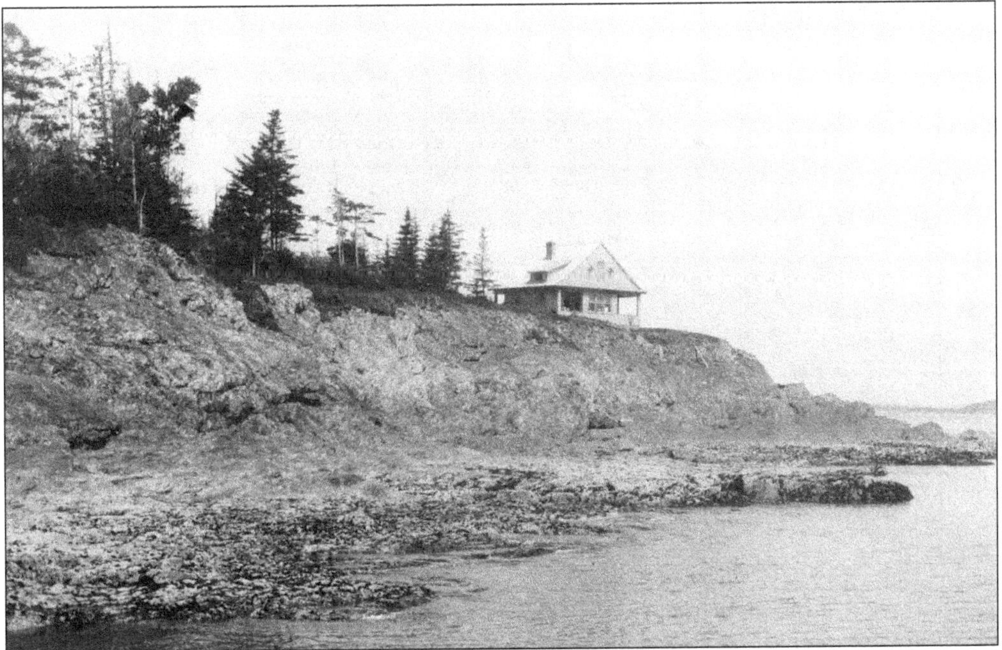

This is a perfect view of the cottage as it was originally designed and built in 1904. Both the front and two side porches are open to the weather and would be glassed in soon. The two diamond windows on the second floor had colored glass panels that add much-needed light in the upstairs bedrooms since shed dormers let in very little light.

Know all Men by these Presents, That

I George W. Curtis of Harpswell in the County of Cumberland and State of Maine, in consideration of Two Hundred Dollars paid by Robert E. Peary of Washington, in the District of Columbia the receipt whereof I do hereby acknowledge, do hereby give, grant, bargain, sell and convey unto the said Robert E. Peary his heirs and assigns forever, a certain lot or parcel of land situated in said Harpswell, in Casco Bay, and known as Eagle Island and lying on the Easterly side of Broad Sound, so called, and adjoining [illegible] containing [illegible] acres more or less. It being the same property conveyed to Paul and Michael Curtis by Enoch [illegible] by deed dated July 12th 1768 and recorded in the Cumberland Registry of Deeds Book 7 Page 100 to which reference is hereby made, the title to which I have acquired by descent and purchase.

Curtis
to
Peary

To have and to hold the aforegranted and bargained premises, with all the privileges and appurtenances thereof, to the said Robert E. Peary his heirs and assigns, to their use and behoof forever. And I do covenant with the said Grantee his heirs and assigns, that I am lawfully seized in fee of the premises; that they are free of all incumbrances; that I have good right to sell and convey the same to the said Grantee to hold as aforesaid; and that I and my heirs shall and will warrant and defend the same to the said Grantee his heirs and assigns forever, against the lawful claims and demands of all persons.

In Witness Whereof, I the said Grantor ~~and~~ ~~of the said~~ ~~in testimony of~~ ~~relinquishment of~~ ~~right of dower in the above-described premises~~, have hereunto set my hand and seal this Twenty second day of July in the year of our Lord one thousand eight hundred and eighty One

Signed, Sealed and Delivered in presence of

Edw. C. Reynolds — George W. Curtis Seal

State of Maine, Cumberland, ss. Aug. 4 1881 Personally appeared the above named George W. Curtis and acknowledged the above instrument to be his free act and deed.

Before me, Edw. C. Reynolds Justice of the Peace.

Received Aug. 4th 1881, at 5 o'clock 40m., P. M., and recorded according to the original.

Attest, Frank G. Stevens Register.

This is a copy of the deed from George W. Curtis of Harpswell, Maine, to Robert E. Peary of Washington, DC, conveying Eagle Island to Peary on July 2, 1881; it was recorded in the Cumberland County Registry of Deeds on August 4, 1881. Eagle Island was only one of several islands Admiral Peary owned during his lifetime. Among the others were Upper Flag Island, Shelter Island, Crab Island, and Pettengill Island. He bought the small island Pound of Tea in Freeport for his daughter, Marie.

Local Harpswell workers were contracted to Harpswell builder Leon Merriman, and they lived in tents on the island during the construction project. Some material arrived by barge from Portland, was floated onto the island at high tide, unloaded at low tide, and the barge sent back to Portland for more material during the next high tide. Other material was rowed out to the island from Potts Harbor, Harpswell, Maine, or was found on the island itself.

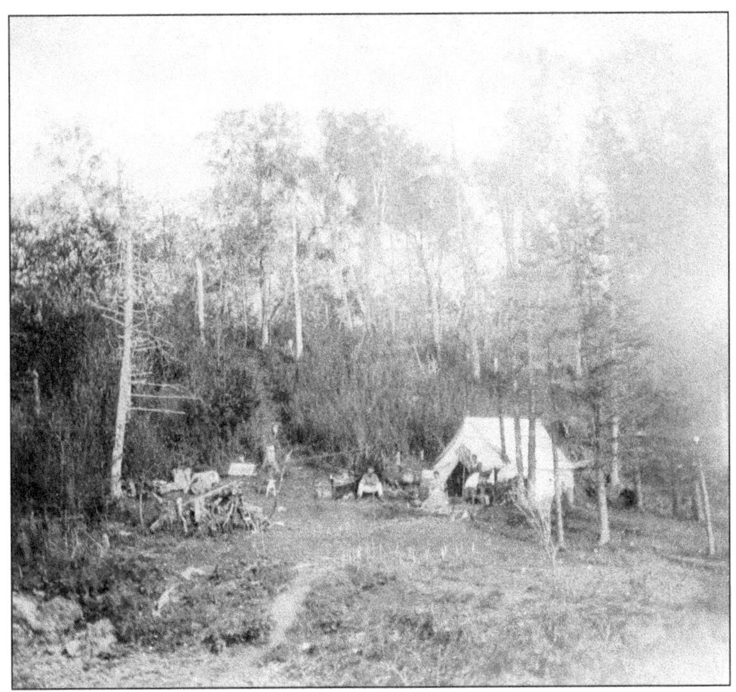

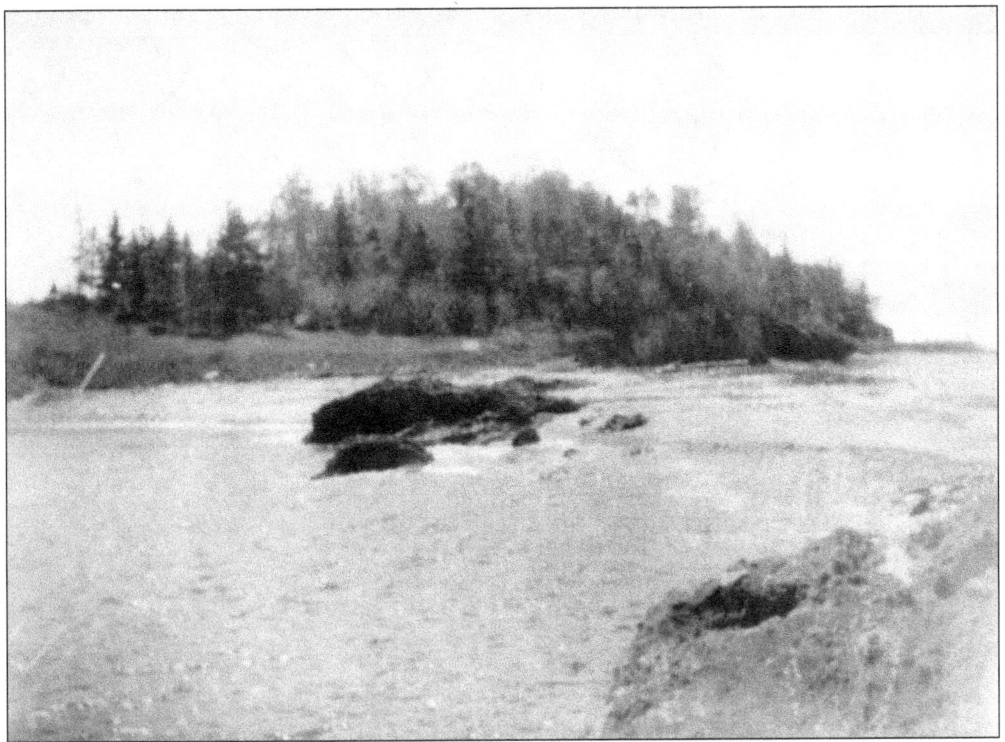

The campsite and location of the caretaker's cottage can be seen at far right in this photograph of Eagle Island. The photograph was taken by Emil Diebitsch (Josephine's brother) while standing on rocks to the west of what would be the sandy cove beach where the family boated and swam. (Courtesy of PMAMBC.)

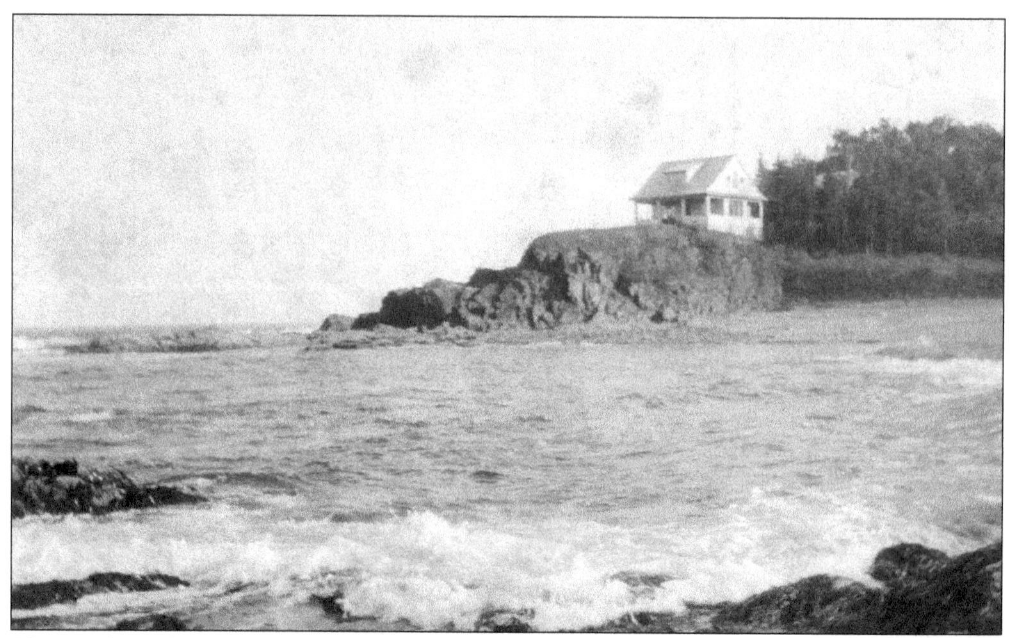

This was how the cottage on Eagle Island looked in the early years. By 1906, Peary realized that the house needed updating, including a kitchen, but this quaint cottage and the caretaker's cottage filled the vision that Peary had had for a house on Eagle Island. (Courtesy of PMAMBC.)

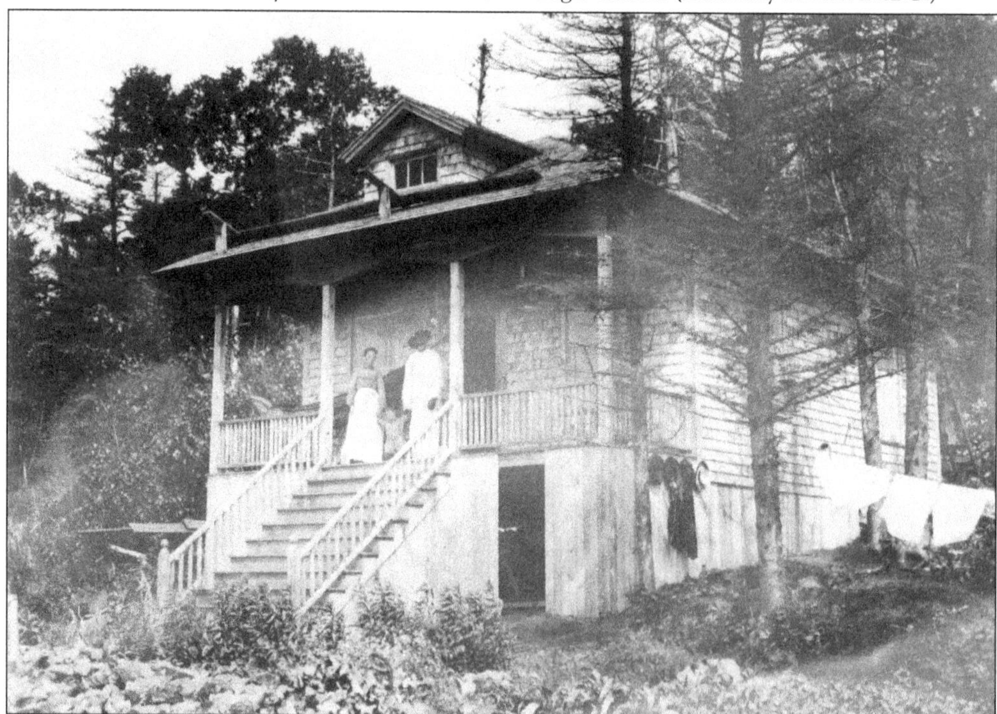

This was the caretaker's cottage as it was in the early 20th century. The long steep staircase is no longer there, but visible here at the bottom of the stairs are the edges of the vegetable gardens. These gardens were quite extensive and closely monitored. Records were kept noting the time of planting, sprouting, harvesting, and yield.

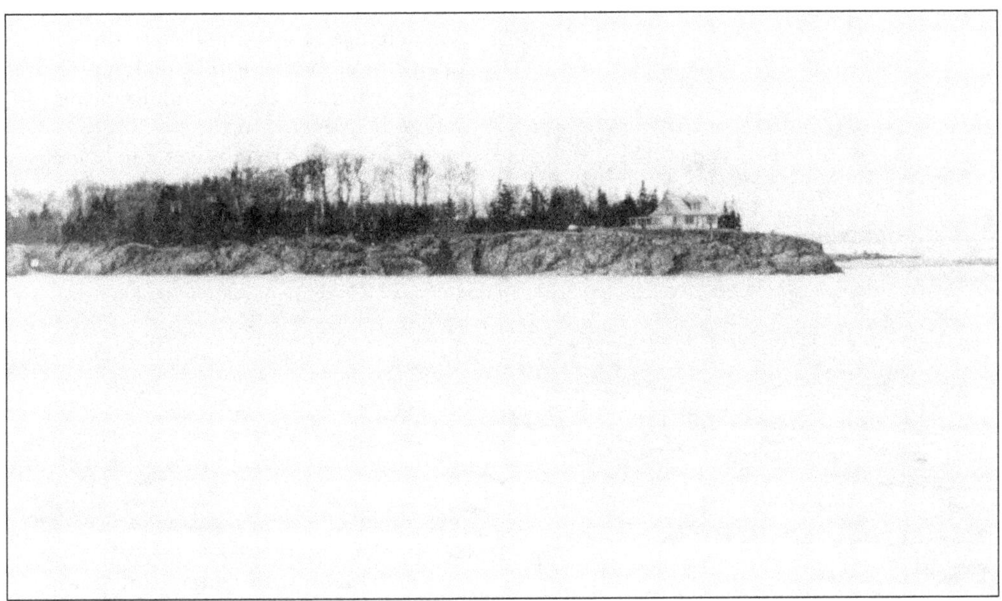

This c. 1908 photograph taken from the east shows the area of the island just south of the cottage and is evidence of the number of the island's trees harvested to build the house. In 1928, Josephine replenished this area with a purchase of 1,200 various trees and shrubs. Receipts for flower seeds purchased at E.J. Harmon & Co. in Portland, Maine, can be found in a bookcase in the dining room.

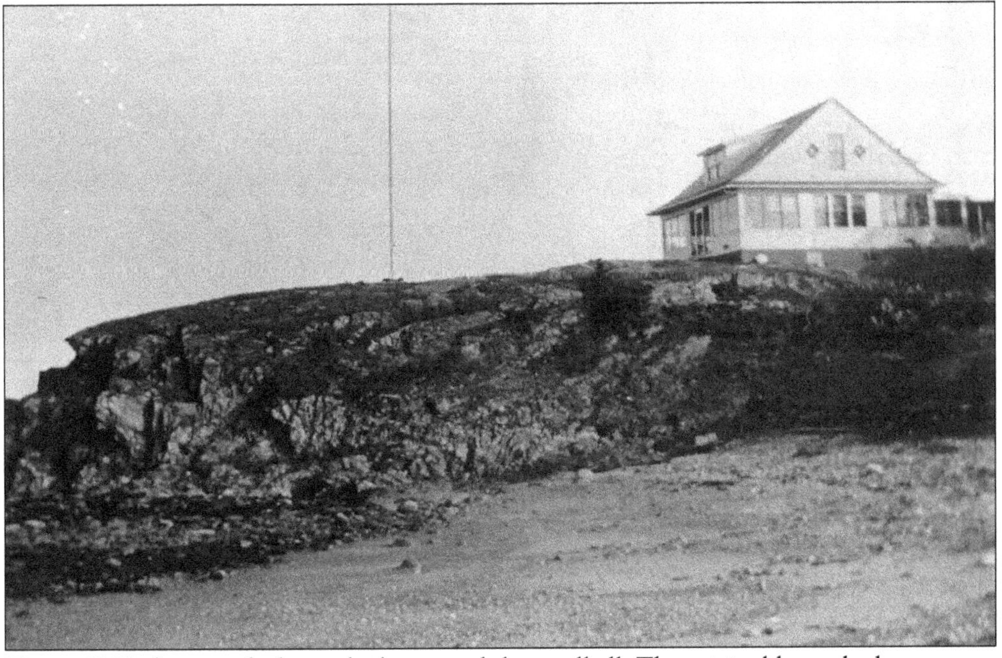

This c. 1905 photograph shows the house and the small ell. The original house had two rooms on the first floor, with three bedrooms above; the ell added a dining room and kitchen. Windows on all four sides of the house allowed for unobstructed views of the Atlantic Ocean on the east and of Casco Bay to the west and north.

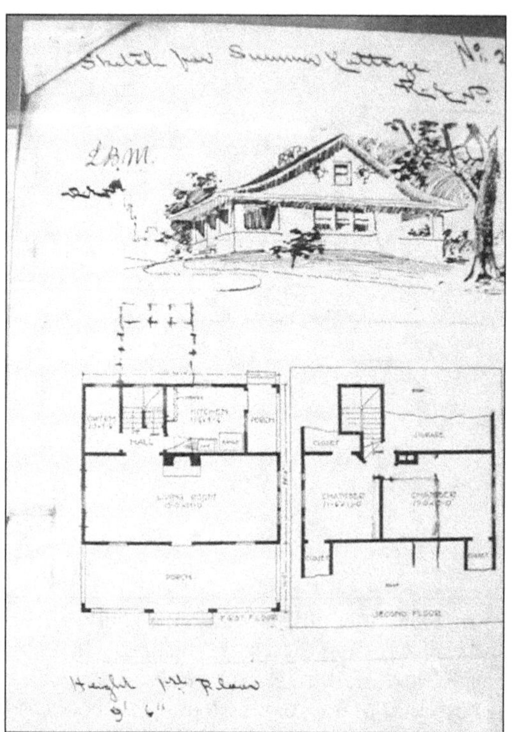

Peary changed the original plans drawn for the initial house plan by eliminating the kitchen and a closet. Initially, meals were to be prepared in the caretaker's cottage and delivered to the main house.

The caretaker's cottage is a one-story-high rectangular structure about 20 feet by 36 feet based on the original plan drawn for Admiral Peary. It is wood-framed with wood shingles on the exterior. The front of the caretaker's cottage faces the ocean to the west and allows late-day sun to warm it before evening.

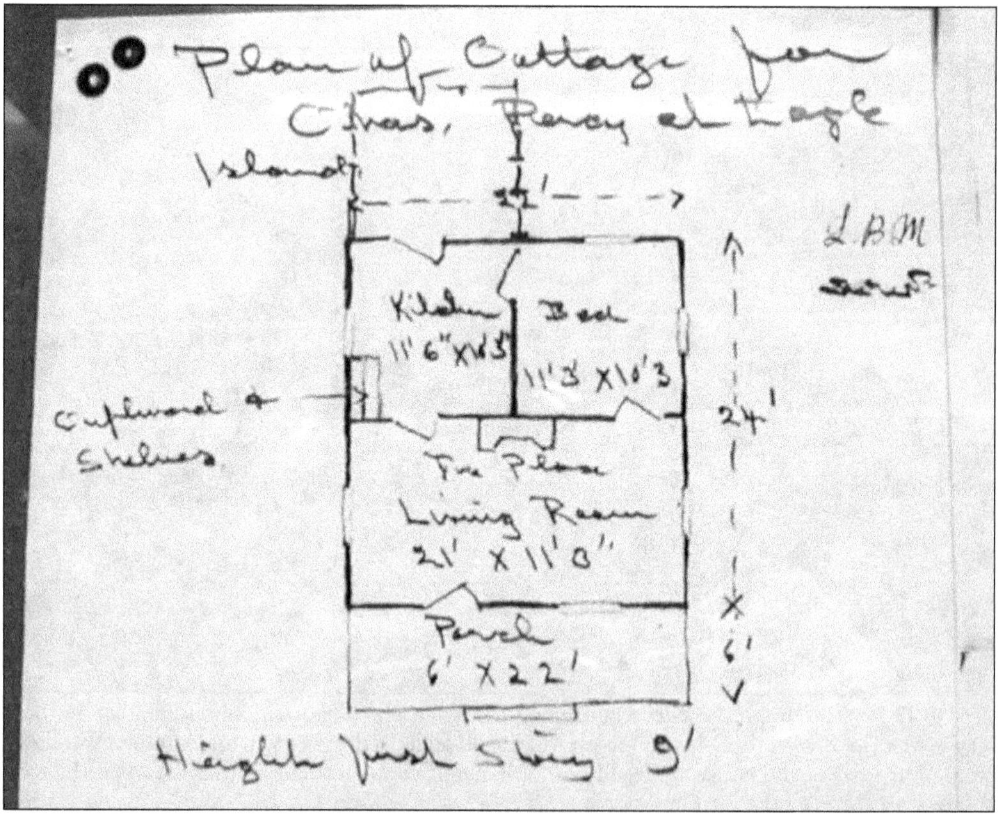

The contract between Admiral Peary and Leon Merriman, shown in parts here, indicates the level of detail requested of the contractor. Dated May 1904, the contract states the cottage is to be built by July 1904. Peary wanted to celebrate Fourth of July that year "on island." Workers and supplies came in from the mainland, and many of the construction workers camped on the island during the building process (see page 17). (Both, courtesy of GJMBC.)

THIS AGREEMENT made this twenty eighth day of May, A. D. 1904, between Leon B. Merriman of Harpswell in the County of Cumberland, in the State of Maine, contractor; party of the first part, and Robert E. Peary, U. S. N. of Washington in the District of Columbia, owner; party of the second part;

WITNESSETH that the said party of the first part, or and in consideration of the payments to be made to him y the said party of the second part, as hereafter provided oes hereby covenant, contract and agree to erect two cot-ages on the site designated on Eagle Island in Casco Bay in the Town of Harpswell n said County of Cumberland, furnishing all labor and materials therefor, all labor to be skilled and competent, nd all materials to be as specified in the plans and speci ications, in accordance with which said materials are to e furnished, which plans and specifications are here re-erred to and made a part of this contract. Said work is o be done in a good, substantial and workmanlike manner, o the satisfaction of the owner or his agent.

IT IS further mutually agreed between the parties hereto that no certificates given, or payment made under this contract, except the final certificate or payment, shall be conclusive evidence of the performance of this contract, either wholly or in part, against any claim of the owner, and no payment shall be construed to be an acceptance of any defective work.

IT IS also agreed that said first party shall pay laborers and material men all sums due them, for labor performed and materials furnished under this contract, before entitling himself to demand any of the payments herein stipulated.

IN WITNESS WHEREOF, the said parties have hereunto set their hands and seals the day and year first above written.

IN PRESENCE OF,

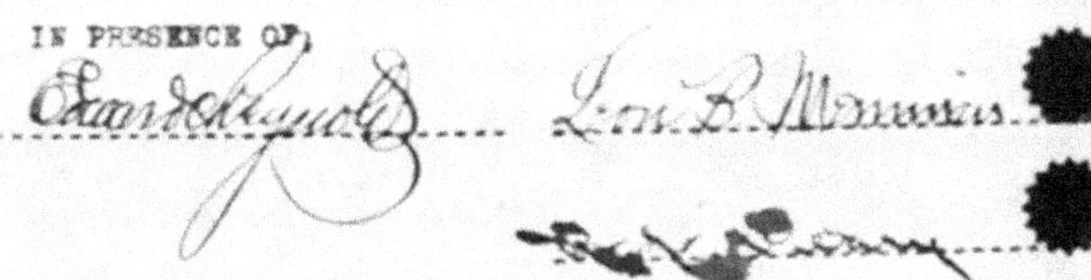

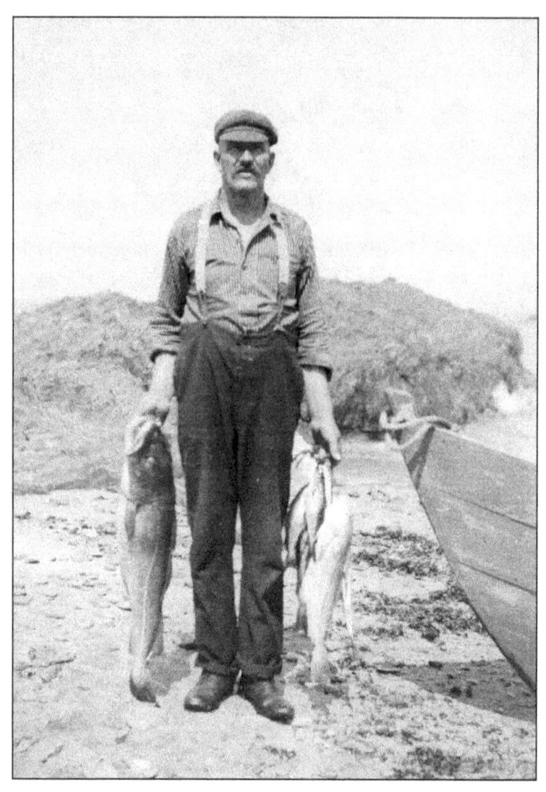

Charles Percy, called "the old man" by the family, was one of the first caretakers the Peary family had on Eagle Island and was also the steward for Peary aboard the *Roosevelt*. He is shown here in 1910 with a nice fresh catch of codfish caught off Eagle Island. Codfish of this size are no longer found in Maine waters near the shore in Casco Bay; today, only commercial or deep-sea fishermen catch this size fish well offshore.

The waters around Eagle Island are an excellent area for lobster; ledges under the water are steep and deep—perfect for lobsters. Charles Percy is shown here pulling a lobster trap. Often during storms, traps and buoys are torn free and find their way to the shores of Eagle Island. Some are salvageable, but many are given up as casualties. The colors of the buoys make for a bright display, and hundreds of buoys can be seen every day dotting the waters nearby.

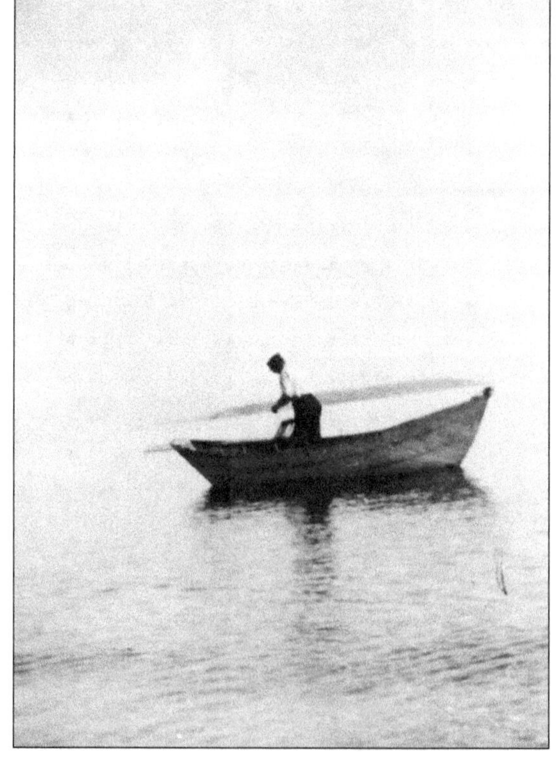

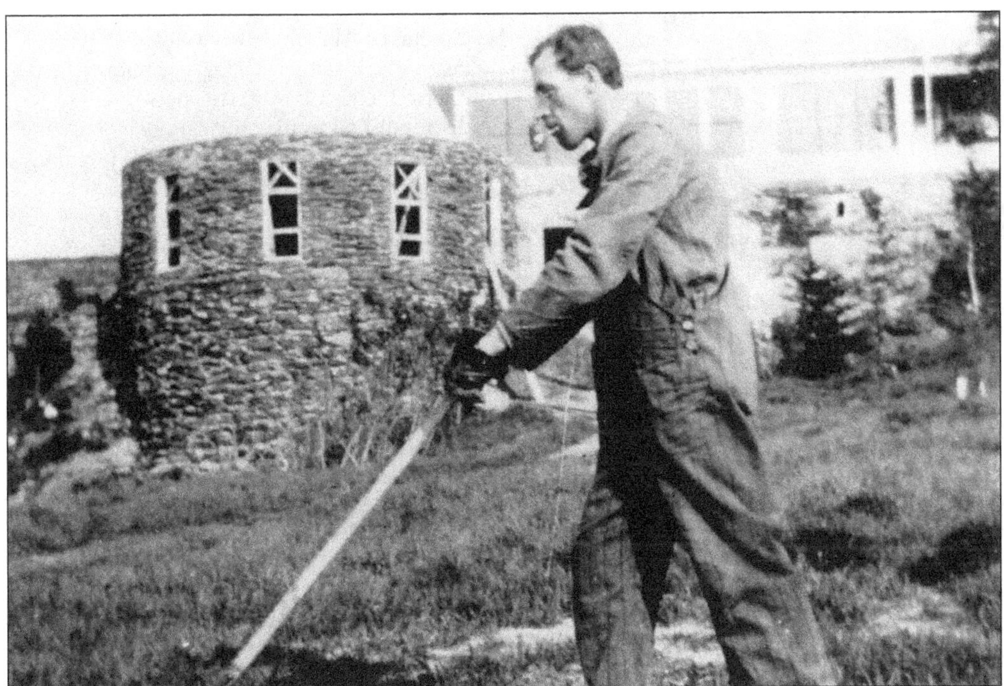

Charles Percy's son, also Charles, is seen here performing a regular chore—mowing the very large front lawn. At the beginning of every season, the weeds and grass in this lawn could be over a foot tall. Note the corncob pipe and the coveralls he is wearing to perform chores around the island.

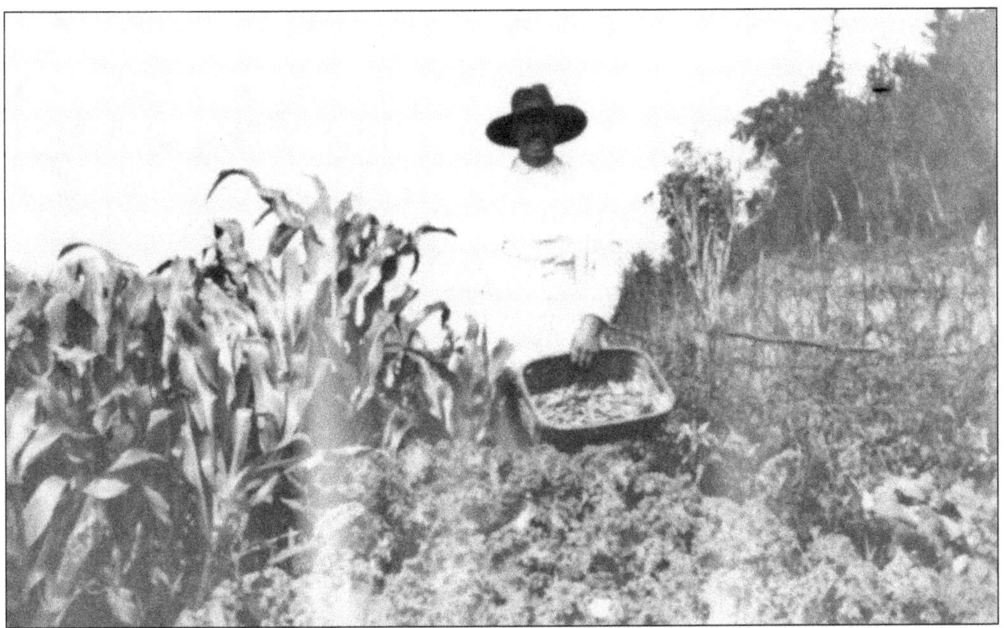

Charles Percy and the other caretakers throughout the years helped the ladies of the family plant and maintain vegetable gardens. Living on an island, one either grows food or brings it by boat from the mainland. Here, Percy is working in the garden; the corn is knee-high.

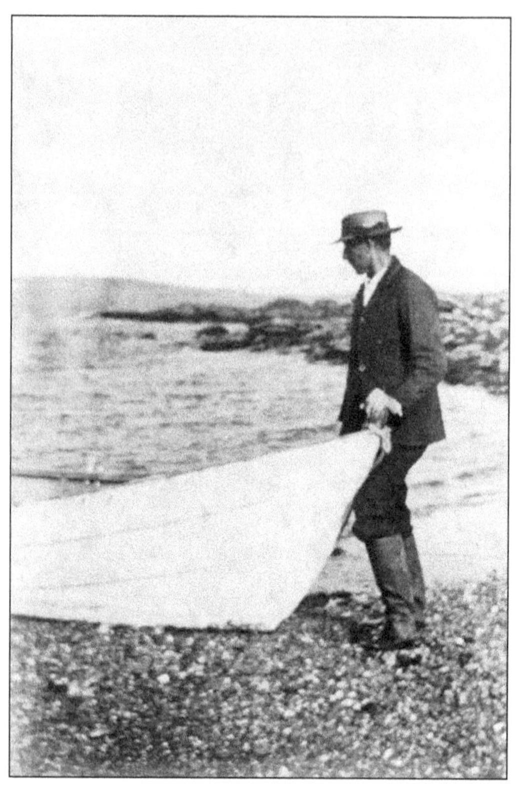

Caretaker Abiijah Stove was one of Peary's boatswains. Today, commonly referred to as a bosun, this person is distinguished from other sailors by having a more supervisory role. They are familiar with all of the duties of running a ship, including regular inspections, and are skilled in many tasks required of sailors.

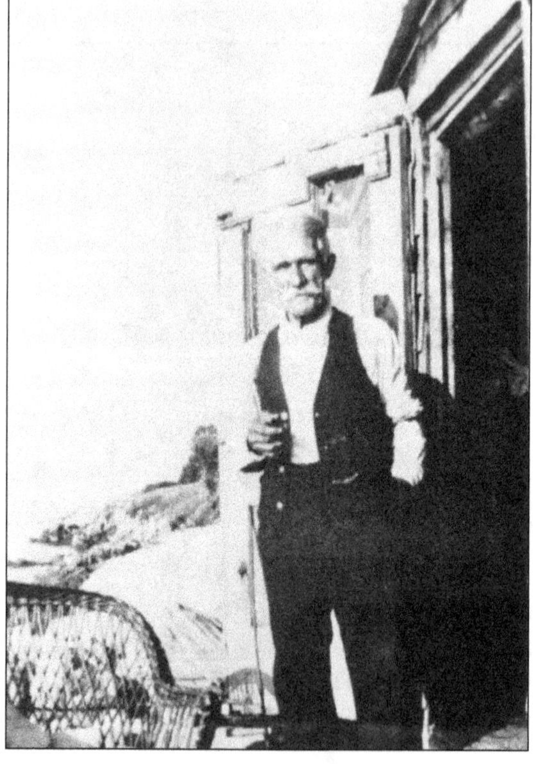

Antonio "Tony" Gomez was another of the Eagle Island caretakers/staff. He was a Spaniard by birth and served in the Spanish navy as a noncommissioned officer. Gomez would make daily trips to South Harpswell, mostly at Josephine Peary's request, to gather supplies and retrieve mail that might have a letter from her husband hundreds of miles away to the north. Gomez is pictured here outside the Igloo (see page 53).

So. Harpswell E. I.
Jan 31, 1916

Dear Admiral...
I have been expecting to hear from you since the 10th I have been anxious to get the check as we are all out of dog bread and corn and cant get any untill I hear from you if it is convenient to you I would like to have my check every month. every thing is alright on the Island and we are both well. Hope to hear from you soon I remain

Yours Truly
Doughty

Ans. with check for $100. —
Feb. [illegible]

The next two pages show correspondence from M.J. Doughty, a caretaker on the island during the winter and summer of 1916. In the note, he is looking for money to purchase dog food and advises that everything is fine on the island. This is very formal correspondence for the caretaker; Peary's notes at the bottom indicate that he forwarded a check to the caretaker in early February. (Courtesy of GJMBC.)

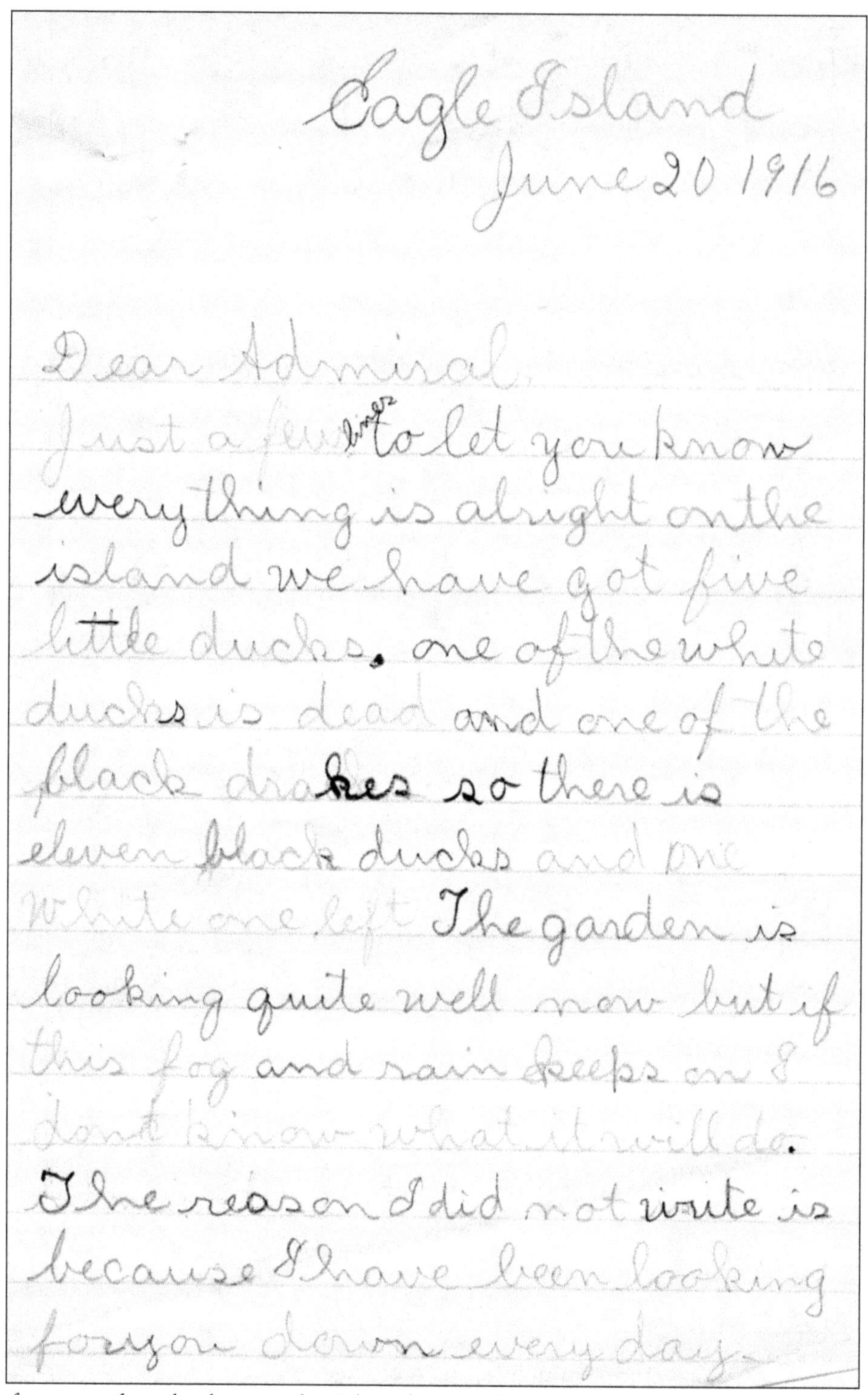

Eagle Island
June 20 1916

Dear Admiral,
Just a few lines to let you know
every thing is alright on the
island we have got five
little ducks. one of the white
ducks is dead and one of the
black drakes so there is
eleven black ducks and one
white one left The garden is
looking quite well now but if
this fog and rain keeps on I
dont know what it will do.
The reason I did not write is
because I have been looking
for you down every day.

The first page of another letter to the Admiral in June 1916 apprises Peary of the status of things on the island. New ducklings have hatched, and the garden is doing well despite the weather. (Courtesy of GJMBC.)

Two

The Family and Children

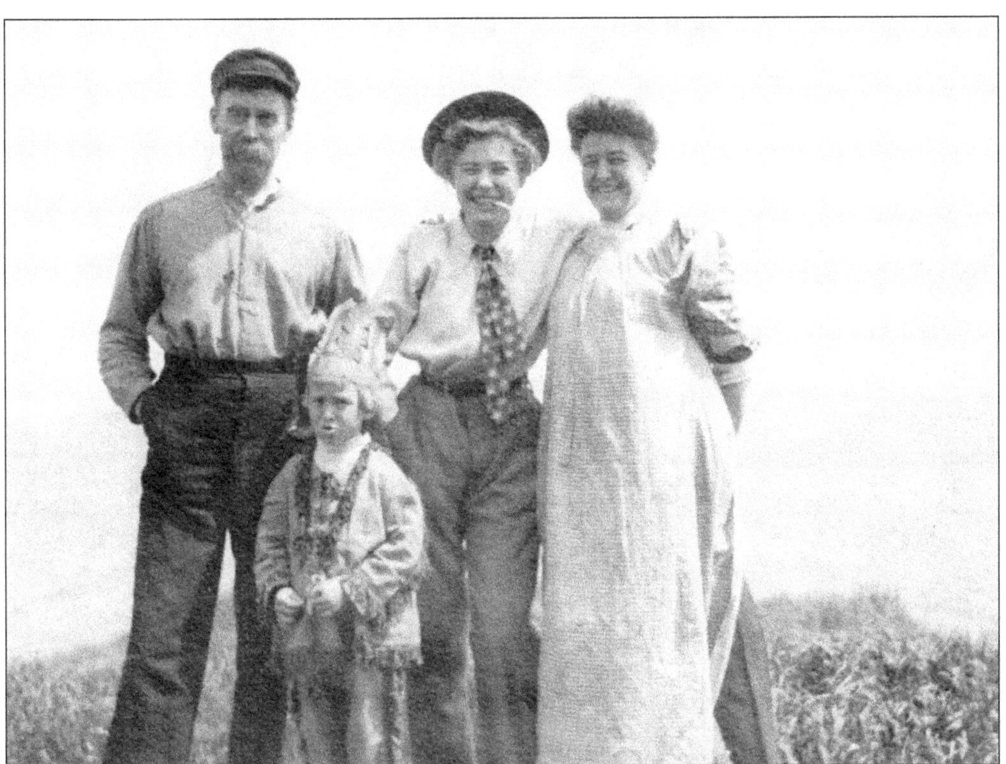

By 1907, the Admiral, Josephine, Marie, and Robert Jr. were very much at home on Eagle Island, as evident in their relaxed attitudes in this photograph. Note the bit of a smile from the Admiral, which apparently was about as much expression as one could expect from him.

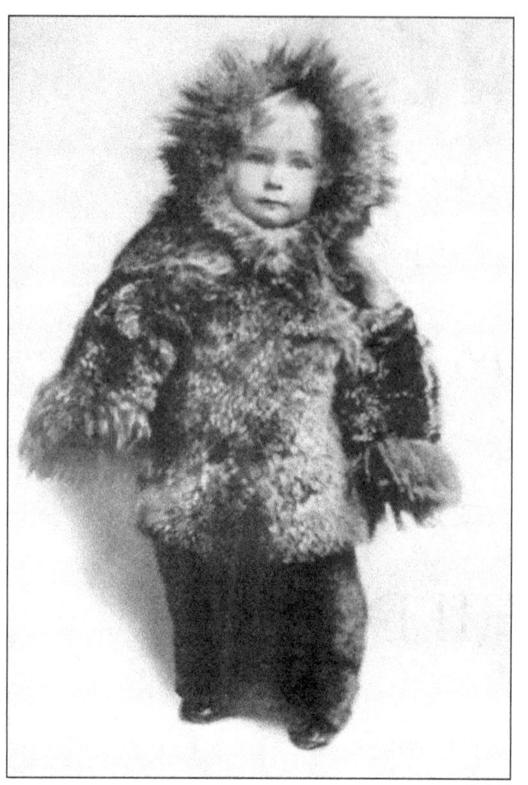

Marie, the Peary's eldest child, was born in Greenland in 1889 during one of the two expeditions on which Josephine traveled north with the Admiral. Marie was born less than 13 degrees latitude from the North Pole and was the first white child seen by the local Inuit. She became known as "snow baby," and her middle name Ahnighito was Inuit.

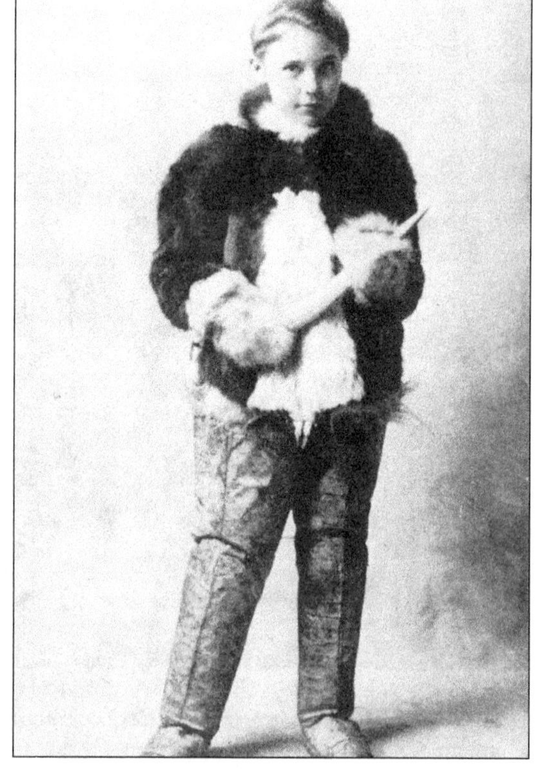

Here is Marie at the age of seven posing in Arctic clothing and carrying part of a narwhal tusk. Peary learned early in his Arctic explorations to follow the lead of the native population, and he and his crew dressed in fur just as the Inuit did.

Robert E. Peary Jr., who was called Bob to differentiate him from his father, was the Pearys' only son and the third-born. The Pearys lost a child named Francine in 1899, under one year of age (see page 35). Here, Bob is seen with his father in a formal picture, which was shared with then president Theodore Roosevelt, a fan of Peary.

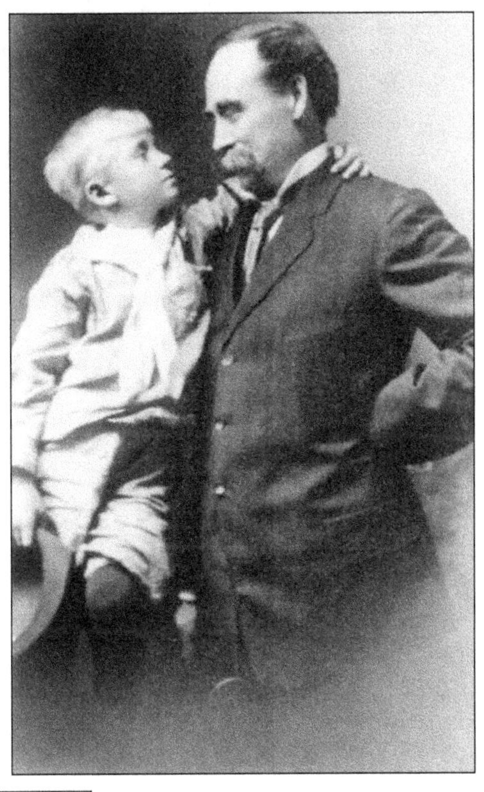

WHITE HOUSE
WASHINGTON

March 13, 1908.

My dear Commander Peary:

I am touched by your letter, and I love the photograph of your small son. Give him my good wishes. If he takes after his father he will think quick, shoot straight, not strike at all until he must, and then strike as hard as any human being can.

Wishing you all good fortune,

Faithfully yours,

Theodore Roosevelt

Commander Robert E. Peary, U.S.N.,
Grand Union Hotel,
New York.

In this letter from President Roosevelt responding to the previous picture of the Peary men, one gets the sense that both the president and Peary, a commander in the US Navy at the time, shared the same sense of exploration, adventure, and doggedness.

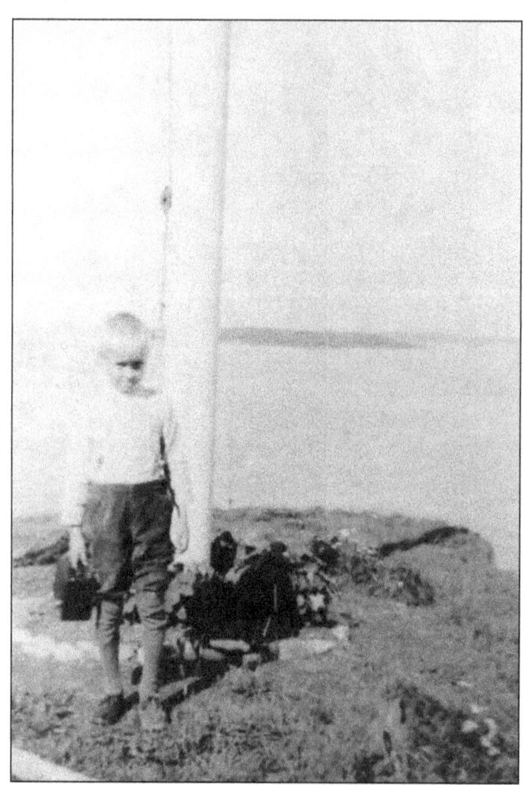

Robert E. Peary Jr., at about eight years old, on the north lawn of the island, stands near the edge of the northern bastion. Bastions were used to fortify the island against the enemy—the Atlantic Ocean and its tides, swells, and heavy weather. By the time Bob reached his early teen years, he was already an old hand with boats, building them and sailing them. He is pictured here at the stern of one.

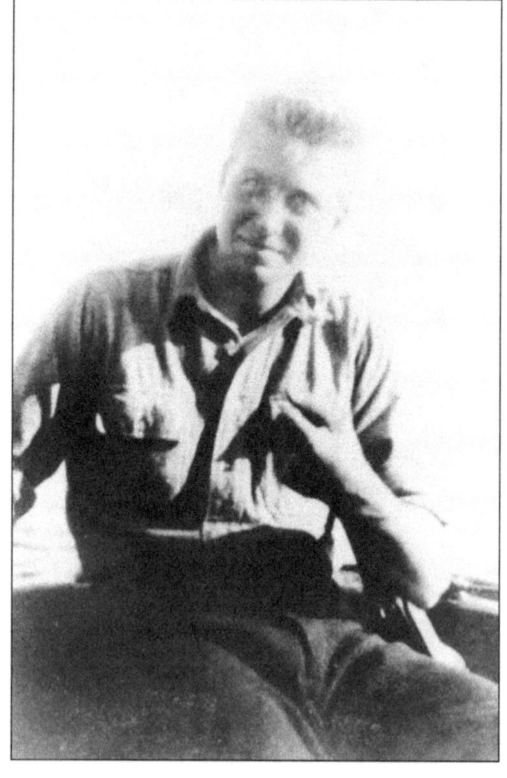

Dogs were an ever-present part of the Peary family on Eagle Island. Here, Josephine is pictured with Rex, a Saint Bernard mix and one of the family's pet dogs. She stands on the boardwalk, or open deck, that surrounded the cottage on all four sides.

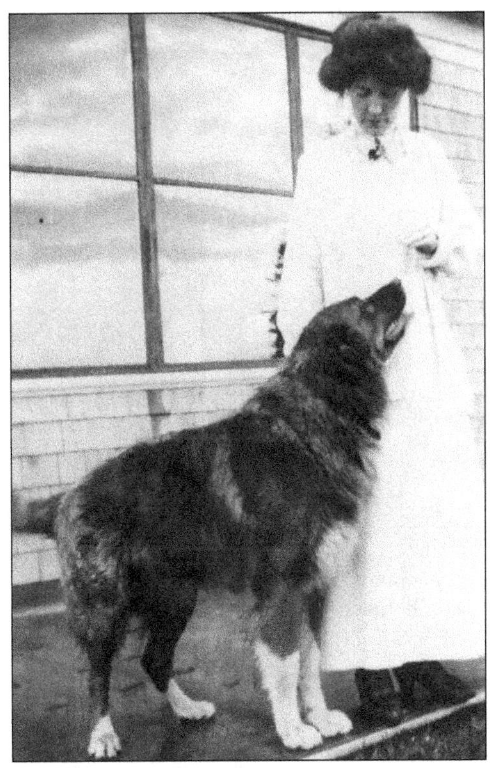

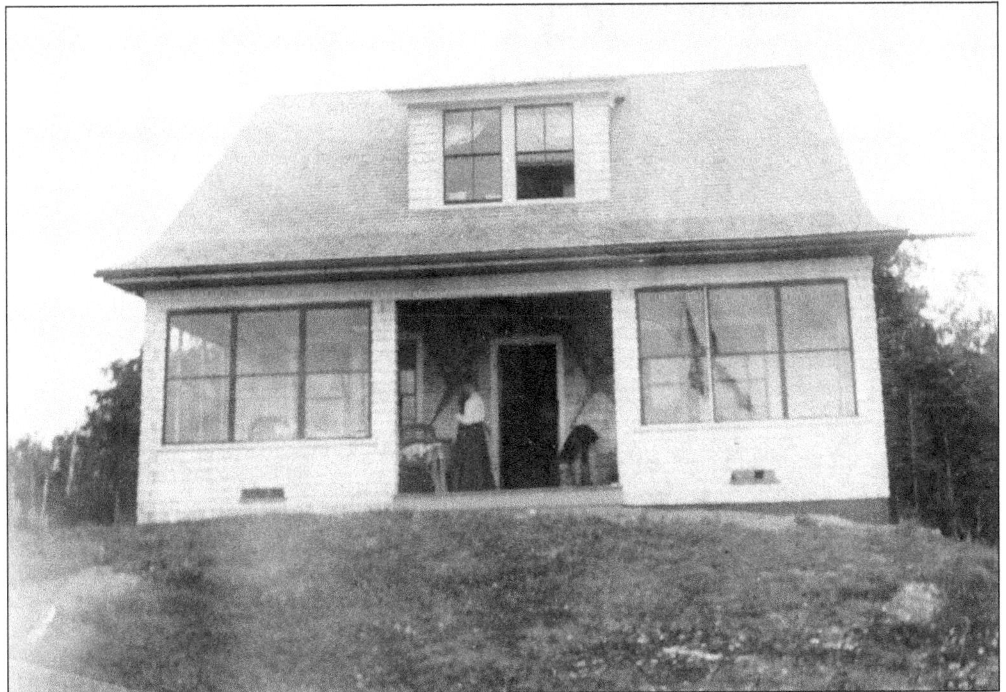

Josephine is working on the north front porch of the cottage. Initially, this porch was completely open; however, after experiencing the weather on the edge of the Atlantic, the Admiral enclosed it with windows on all sides.

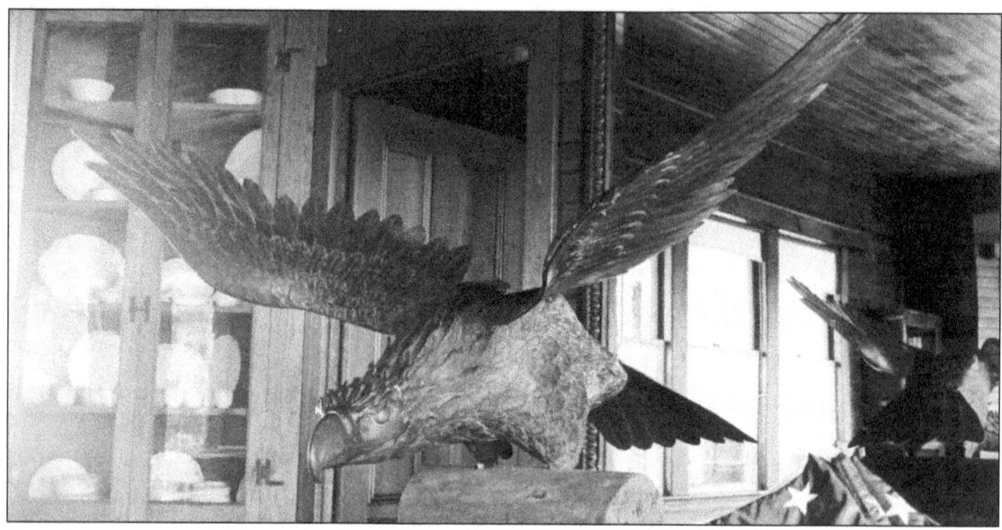

This brass statue of an American bald eagle was affixed to the north bastion (see page 51) every summer when the Pearys were on Eagle Island. It is now on display in the Admiral's Eagle Island library.

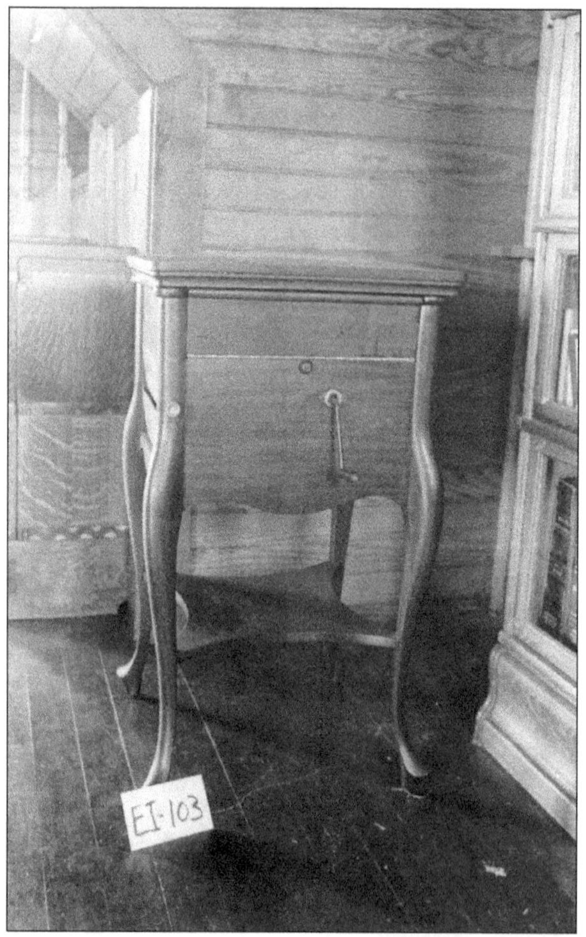

The graphophone pictured here is tucked away in a corner of the living room. The EI-103 indicates the number the State of Maine used when it inventoried the home after the Peary family donated it to the state. There was no electricity in the house early on, and music was a big part of the entertainment for the family and their visitors.

Initially, the cottage had two rooms on the first floor, one of which had this fireplace using a central chimney that was made with bricks from Maine brickyards. It warmed the downstairs and was the main source of heat. Summer evenings on Maine coastal islands can get very cool.

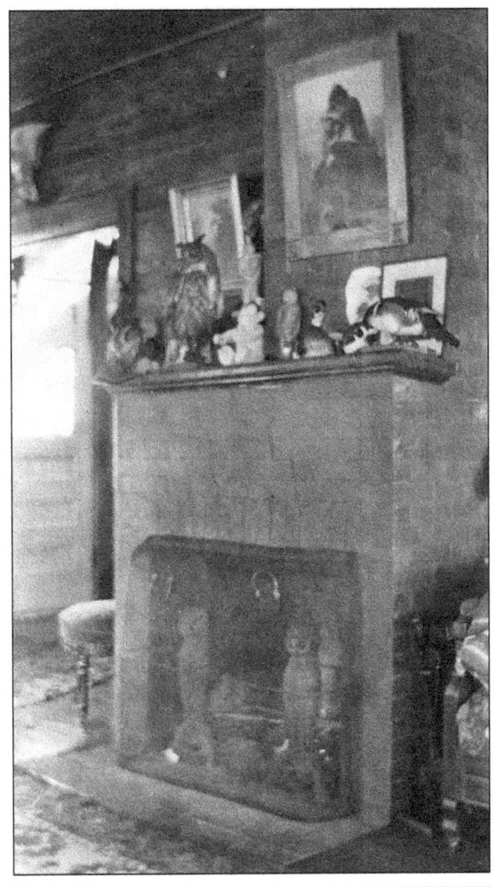

Carried to and fro from Maine to New York to Greenland and back, Admiral Peary's valise clearly took a beating. The leather has seen better days. It remains on display in the cottage.

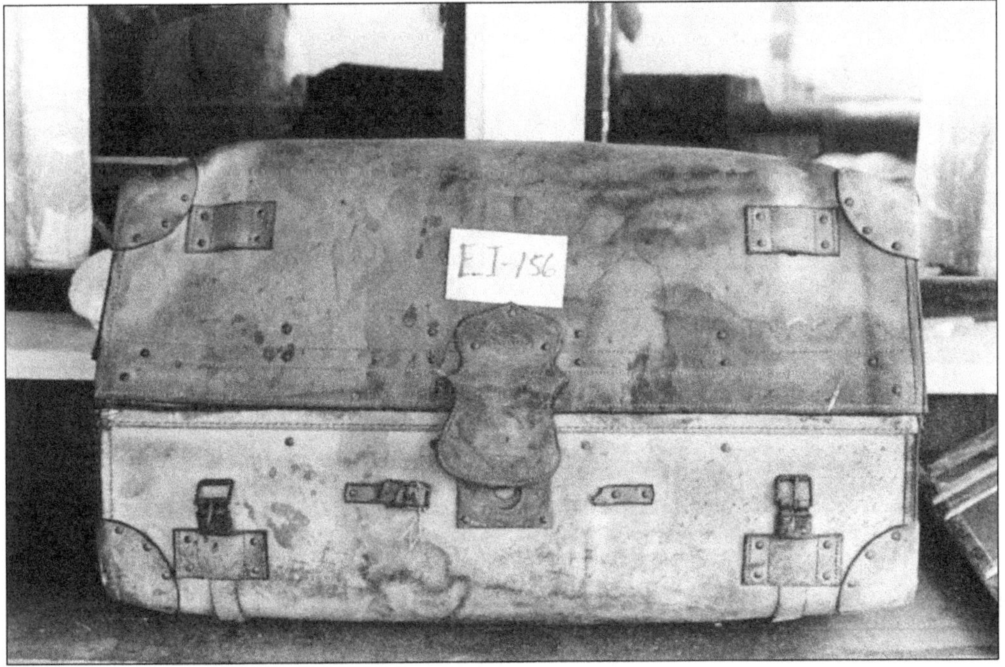

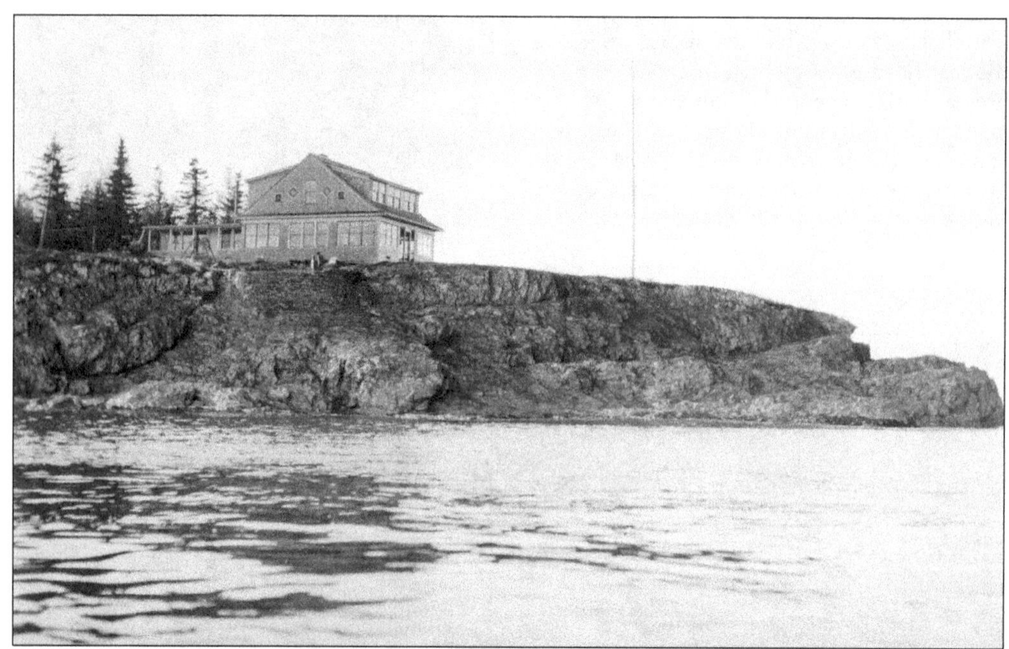

By 1906, the Peary family realized their initial cottage was too small for a family with two children and many visiting family members, crew members, and caretakers. One of the first steps was to add an ell to the back of the house, which is visible in this photograph. Construction of the bastion on the east side of the house, to protect the rock face and island from the beatings of winter weather off the Atlantic coast, was begun.

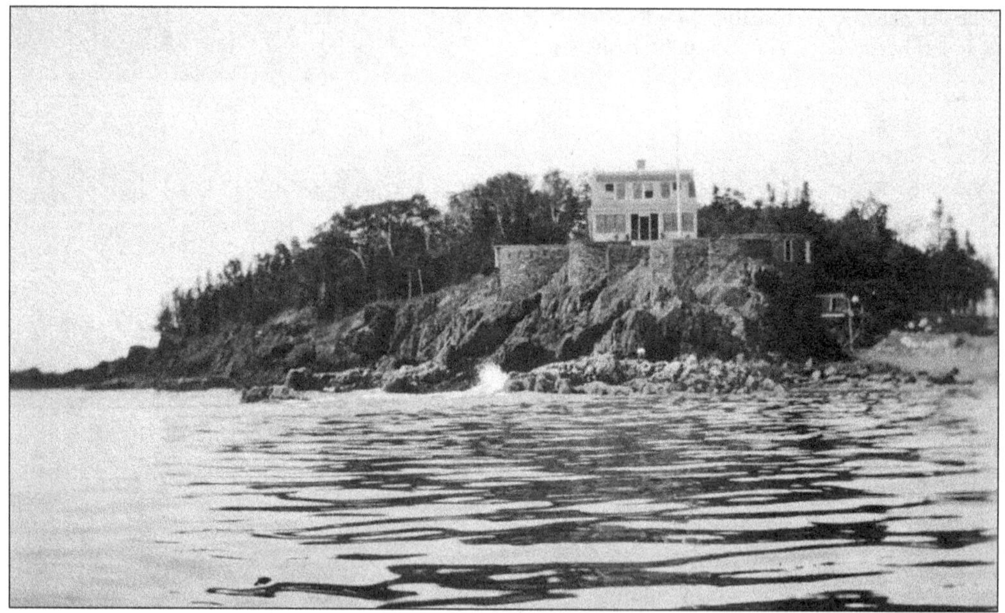

Bastions were built onto the house as part of the seawall system to protect the northern portion of the island and the cottage from the sea. To Peary, the northern bastion and seawall system served as the prow of the ship; the east and west bastions formed the bridge wings (narrow walkways extending from the interior of the bridge of a ship to allow those sailing the vessel to have greater visibility when maneuvering the vessel).

Three

EXPLORATION

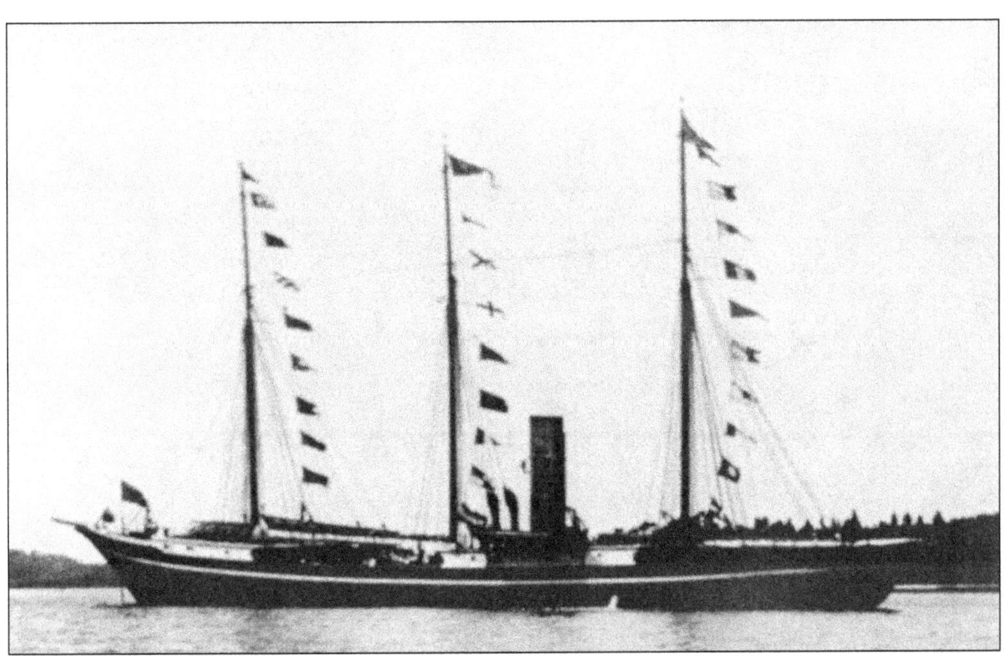

Built in Bucksport, Maine, on Verona Island, the SS *Roosevelt* was launched in March 1904; when not under sail, it was fueled by coal-fired boilers. Designed by Peary as an icebreaker, it sailed on two expeditions to the Arctic, including in 1908–1909 when he reached the geographic North Pole. As an "icebreaker," it could break through the ice and withstand the pressure of being frozen in Arctic ice for months at time. As the SS *Roosevelt* left for the Arctic in 1908, its last stop in the United States was Eagle Island, where Peary picked up additional parts.

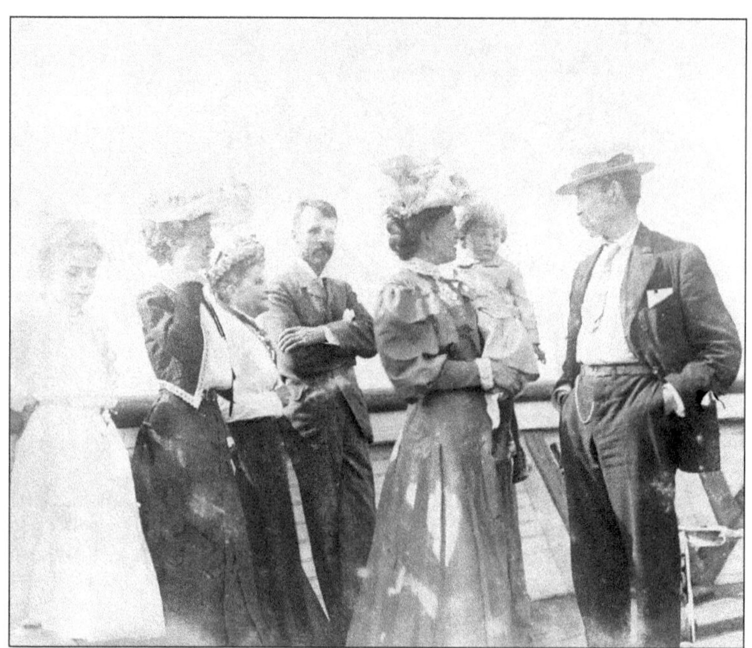

It was a tradition when ships left docks for expeditions or for leisure travel for visitors to come aboard prior to weighing anchor. Here, Josephine and Robert Jr. are talking with the Admiral during one such visit in 1905. Others in the group include, from left to right, their daughter, Marie; Josephine's sister, Marie Flora Diebitsch; and her sister-in-law and brother, Roberta and Emil Diebitsch.

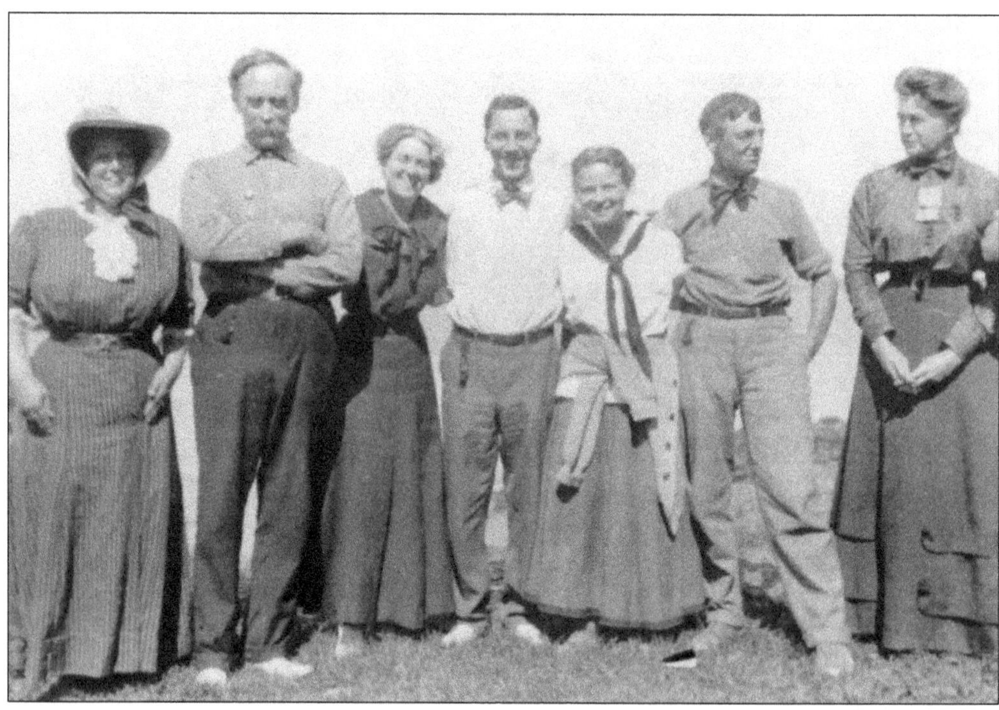

Adm. Robert E. Peary retired from the US Navy in March 1911. Following his great expedition to the North Pole and his retirement, he and his family were more often together on Eagle Island. Extended family spent summers with the Pearys on the island, including Josephine's sister Madge Diebitsch (fifth from left).

2014 – 12th St. n.w.

My Darling, My Husband; March, 1900

For the first time in my life it seems a hard task to write to you as I ought. If only the time since last August has not been as hard for you as it has for me is all I ask & pray for nightly. Surely we ought not both to suffer & I have suffered for both. Our little darling whom you never knew was taken from me on Aug 7. 99 just 7 months after she came. She was only sick a few days but the disease took right hold of her little head & nothing could be done for her. Emil was more than a brother to me & I don't know what I should have done without him both before & afterward. But oh my husband I wanted you so much you will never know. I shall never feel quite the same again part of me is in the little grave. The news of your terrible suffering came soon after. (The Windward getting in a week before the Diana) It nearly prostrated me, but you know I am strong & can bear & bear & bear. Oh sweetheart husband we could have borne it together but alone it was almost too much. You too will carry the scars of your suffering all your life & not only physically.

It will probably be a great disappointment for you to learn that the Windward can not be "re engined & boilered" this year. The hull is being thoroughly overhauled under Capt "Jack's" supervision & she will be fitted up with her old machinery & sent to communicate with you this summer. I do not write particulars as Bridgman probably will, besides I really don't know them. Marie is wild to see you & Mr Jesup says I must go. He & the Club think it will be for our mutual good. I shall probably come (though you never expressed such a wish) but fear it will make a great disturbance in your present domestic life.

Our little Marie was taken down with measles Feb. 1st last & for 3 weeks I watched over her in a darkened room. She came out all right & 5 days later came home from school with scarlet fever. The fever is broken now & the Dr. says nursing & care will do the rest. We are to be quarantined for weeks longer if all goes well. Surely God will not take her from me too. She is all I have left to live for. I mean the only one to whom it makes any real difference. You will find her a big girl. Her

This is the first page of a letter from Josephine to her "darling husband" the Admiral, dated March 1900. She wrote to him about the loss of one of their children, Francine, whom he never knew. Born in January 1899, Francine died in August of that year. Josephine's strong and steady nature is evident in this correspondence where she also discusses their daughter, Marie, having contracted measles (the family being quarantined because of it) and her concern for her husband's suffering over these matters, while at the same time writing about boiler issues on another vessel, the *Windward*. (Courtesy of JDPUNE.)

Associated Press
New York

Stars and Stripes nailed to North Pole.
Peary

Having realized his lifelong goal of being the first man to reach the geographic North Pole, Peary prepared to announce his great achievement to the world. Returning back to civilization in Labrador, Peary sent telegrams, including the two on this page. One was directed to the Associated Press claiming the "discovery" of the North Pole for the United States; another was directed to his supporter and stalwart cheerleader Theodore Roosevelt, letting the former president know that having him in his corner meant the world to Peary and that his support was much appreciated. (Both, courtesy of GJMBC.)

Theodore Roosevelt
Ex President U.S. of America

Your farewell was a royal mascot. The Pole is ours.
Peary

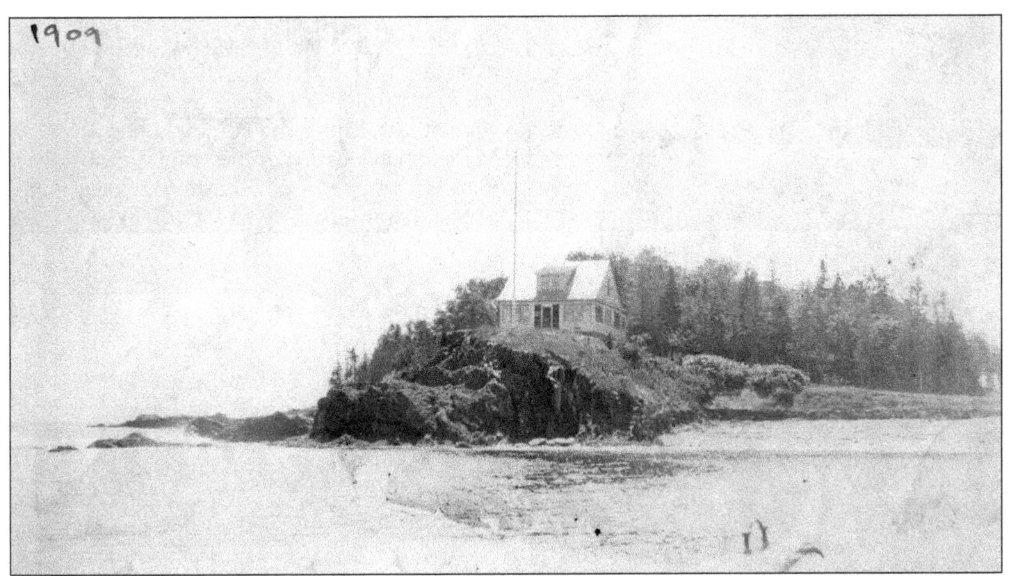

This photograph shows the house as it stood when Peary headed to the Arctic for his last great expedition. It is here that Josephine awaited word about the safety, the success of the trip, and the survival of her husband.

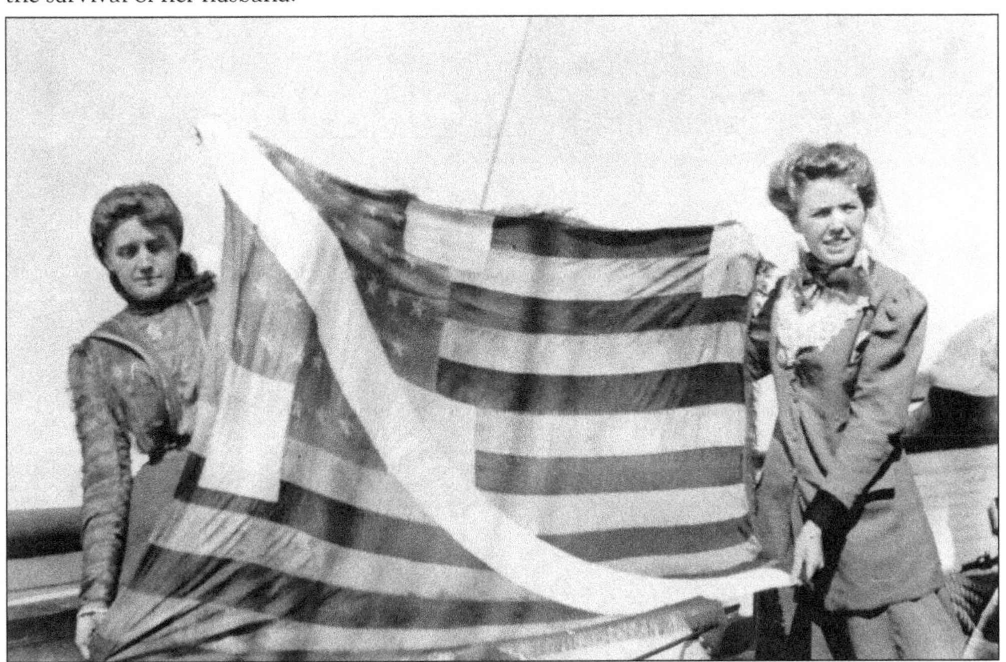

As Peary and his party ventured to the Arctic season after season—as many trips as the US Navy would allow—Josephine made Peary an American flag, which he carried with him on each journey from 1898 onward. Each time Peary reached a "furthest" north latitude, he cut out and left a part of that flag at that point to mark the accomplishment for himself and his country. This flag also flew at the North Pole when Peary was certain he had achieved that monumental task. As parts of the flag were cut and left on the trail, white fabric was sewn in to replace the missing pieces. Here, Marie and Josephine hold up the flag after the 1908–1909 journey. (Courtesy of PMAMBC.)

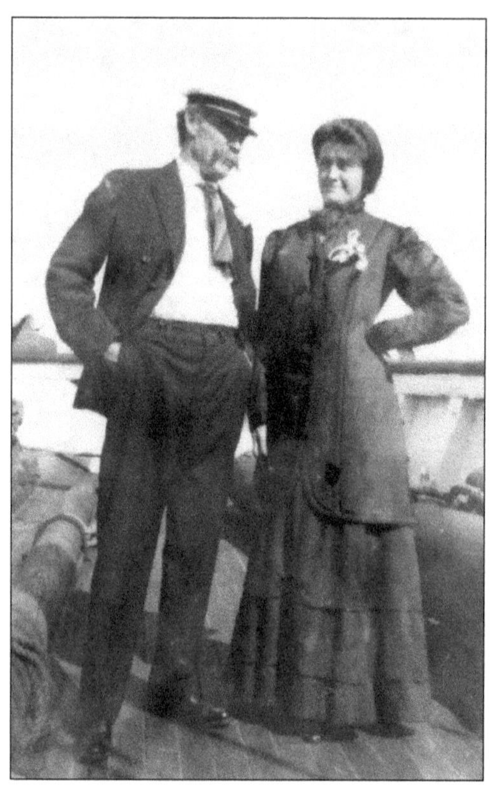

On his return from his successful final expedition in 1909, Peary telegrammed Josephine from Labrador: "Have made good at last. I have the Pole." Josephine, Marie, and Robert Jr. joined him on the *Roosevelt* when it reached Sydney, Nova Scotia. (Courtesy of PMAMBC.)

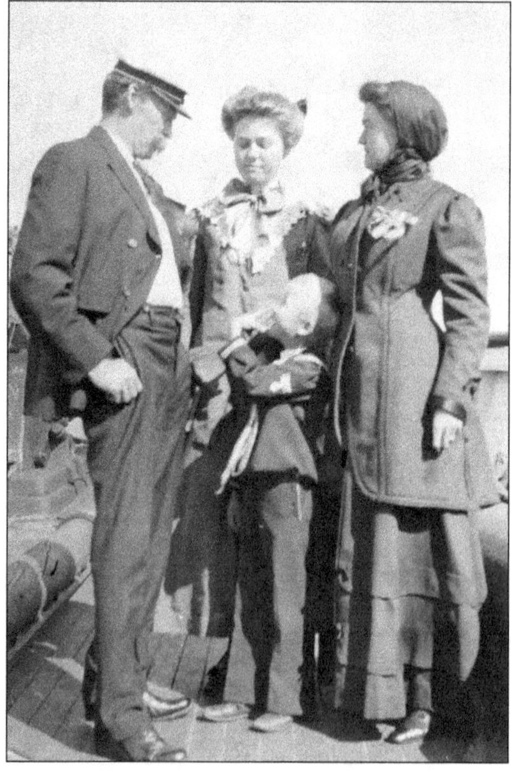

Peary was now ready to retire to Eagle Island. By a special act of Congress, on March 30, 1911, Peary was promoted to the rank of rear admiral in the Navy Civil Engineer Corps retroactive to April 6, 1909, the day he stood at the North Pole. (Courtesy of PMAMBC.)

Here, Peary is seen relaxing on the island with son Bob, wife Josephine, and his wife's niece Madge Diebitsch. They are resting on a spot near the house to the northwest of the front porch, which overlooks Casco Bay and the mainland toward Harpswell and Freeport.

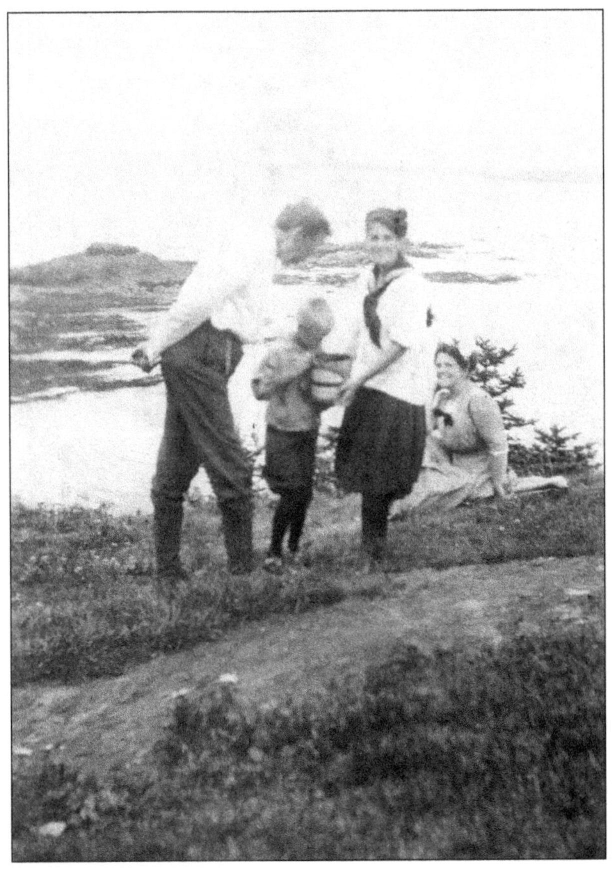

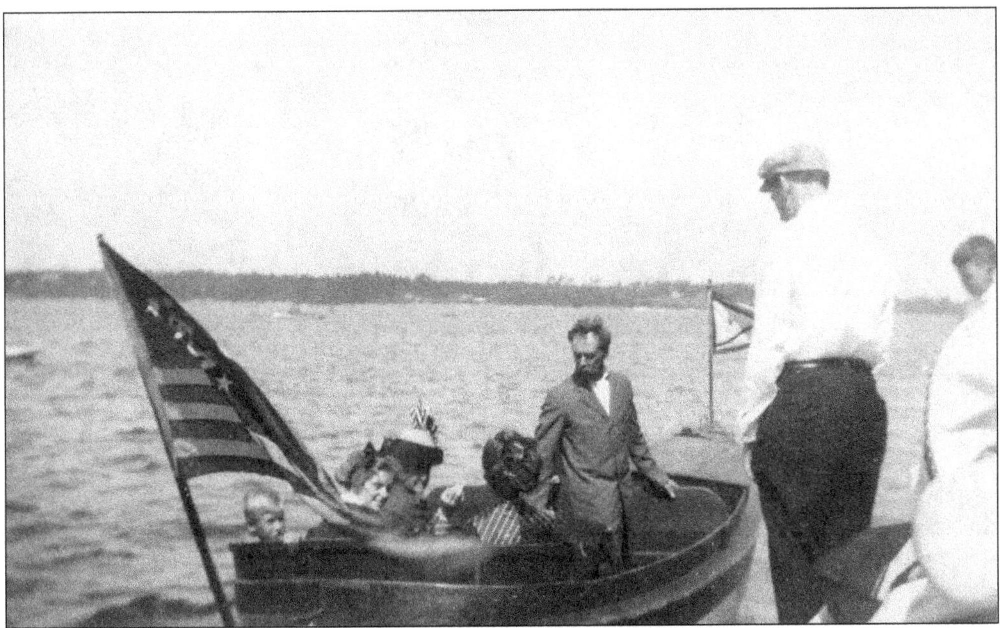

Once a naval officer, always a naval officer. At the helm of the *Ahnighito*, named for Marie, with the American flag at the stern, the family is headed off to the mainland.

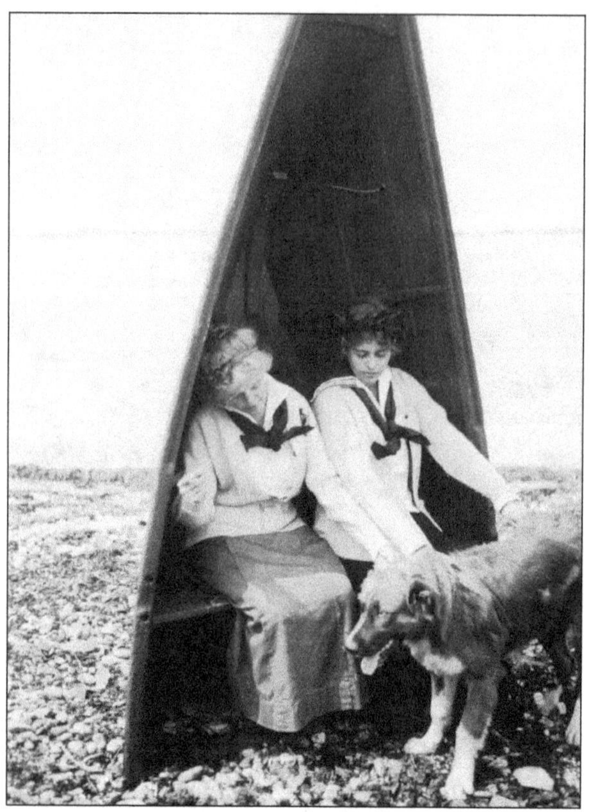

Extended family and close friends were always welcome to spend time with the Pearys on Eagle Island. Emily Stuart (left) was a friend of Marie's and here the two are huddled in a spoonhandler, which was built on the island out of wood that floated up on the beach or was cut out of a rescued boat. Spoonhandlers block the wind and create a comfortable seat to watch the waves despite the weather. Rex, the family dog, has joined the girls for a rest. Note the style of clothing typical of Marie's teenage years.

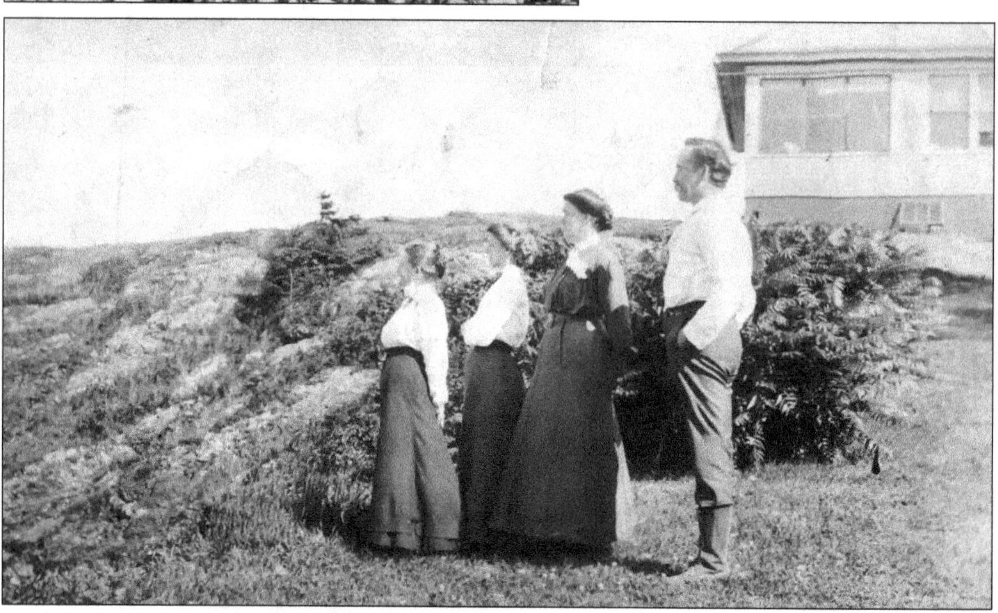

Madge Diebitsch, Marie, Josephine, and the Admiral were a core group of inhabitants on the island. When the Admiral came home to Eagle Island for good and spent each summer there, he continued with his studies, writing his memoirs and vast amounts of correspondence. Josephine's sisters helped with the children and provided Josephine with companionship when the Admiral was away.

Four

EXPANSION

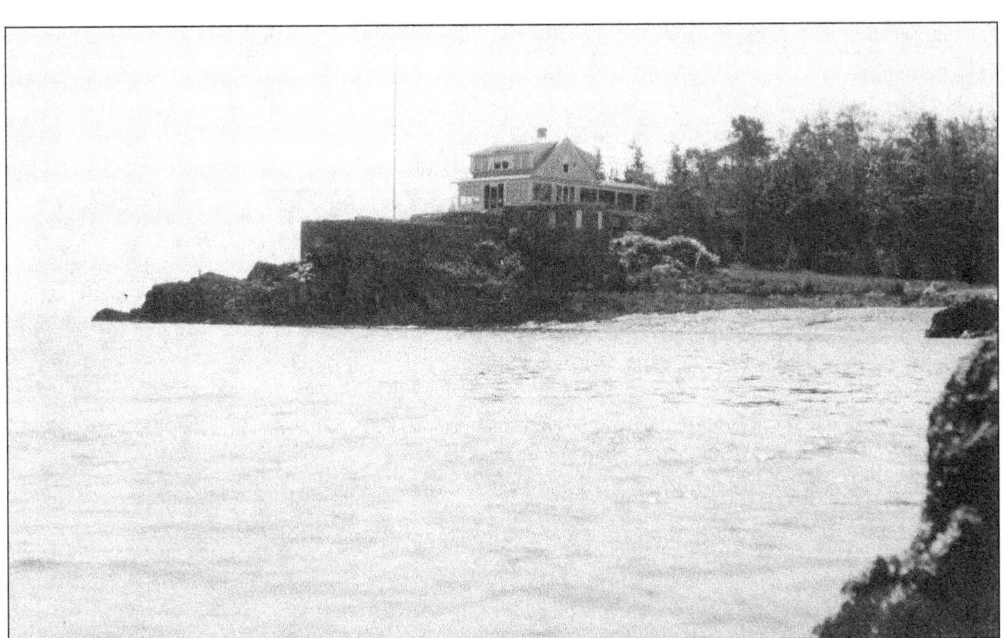

By 1911, Admiral Peary realized that his cottage on Eagle Island was once again not big enough for the family and the number of guests on the island. It was time to expand the cottage into a proper house with the second addition. Shed dormers were made into gables to add space on the second floor for more bedrooms. At the same time, the house was raised a full story, and a foundation was built using the stone on the island. The basement contained a cistern, an icehouse, and, in the west bastion, a pump house. The old ell, added to the house in 1906, was removed and repositioned off the cliffs on the east side of Eagle Island and was used as a guesthouse known as the Igloo. These pictures show the work that was done to make this the house the Peary family came to love and really consider home.

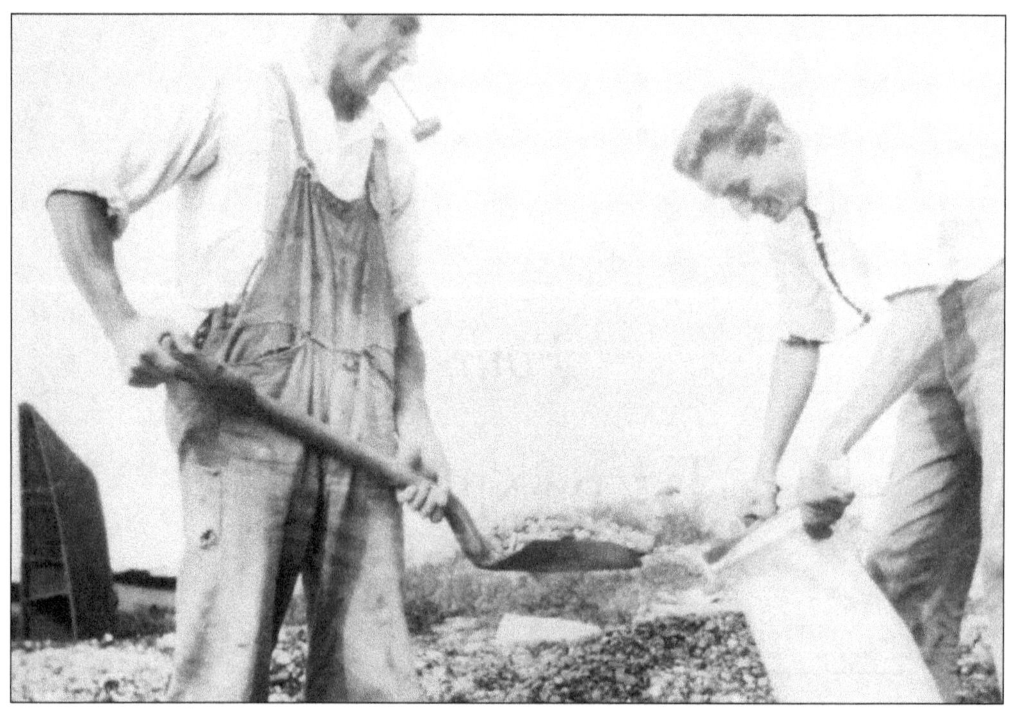

Repairs to seawalls were a regular job on the island, and all hands were on deck with any work done. Here, Jack Miller (right) and John Hummer, family friends, are filling sandbags to shore up seawalls, and Marie and Steve Percy are lugging rocks on a handbarrow. Steve was the son of the original caretakers—Charles Percy and his wife, Martha.

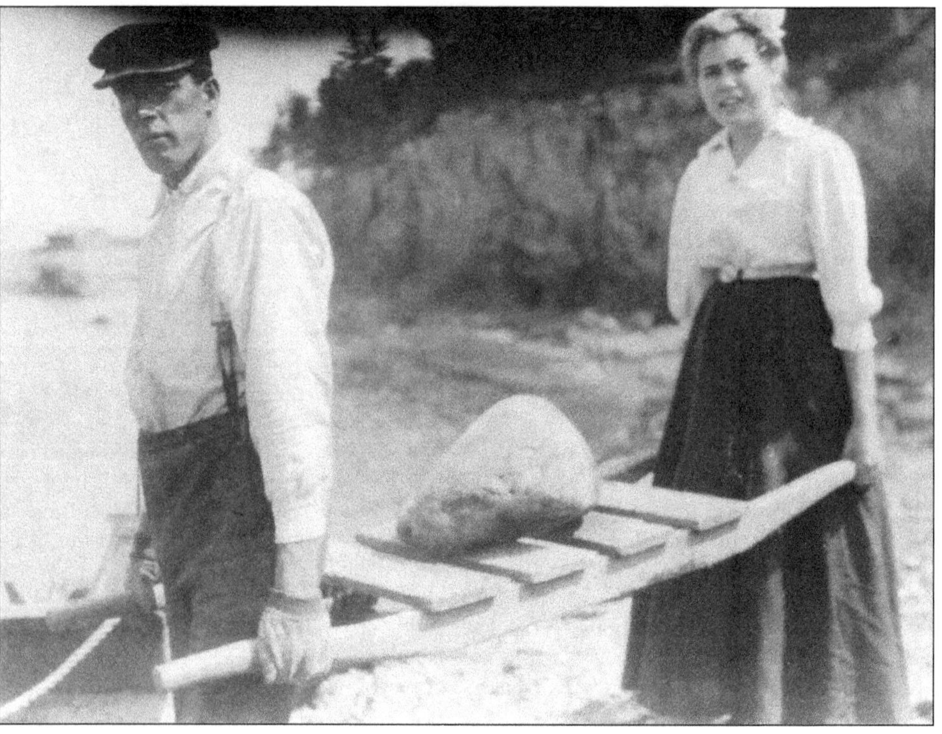

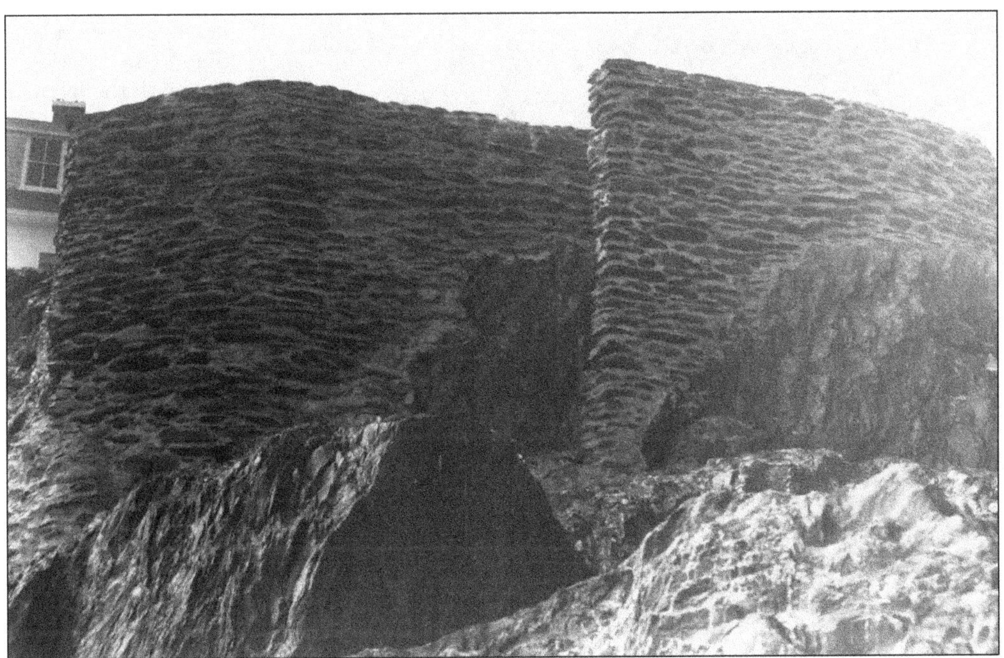

This northern bastion provided protection for the prow of the island and was the center of the seawall system. A staircase was built in this section that allowed for workers to mend and care for the eastern bastion and seawall system as well.

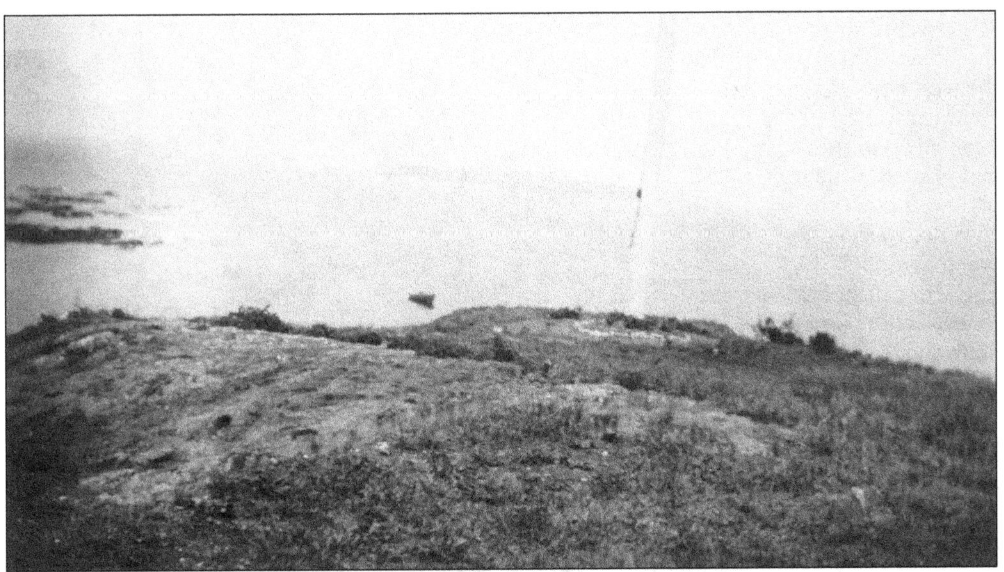

Above the seawall system is a lovely open lawn with the flagpole in the center. This was a place for the family to picnic, relax, read, and play and a great place to watch the boats coming through this part of Casco Bay to Harpswell and Freeport. It was one of the more exposed portions of Eagle Island near the residence itself and had to withstand the constant winds and weather coming in straight off the Atlantic Ocean.

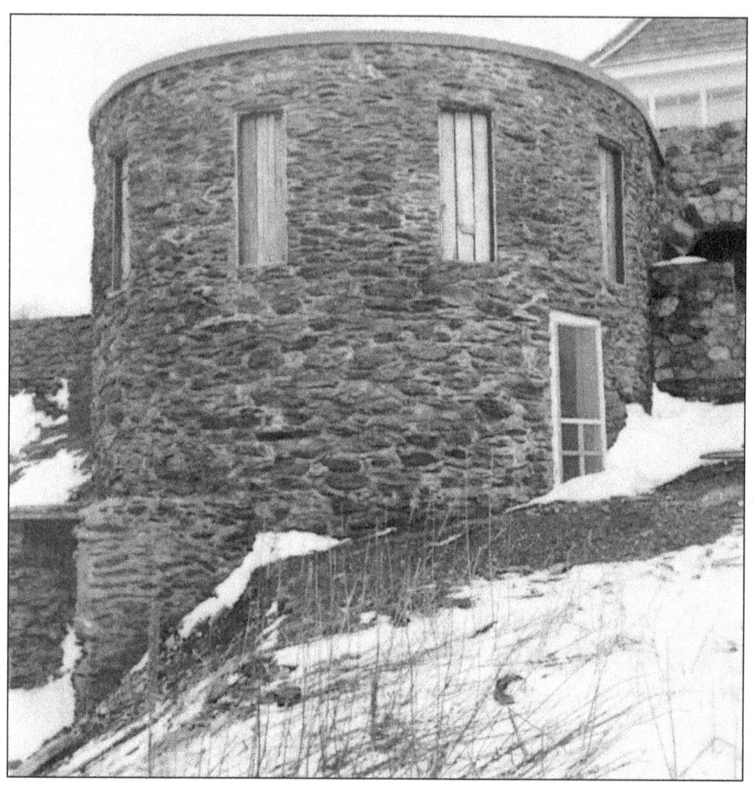

The west bastion is almost three stories high with the pump house in the base, a storage area under the library with a door level with the lawn, and the Admiral's library above. To the south of the west bastion is the stone stairway, which heads to the library towards the left and to the boardwalk towards the right. From the outside, the library windows (shown boarded-up for the winter) contrast with the house because of the decorative glass. Each opens inward, allowing the fresh sea air to circulate.

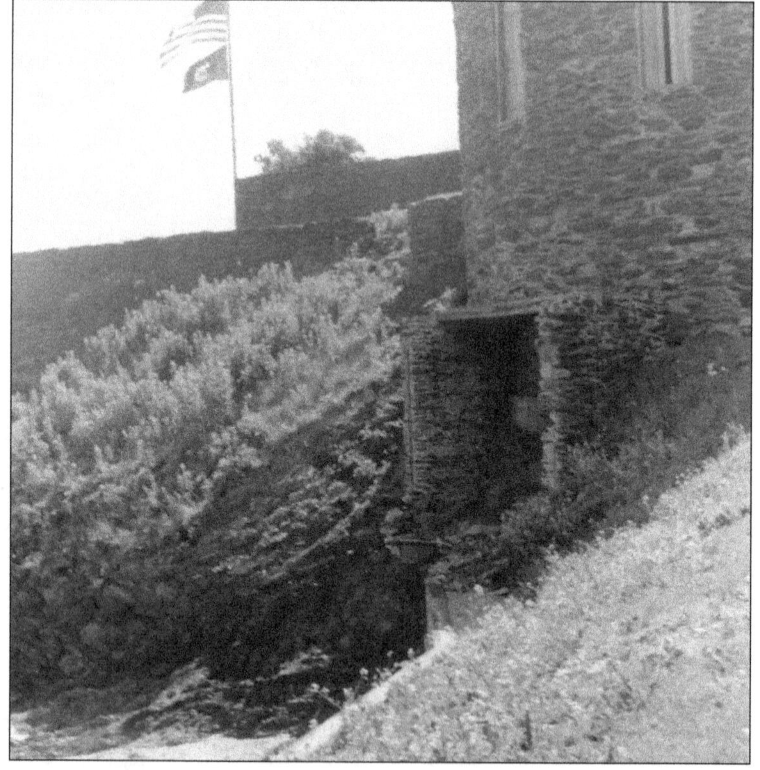

The pump house was attached to the lowest level of the west bastion. Seawater was pumped up to the main house. When no longer used, the entrance to the pump house was filled in with stones to match the bastion. With the sea air comes humidity and dampness, and since the library now holds artifacts and rare books, the storage area underneath it has been cleaned and ventilated to prevent moisture from penetrating the library through the floor.

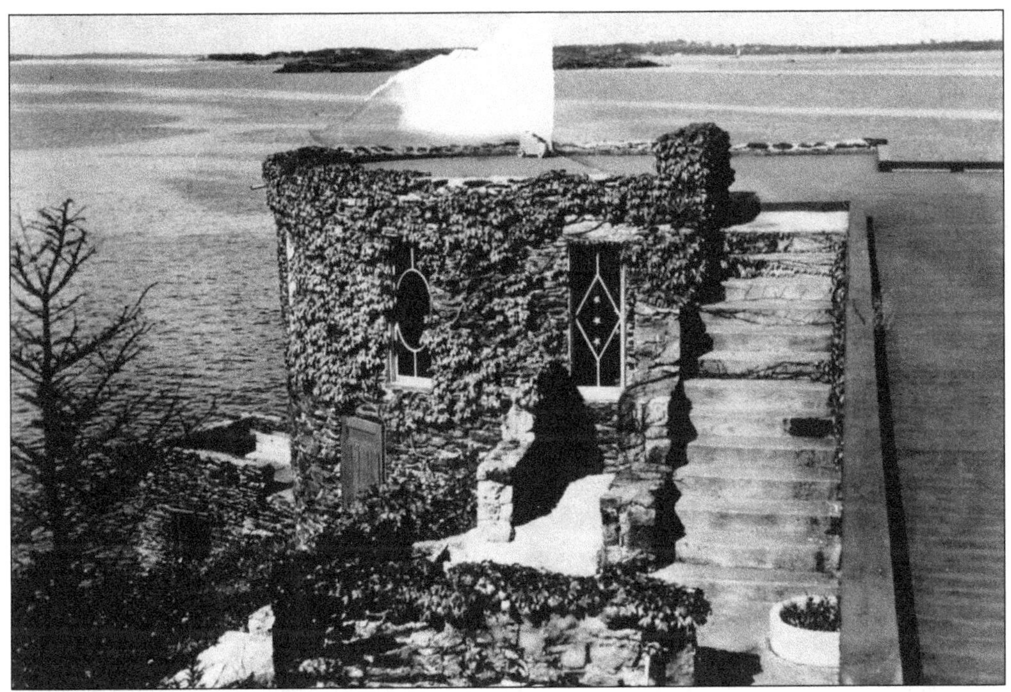

This west bastion holds Peary's library and has seven tall casement windows. The window muntins alternate between diamond and oval shapes. The smaller portions of the windows are yellow stained glass that provides a warming glow when light filters through it.

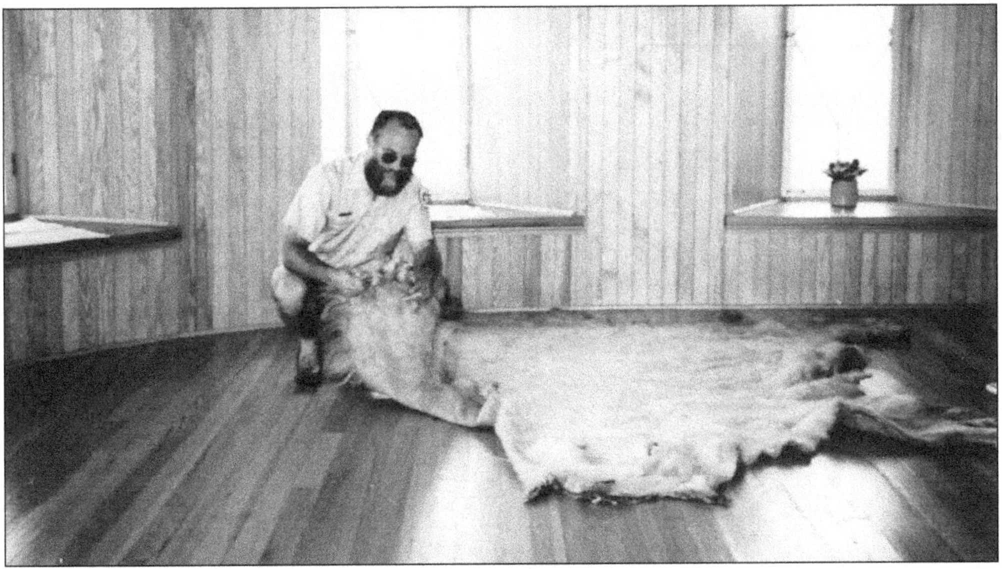

Dave Chaney, a former Eagle Island park manager, holds the polar bear pelt that was usually displayed vertically behind the Admiral's desk in the library (see page 123). This one is about eight feet wide and nine feet long but had to be destroyed due to a serious bug infestation. The polar bear pelt has since been replaced with another one that has been chemically treated to protect it from bugs and weather. It is displayed horizontally in the library to avoid sagging and gives visitors a better idea of the immense size of these animals.

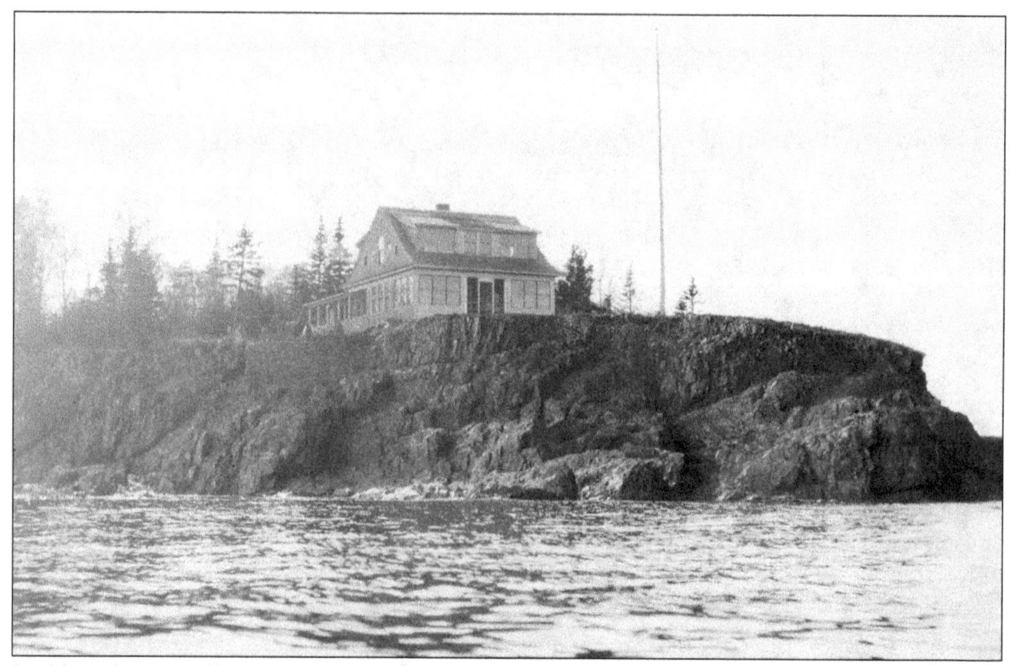

Building the seawall system, including the east and west bastions, began around 1906. Here, two stone masons are building the east bastion walls. This must have been a slow, tedious process. The other improvements to the house that are pictured here are the gables added to the roof and the ell at the back of the house to include a much-needed kitchen. Still, the original cottage is the center, or keystone, of the house.

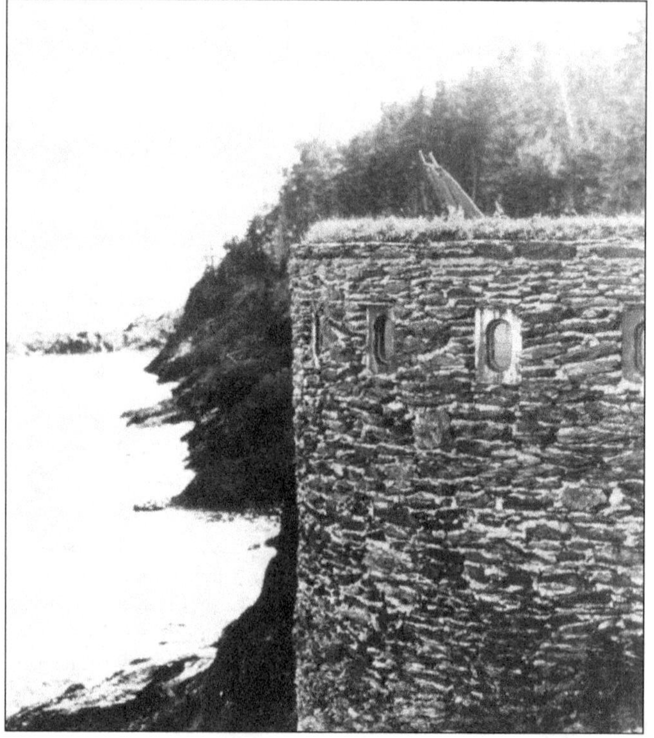

After improvements to the house proper were completed, Peary finished the east and west bastions. The east bastion had small oval panes of glass mounted in wood frames like portholes on a ship. It is semicircular with the top of the bastion floor level with the house. The roof was made of a wooden frame over steel beams and covered with sod. The design is quite different from the west bastion because it faced more extreme conditions from severe ocean storms. The east bastion windows faced the sea and allowed light to penetrate this structure. The east bastion was used initially to store artifacts and equipment from the Arctic. The sledge on the roof was one such artifact.

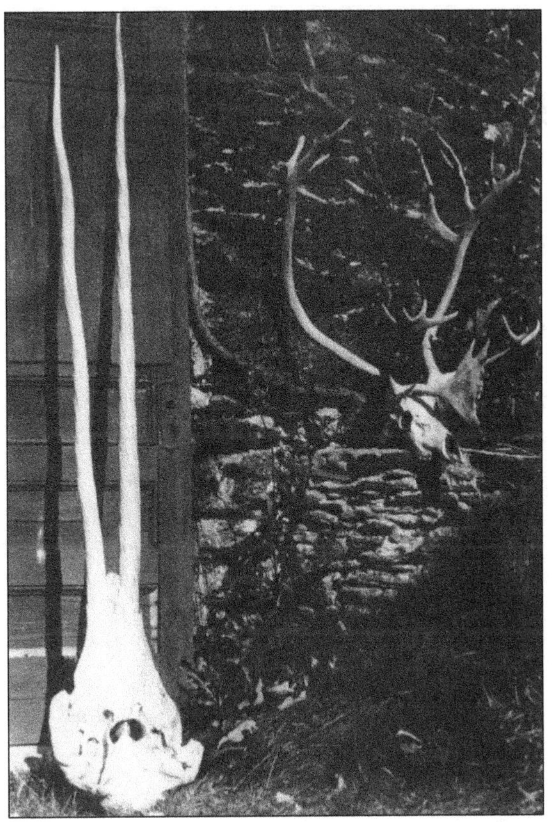

Artifacts and souvenirs from Peary's Arctic trips ranged from clothing to weapons to animal furs to trophies, such as these two items. Antlers were a popular item to display, but having a narwhal skull with "two" tusks was extremely rare. A narwhal is a medium-sized toothed whale that lives in the Arctic waters off the east coast of Greenland. Usually, the canine tooth on the left side of the upper jaw becomes a tusk. The tusk grows throughout the narwhal's life and reaches lengths of 4 to 10 feet and typically weighs around 20 pounds, is hollow, and forms a spiral shape. Shown below on the east bastion is one of Peary's sledges.

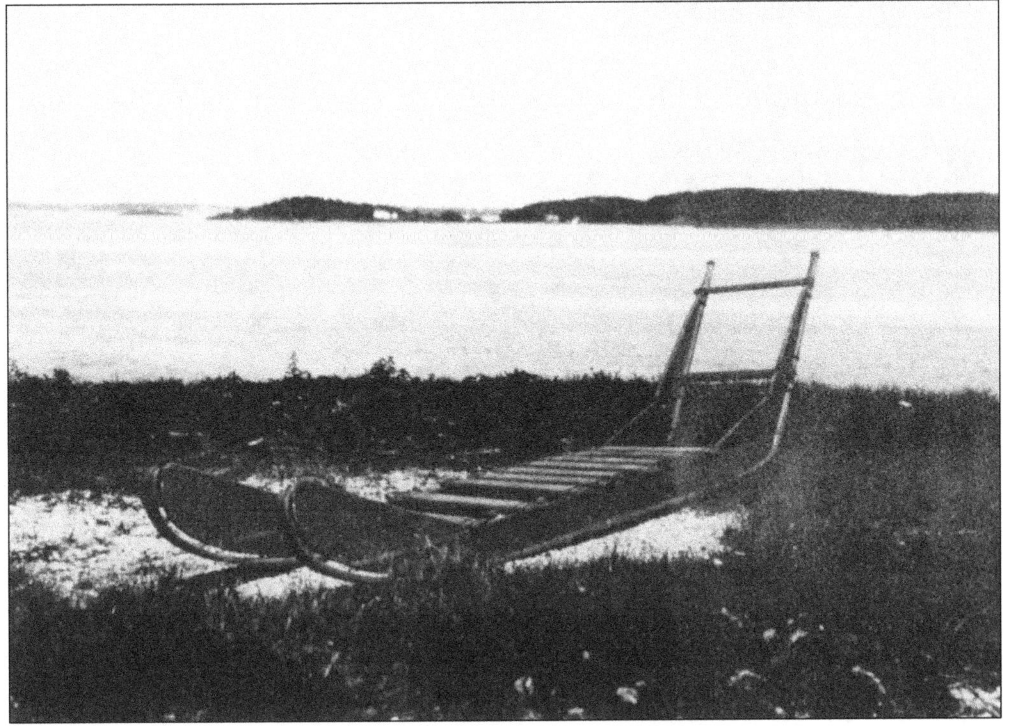

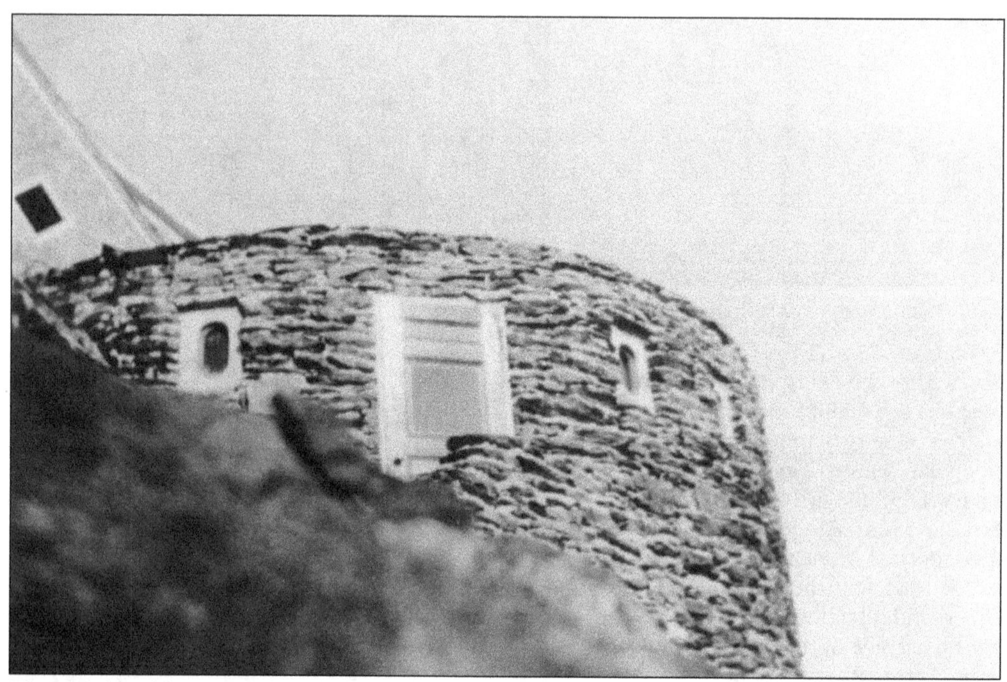

The final build-out of the east bastion included heavy panes of glass in windows resembling portholes and a solid, single-light door. The bastion bore the brunt of the ocean's weather and therefore was very sturdily built. Despite this, all that remains of the east bastion are the walls as depicted in the photograph below.

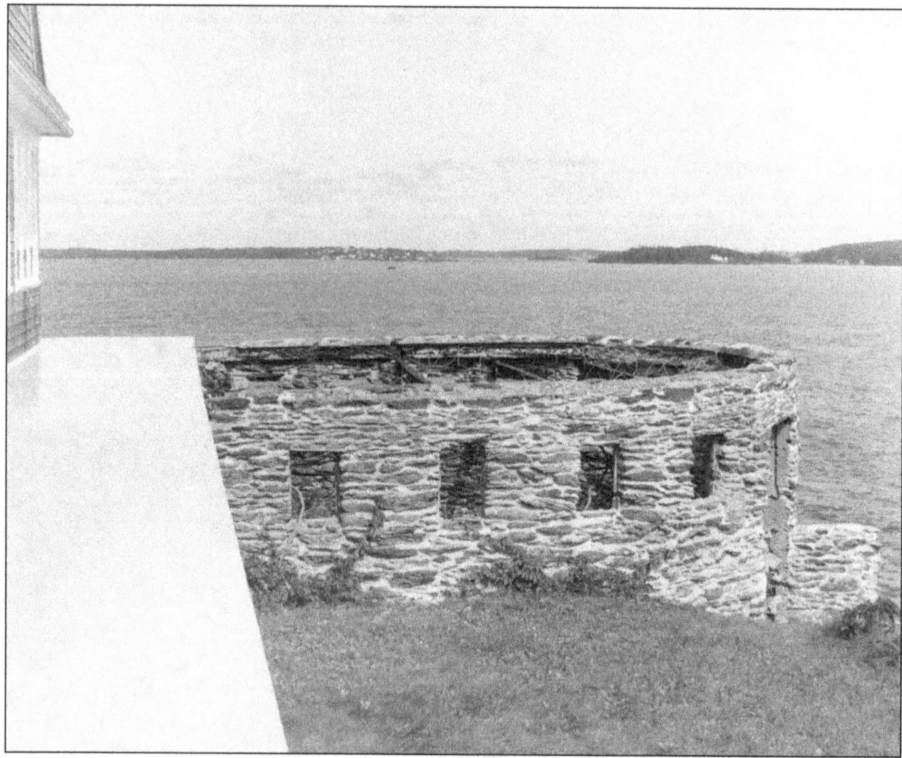

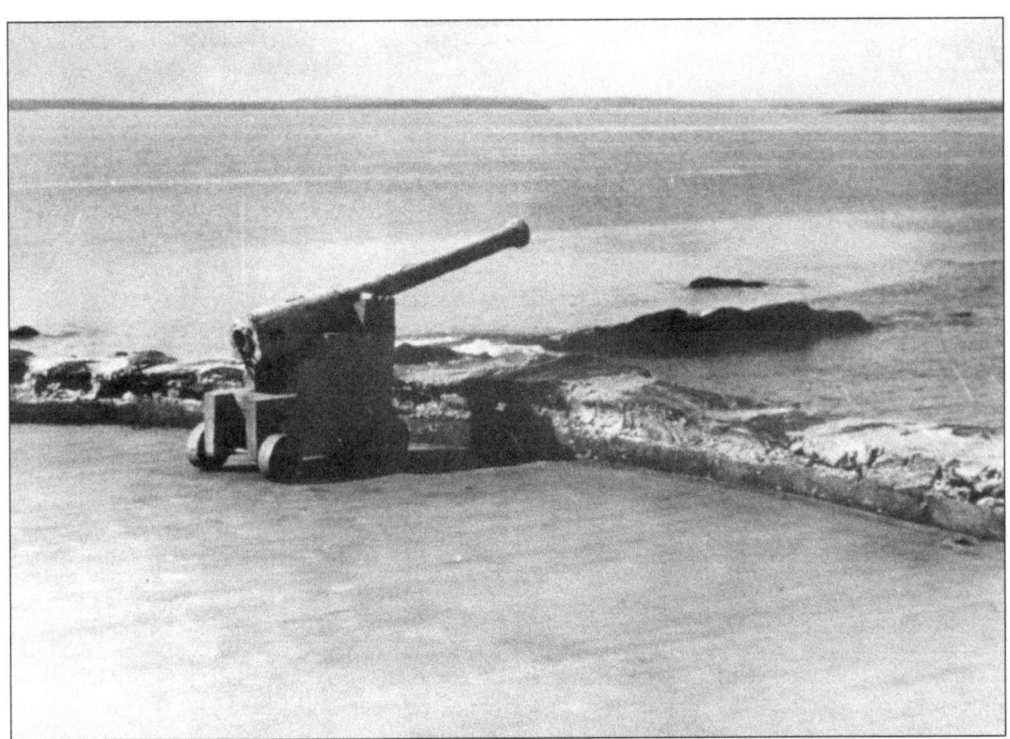

Every summer the Admiral was on Eagle Island, this Spanish swivel cannon was mounted to the west bastion roof. On the north bastion, the eagle displayed below was affixed every summer as well. The eagle sculpture is now on display in the library in the west bastion of the house.

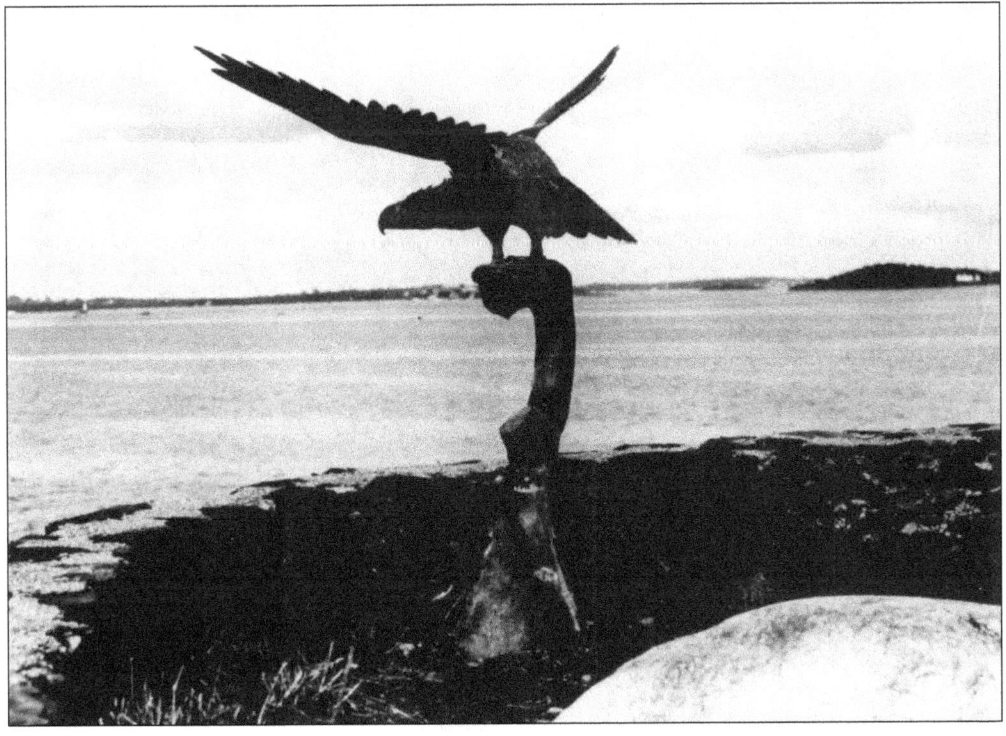

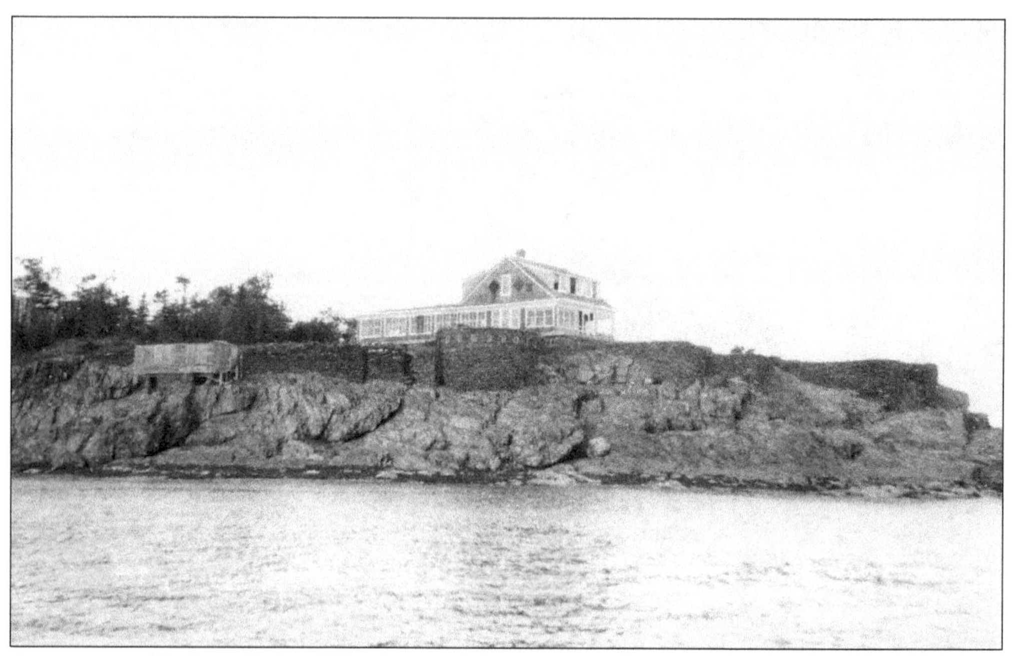

As mentioned before, the small kitchen and dining room, about 20 feet by 36 feet and added in 1906, was removed from the house, moved back about 200 feet, and secured on the east side of the island. This structure was called "the Igloo" by the family.

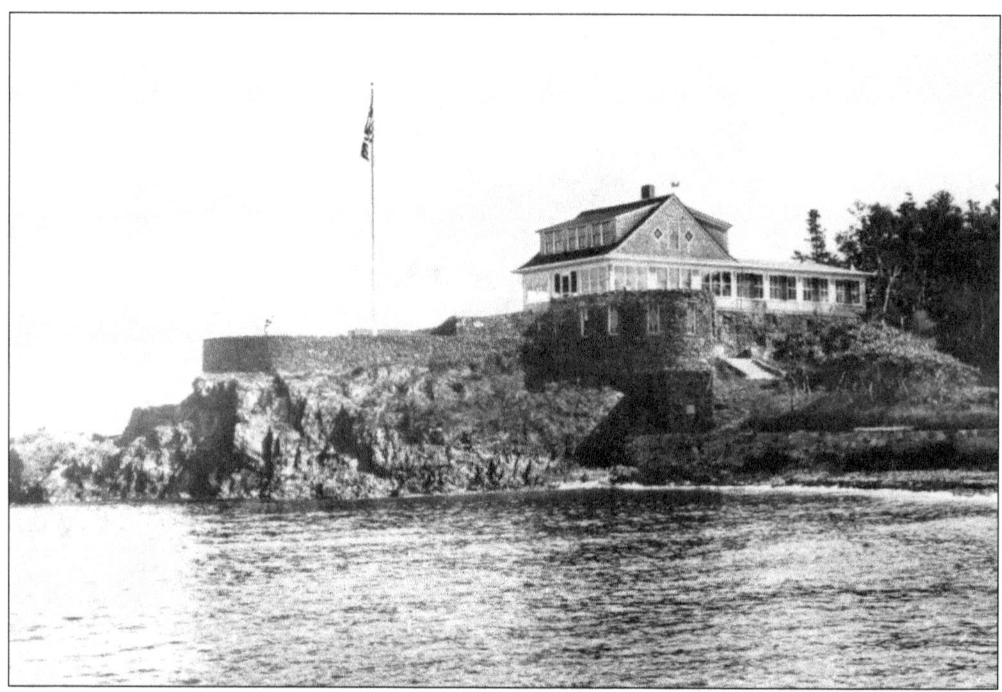

Because the stonework used in the foundation of the house is built in part with island rocks, it makes the house appear to rise out of the rocks. The turret-like bastions and the seawalls make the house appear almost like a castle.

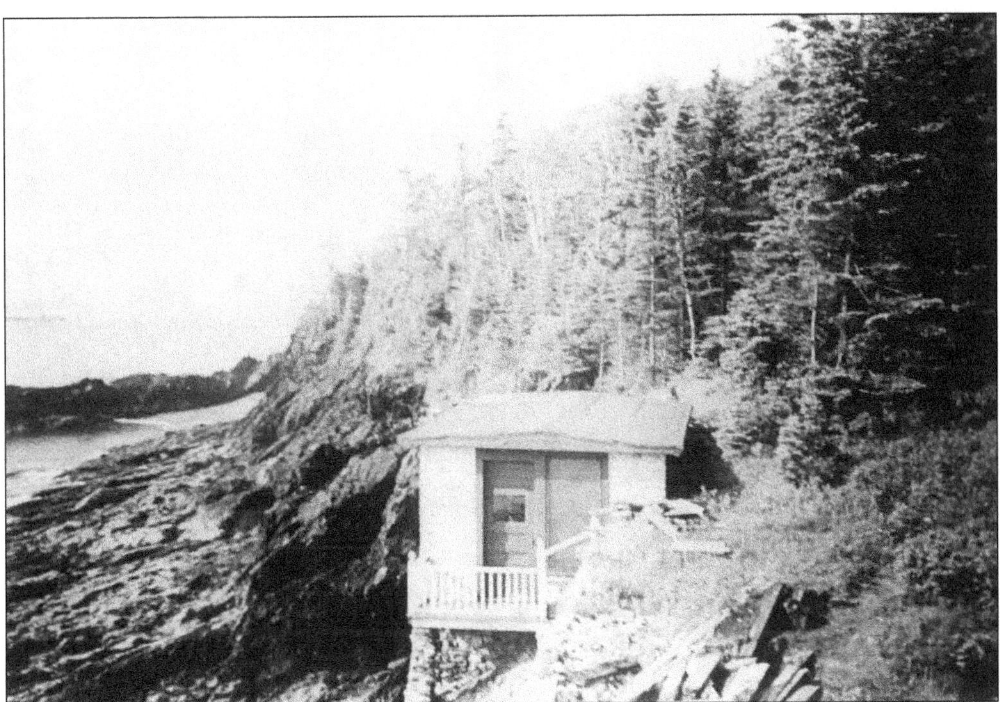

The Igloo, seen here in the summertime, sat perched on a narrow ledge facing the thundering force of the Atlantic Ocean. Never having heat or electricity, the Igloo was a rustic yet exciting place to spend an evening.

The Igloo initially was the first ell added to the house in 1906. During the 1912 expansion took place, the ell was removed from the house largely intact. Attached to the rock face on the east side of Eagle Island just behind the house, it served for years as a guesthouse. Eventually, it was in such a state of disrepair, it was allowed to fall into the sea. Here is a photograph of the Igloo late in the season and boarded up for the winter. Visible is a small rock support tower holding the Igloo in place.

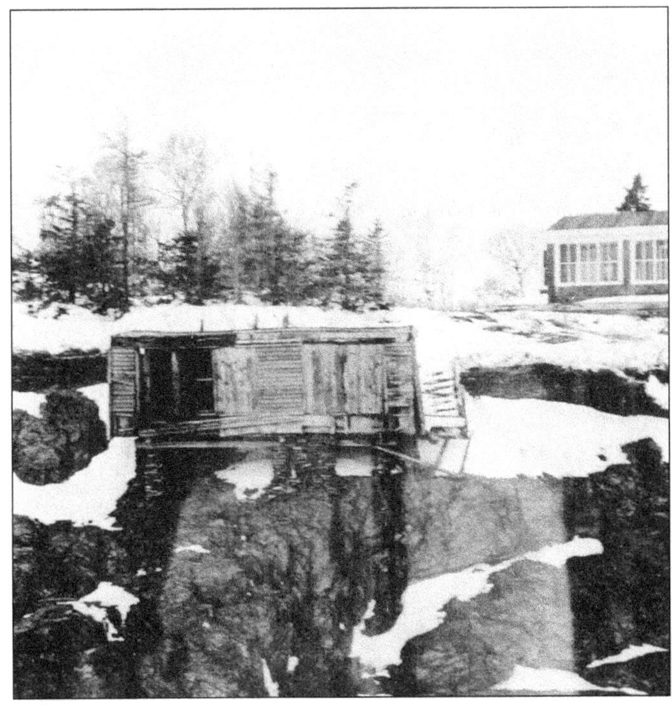

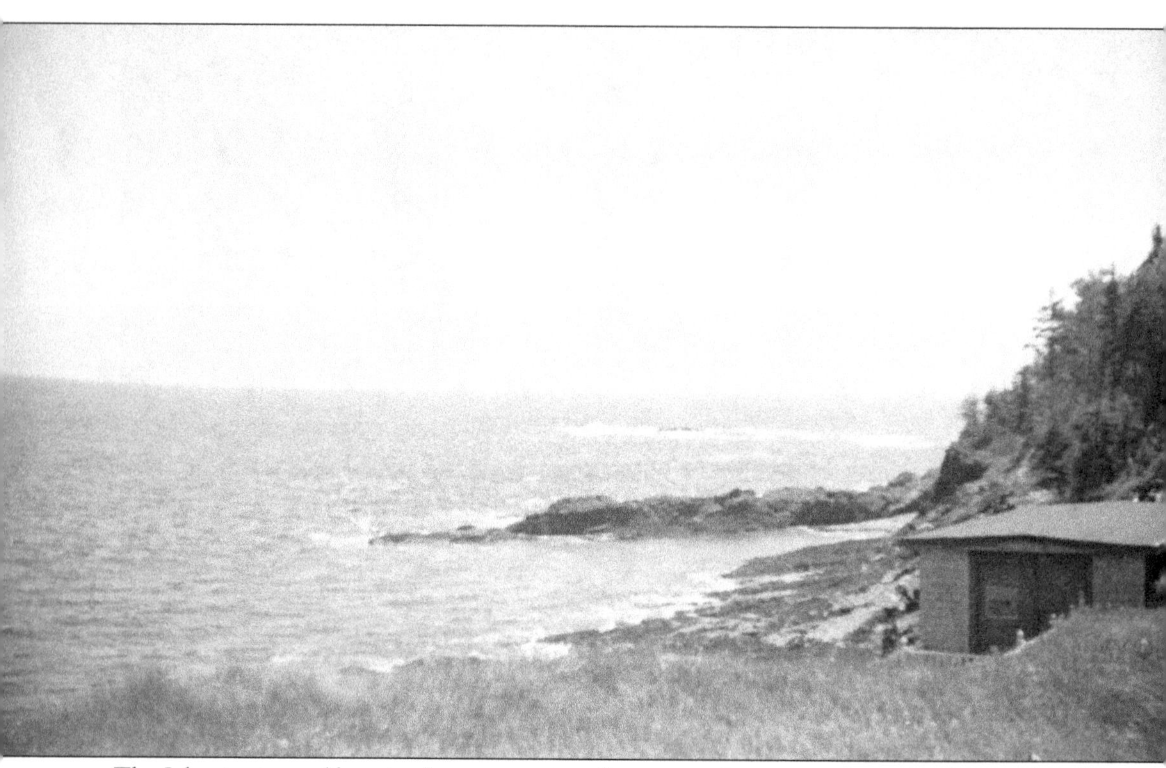

The Igloo is pictured here in the summertime. Imagine waking up to this view. Geographically, just behind the Igloo was the black forest where the Admiral would sit and read. South of the Igloo is a small protected beach that the family frequented. In between the two is a cave that penetrates over 20 feet into the rock ledge.

The kitchen spans the entire width of the house and has windows and doors on the east and west walls. On the north wall is a cast-iron stove made in Portland, Maine, by the makers of the Queen Atlantic. On either side of the stove are built-in cabinets.

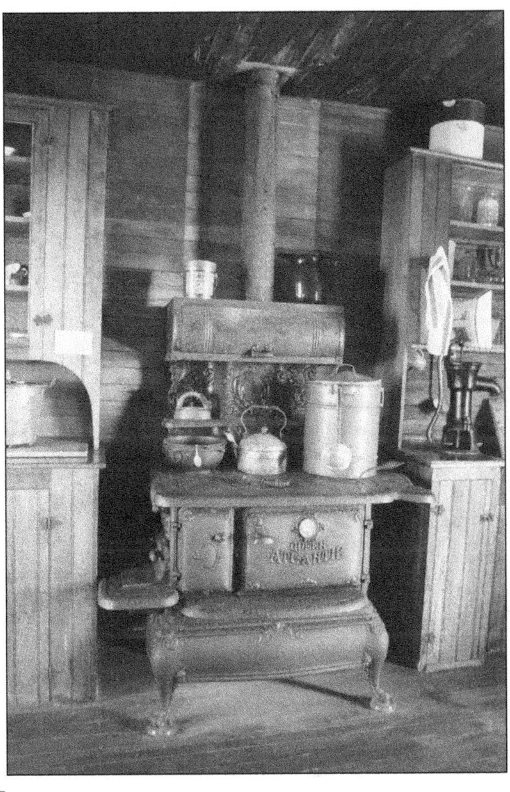

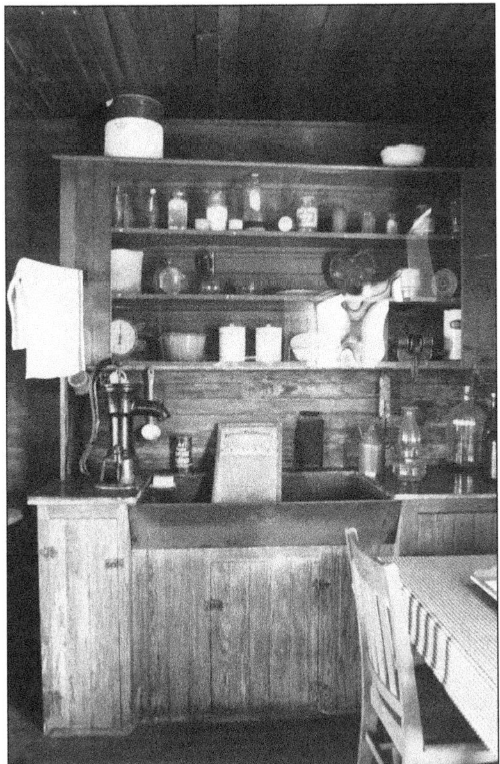

The stone sink to the right of the stove was made by the Portland-Monson Slate Company. Water from the cistern in the basement was brought up using the hand pump.

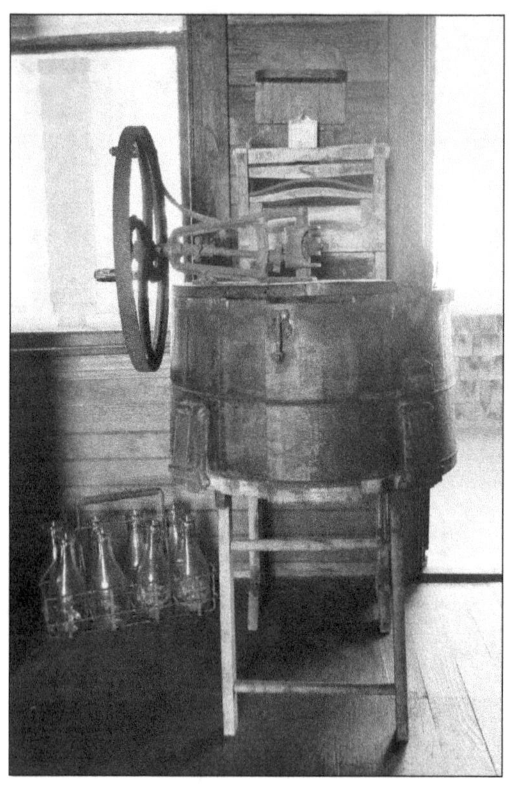

The washer was composed of the large wooden barrel (left) and the wooden framed stand with ringers attached (below). The soapy water was agitated by turning the large wheel to the left side. The clothes were then rinsed in fresh water the same way and then pressed through the back ringers before being hung to dry.

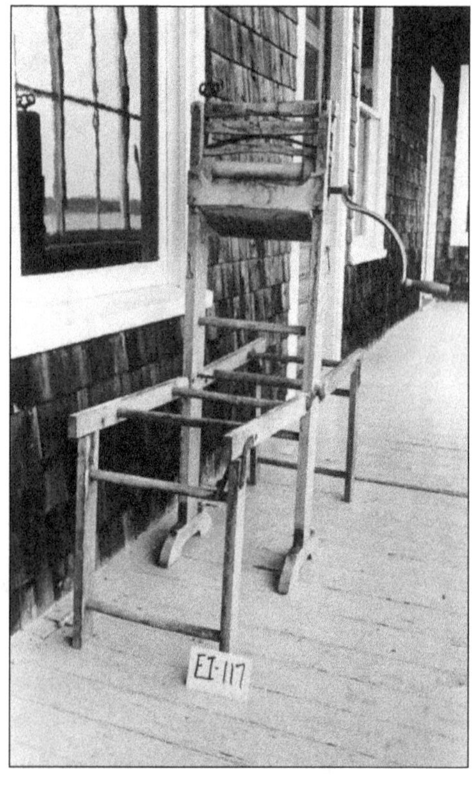

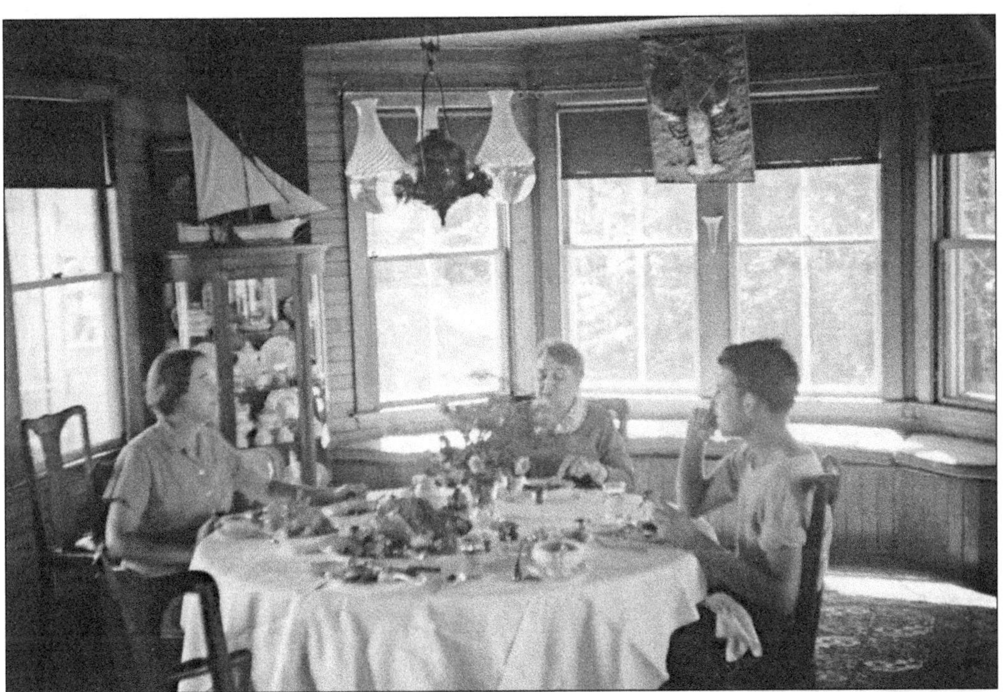

Josephine, Marie, and Robert Jr. are enjoying a meal in the formal dining room. Above them is a three-globe kerosene lamp. As in virtually the entire house, the walls, and ceiling are all made of southern yellow pine and floors of Douglas fir. Three of the four walls in the dining room had windows. The bay window in the background, allowing the southern sunlight to pour in, has a wide window seat in front of it. The sidewalls have windows that open to the glassed-in east and west porches. The north wall of the dining room has two matching built-in corner china cabinets. The Chippendale-style pediments are one of the few things at odds with the Craftsman style of the rest of the house and make the cabinets stand out.

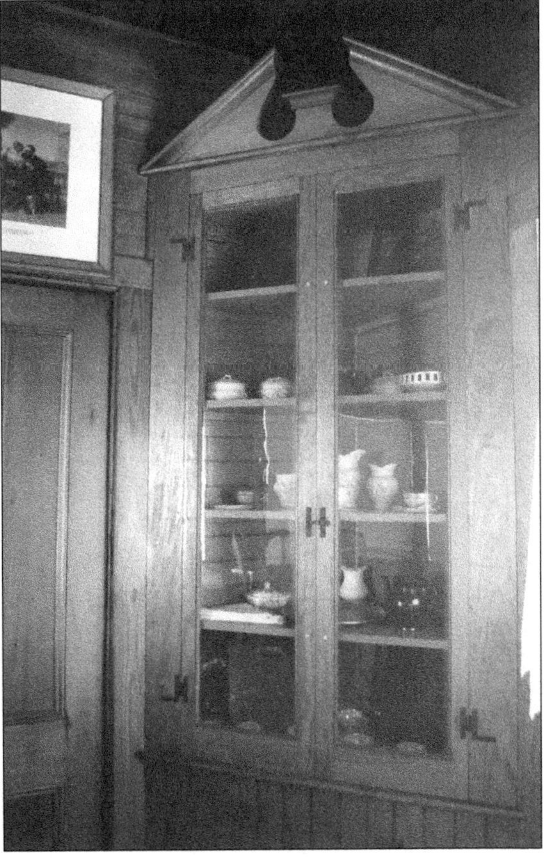

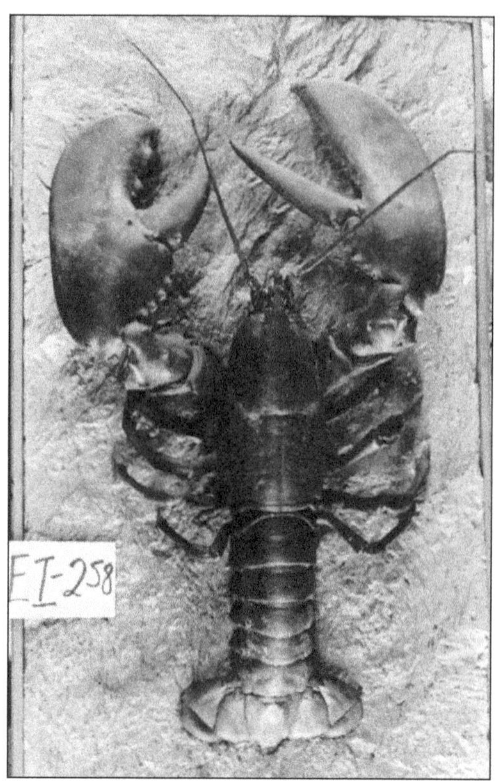

The dining room is decorated with this mounted 20-pound lobster. Legend is that the lobster was caught not in a trap, but holding on to the outside of the trap. To clean the shell, Admiral Peary set the lobster on top of an anthill and allowed the ants to remove any remaining meat and tissue.

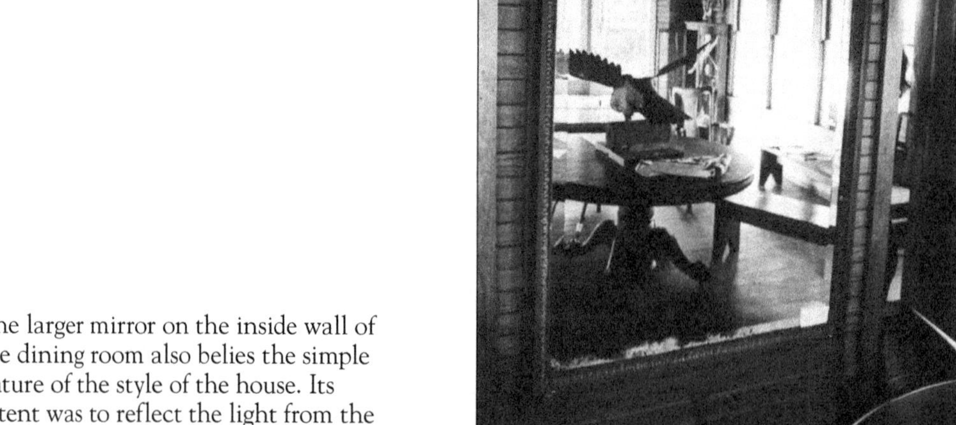

The larger mirror on the inside wall of the dining room also belies the simple nature of the style of the house. Its intent was to reflect the light from the southern end of the room's bay windows.

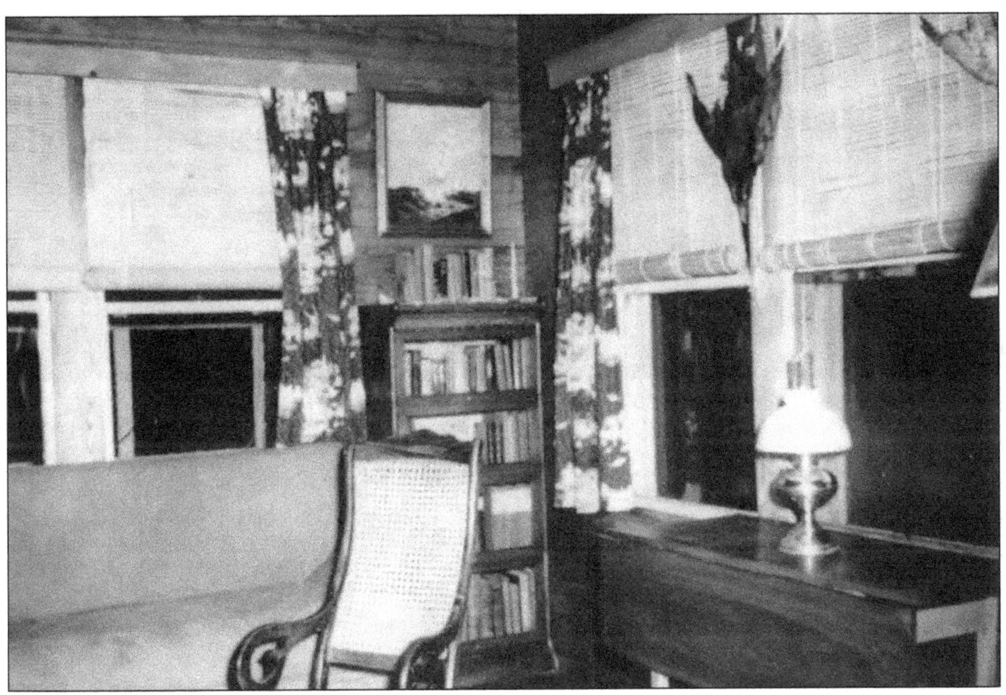

The living room was a central gathering place at night for the family. With the fireplace (see next page), it was the warmest room in the house, but it also had a graphophone for entertainment. This is a large but relaxing and comfortable room with plenty of books to read and many of the Admiral's artifacts and stuffed birds on display.

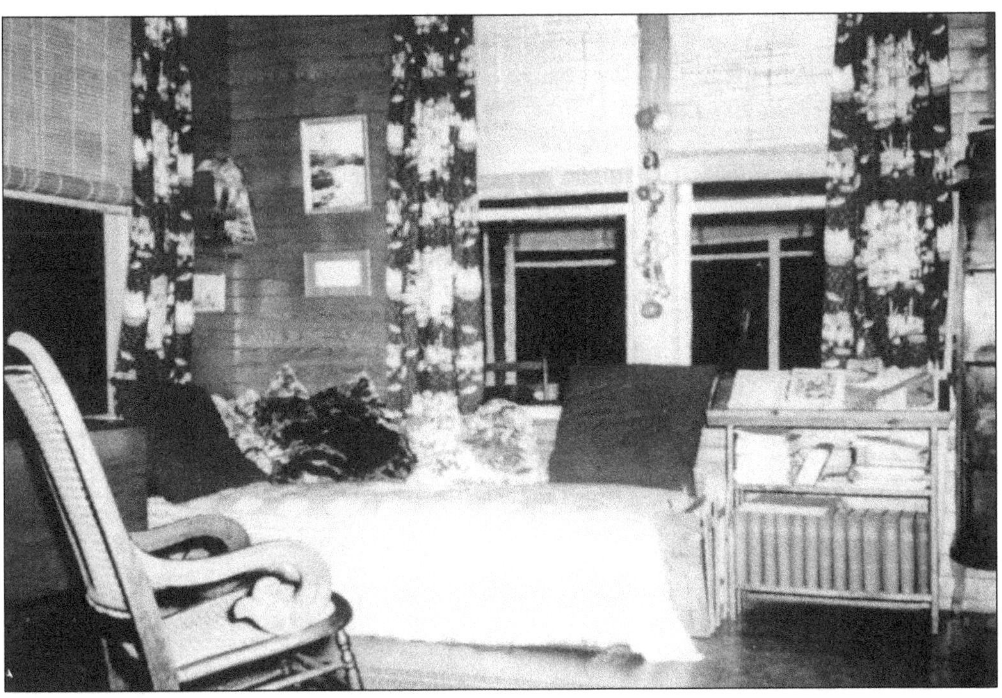

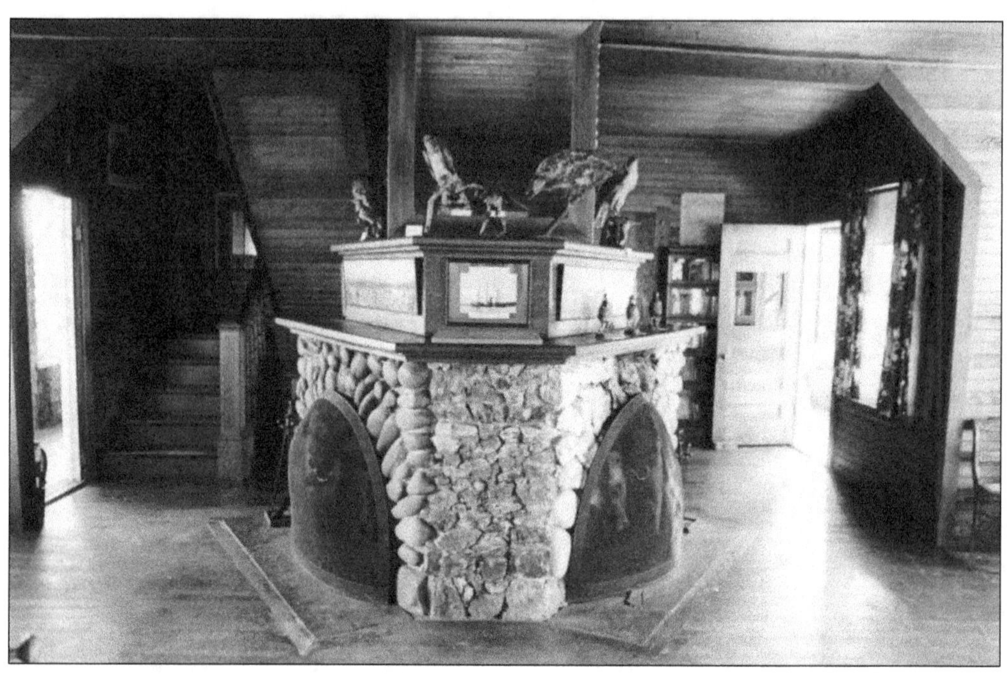

There are three round arched-top hearths to this fireplace in the living room. Two of the hearths are faced with smooth stones, while the third is the same granite stone used in the foundation of the house. Double mahogany mantels on all sides of the fireplace hold birds that were preserved by Peary, who was a skilled taxidermist. The sketch below shows Peary's original ideas for the living room and the placement of this peculiar fireplace. (Below, courtesy of GJMBC.)

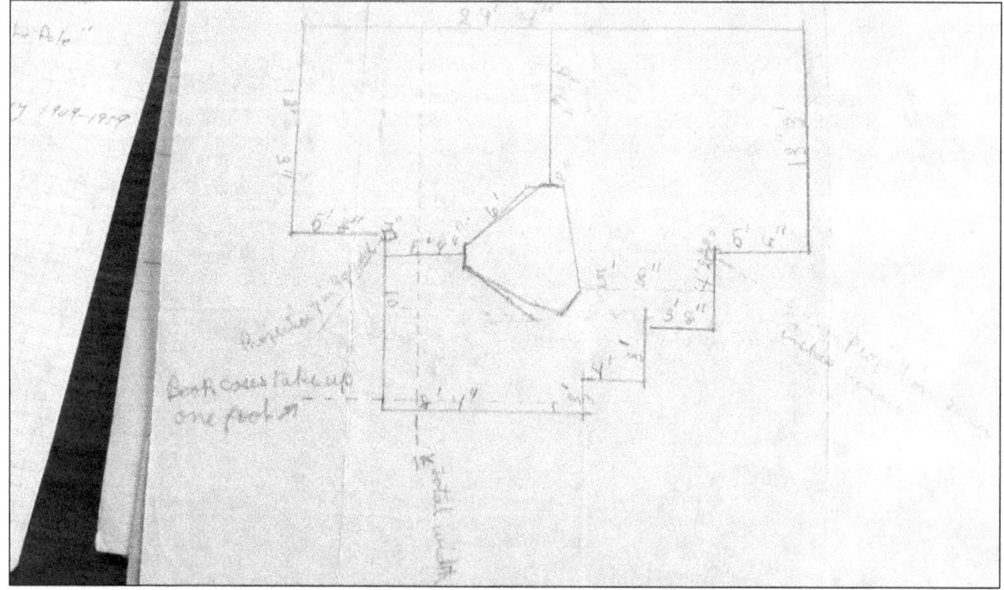

May 30 -1-

Dear Sir;

I prefer the arch ~~pattern~~ style of fireplace shown on the enclosed postal.

Referring to our conversation of a few days ago, & your statement of the cost of various fireplaces & chimneys built by you, I will ~~make~~ give you $150 - for an ornamental stone fireplace & brick chimney as per the following particulars you to furnish all material & labor except the ornamental stone which latter I will furnish & deliver at the cottage.

These two photographs show a letter from the Admiral to the masons who were going to construct the three-hearth fireplace. One can see in this letter, dated May 30 (around 1910–1912), and the drawing on the previous page that he had very specific ideas for this fireplace. (Both, courtesy of GJMBC.)

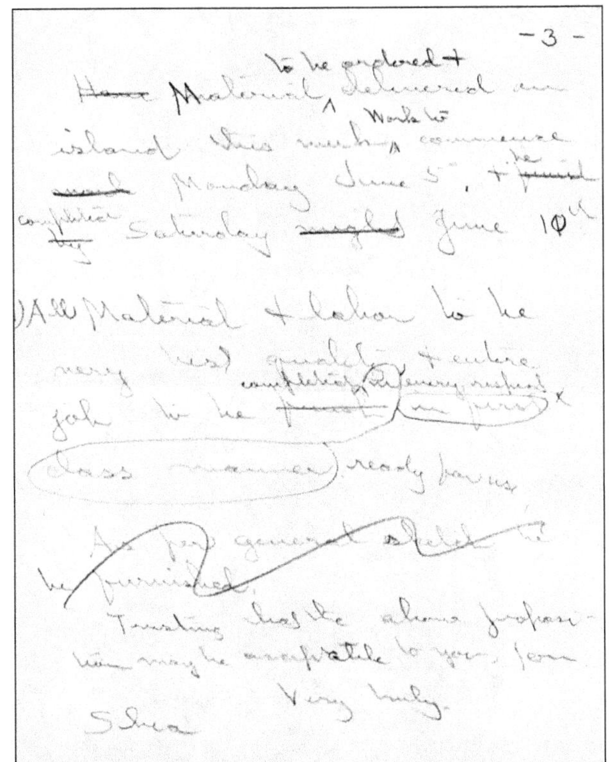

-3-

~~Have~~ Material to be explored & delivered on island this week Work to commence ~~week~~ Monday June 5th, & be ~~finished~~ completed by Saturday ~~night~~ June 10th

All Material & labor to be very best quality & entire job to be ~~finished~~ completed in every respect in first class manner ready for use

~~As per general sketch to be furnished.~~

Trusting that the above proposition may be acceptable to you, I am

Very truly

Shea

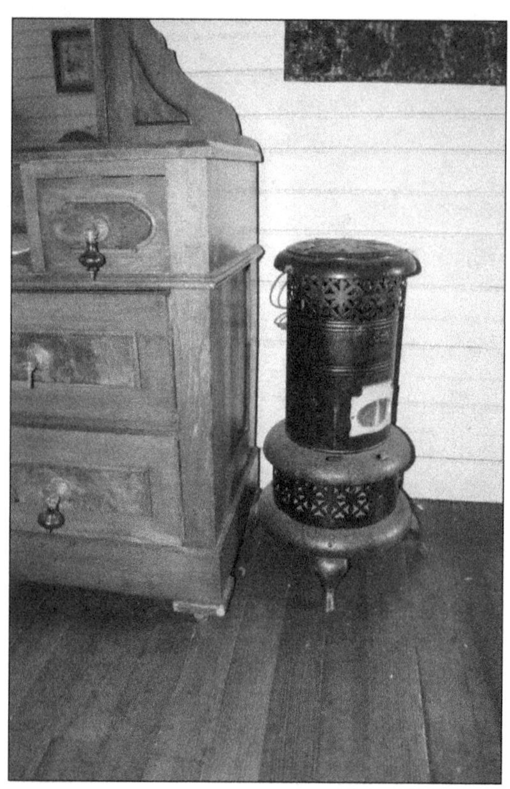

At left, small heaters in each of the upstairs rooms kept the bedrooms warm. Below, the Admiral's desk chair sits in what was once Marie's bedroom and later a guest room.

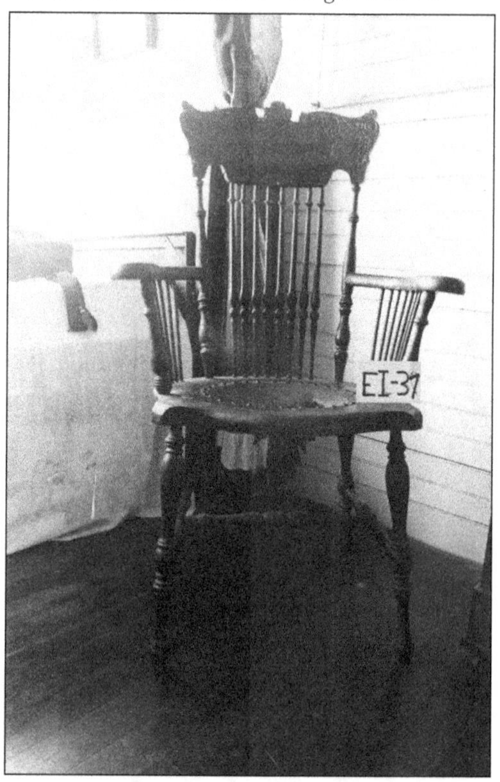

Diamond-shaped windows were uniformly built into the east and west sides of the second story. Their large center pane of glass let in considerable light and the surrounding smaller yellow-glass panes created a warm glow.

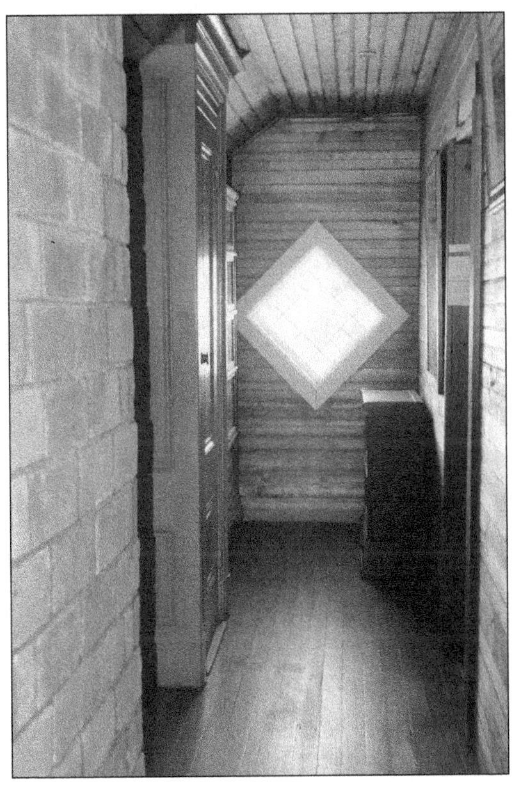

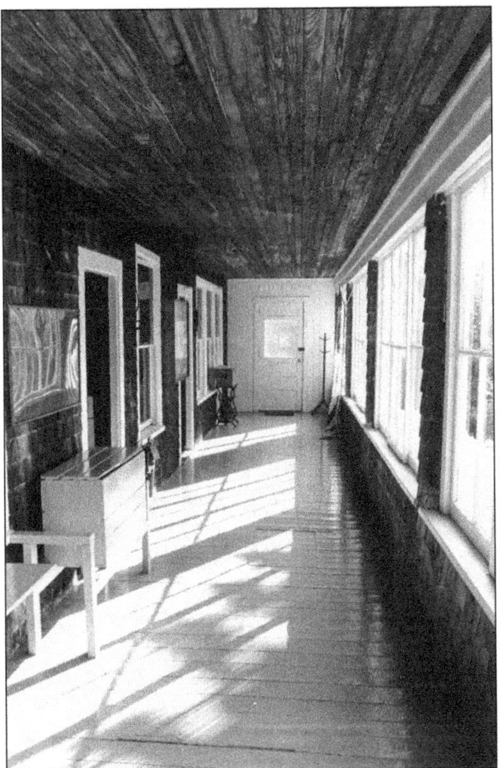

Open side porches were initially added to the house as early as 1906. Glassed-in porches run the full length of the west and east sides of the house.

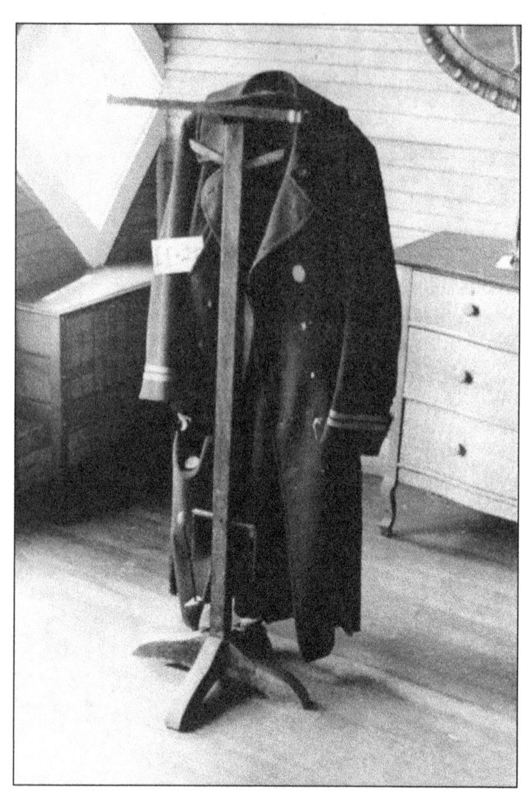

Admiral Peary's formal bridge coat is now in a protected glass case and is on display in his bedroom on the second floor of the house. Below, this men's dressing table is quite an elaborate piece of furniture for its day. The lid closes to provide a smooth surface for writing.

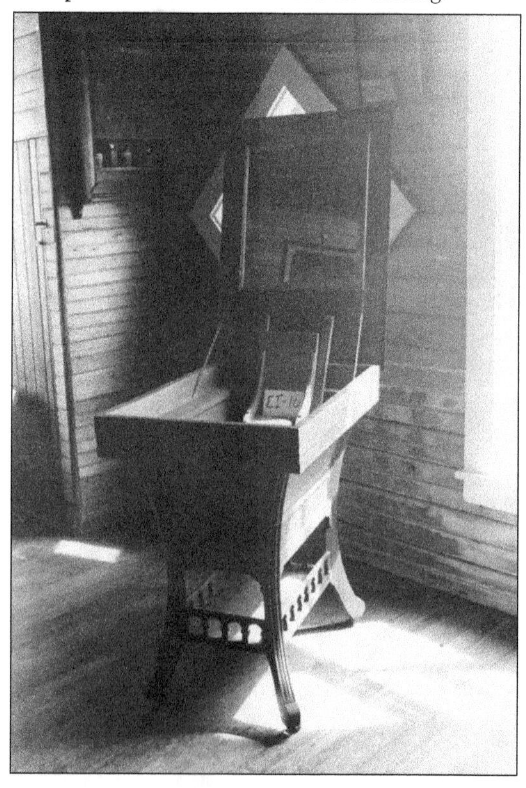

Books are plentiful throughout the Peary household on Eagle Island. A library of over 800 books remains on the island today. Titles range from *Anne of Green Gables* to books and journals about mixing concrete and bridge building. Admiral Peary was studious and read everything he could on whatever subject matter he was pursuing.

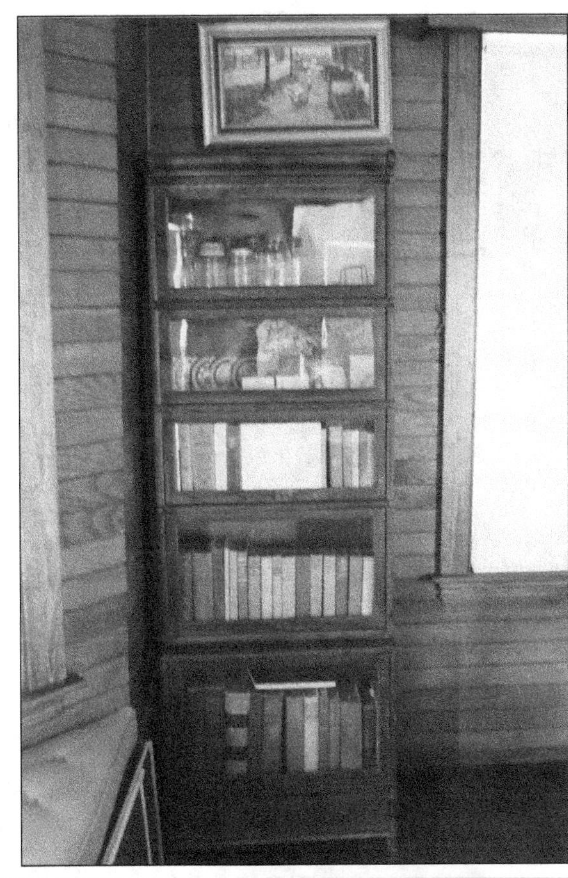

Imagine being tucked away in this bed as a child on a stormy summer's night with the waves crashing just outside the window and being read to by mother or an aunt or a big sister. These are the spaces in this cottage that make it a home. The children's room is full of books and games. This window over the bed faces the east, and the first light of day would pour in to wake them up to another day on Eagle Island.

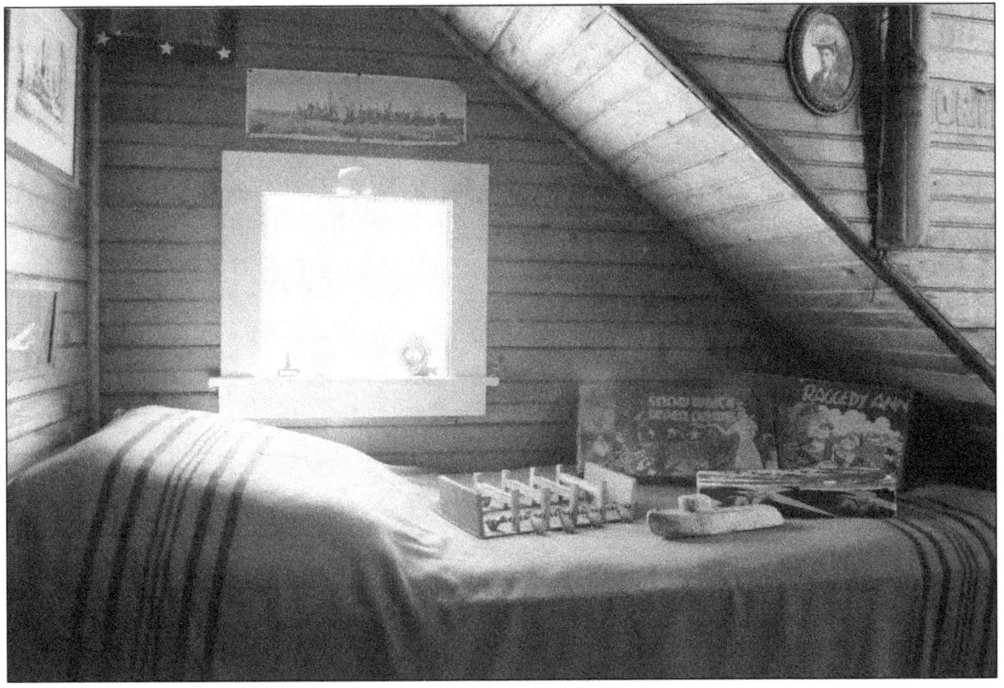

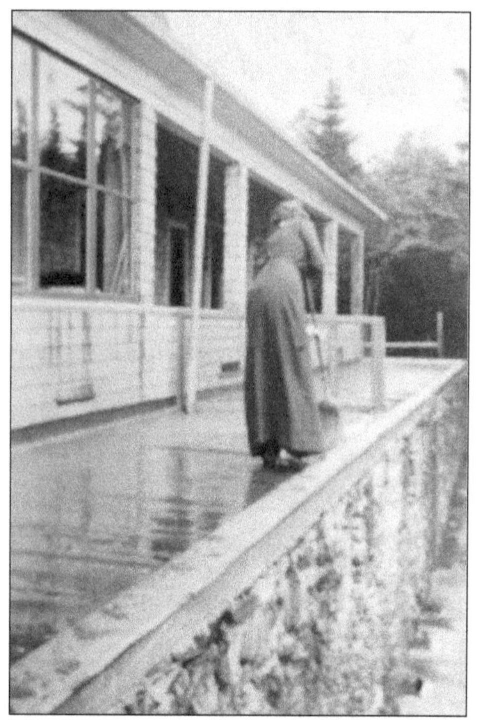

Josephine is pictured here performing what had to be a regular chore at the cottage—swabbing the deck, as the saying goes. With birds constantly overhead and dogs of many sorts running around Eagle Island, the deck got its fair share of dirt and grime. Also note in this picture that porch columns are shingled like the side of the house, and the drainpipe in the middle of the image would direct rainwater from gutters into a cistern in the basement.

This photograph is of the wild rose, *Rosa rugosa*, which is quintessentially Maine and frequently found along coastal beaches, edging sand dunes and beach grass. It adds a natural beauty to the largely green landscape of the island.

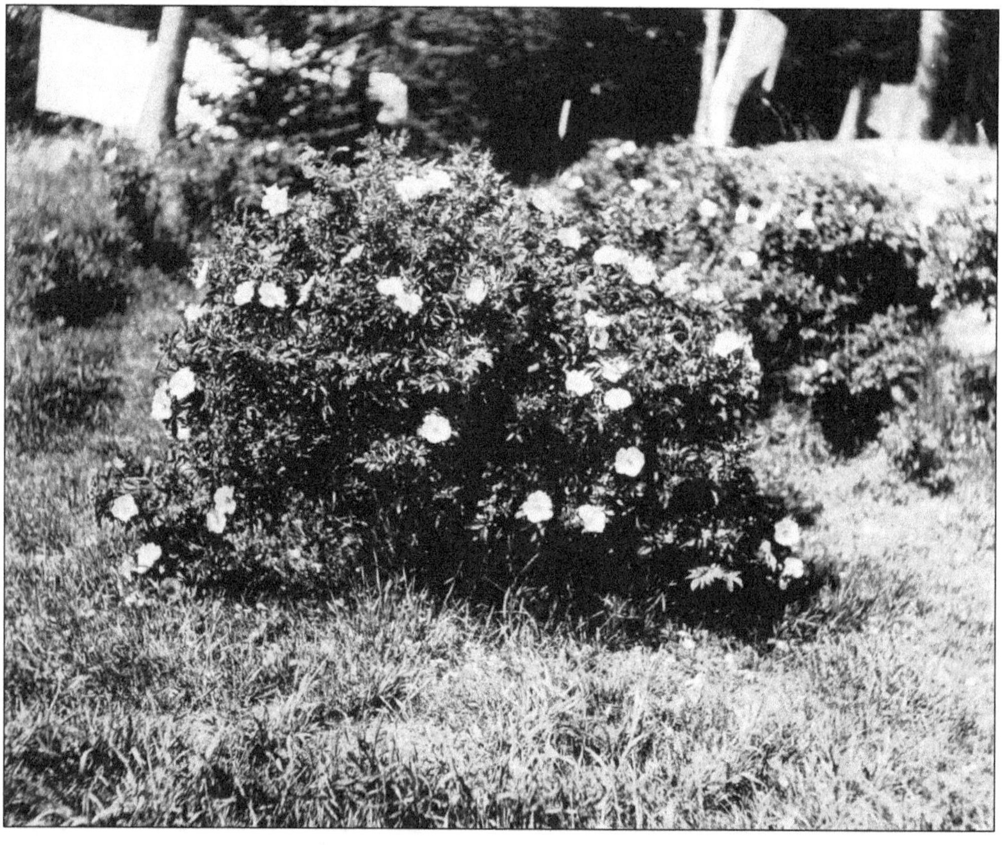

Five

The Middle Years

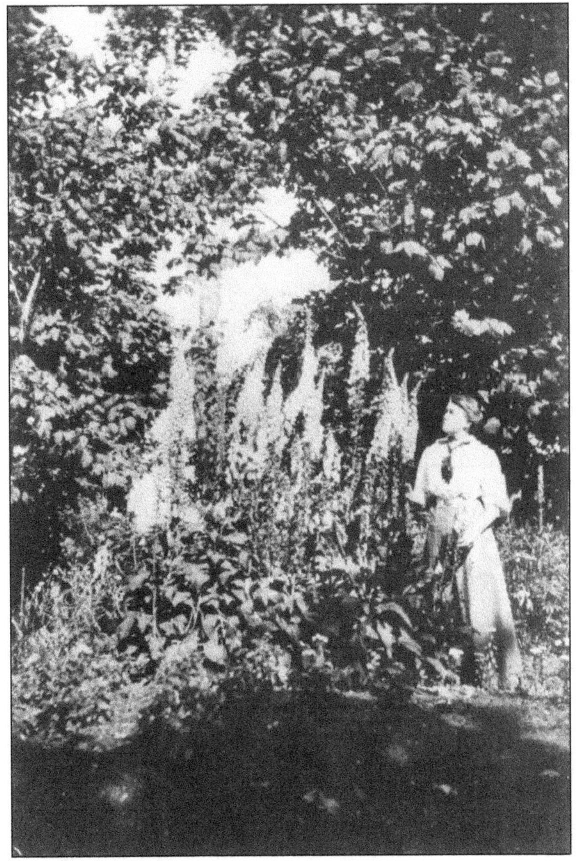

Josephine Peary was known for her love of flowers and gardening. Here, about 1915, Josephine stands by a tall stand of foxglove she planted. Walking the trails today, one might find foxglove all over the island in single blooms or little bunches. Several of Josephine's original small gardens remain on the island, along with gardens planted by Marie and Inez, Robert Peary Jr.'s wife. The gardens are diligently cared for and preserved by park managers and the Friends of Peary's Eagle Island.

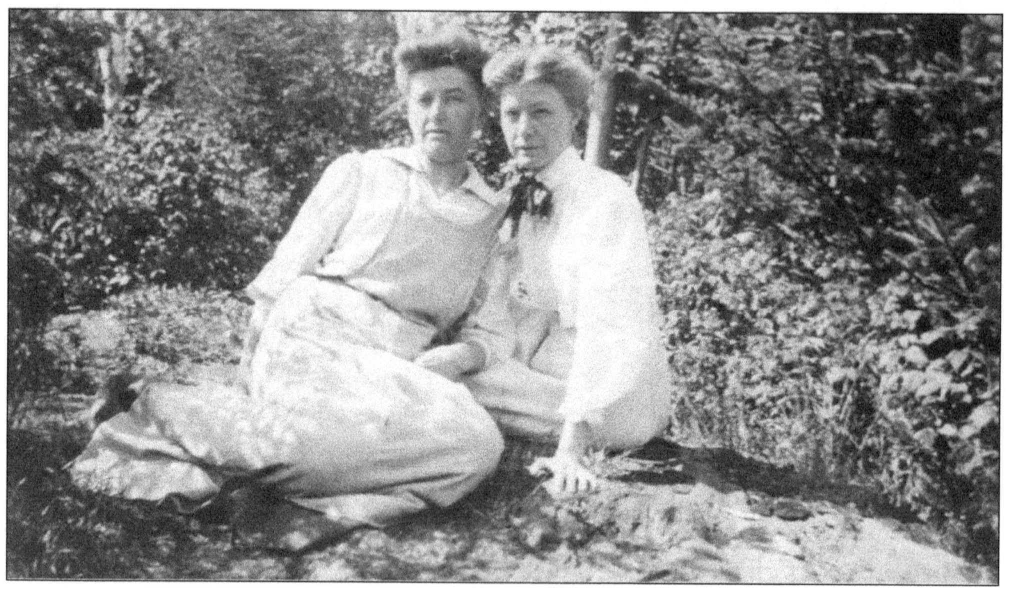

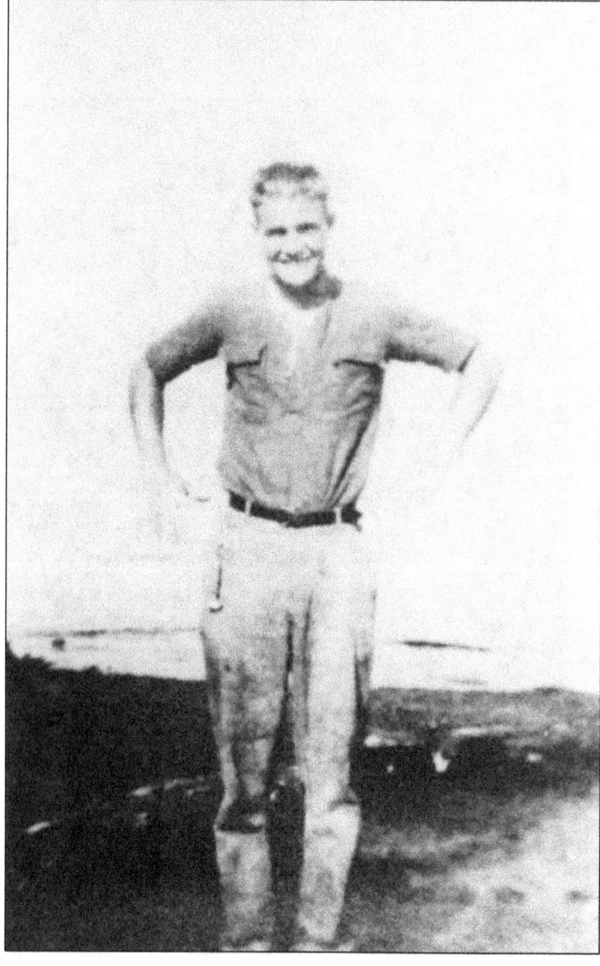

Josephine's sisters were often on Eagle Island and, as mentioned before, helped with the children and the many chores on an island, as well as offering solace and companionship during those summers when the Admiral was in the Arctic. Here, Josephine (left) is with her sister Marie Flora Diebitsch, whom they called "Tod." At left is Josephine's nephew Herman Diebitsch, visiting Eagle Island in 1922. He is seen in his working clothes, pitching in on whatever the project was during his visit.

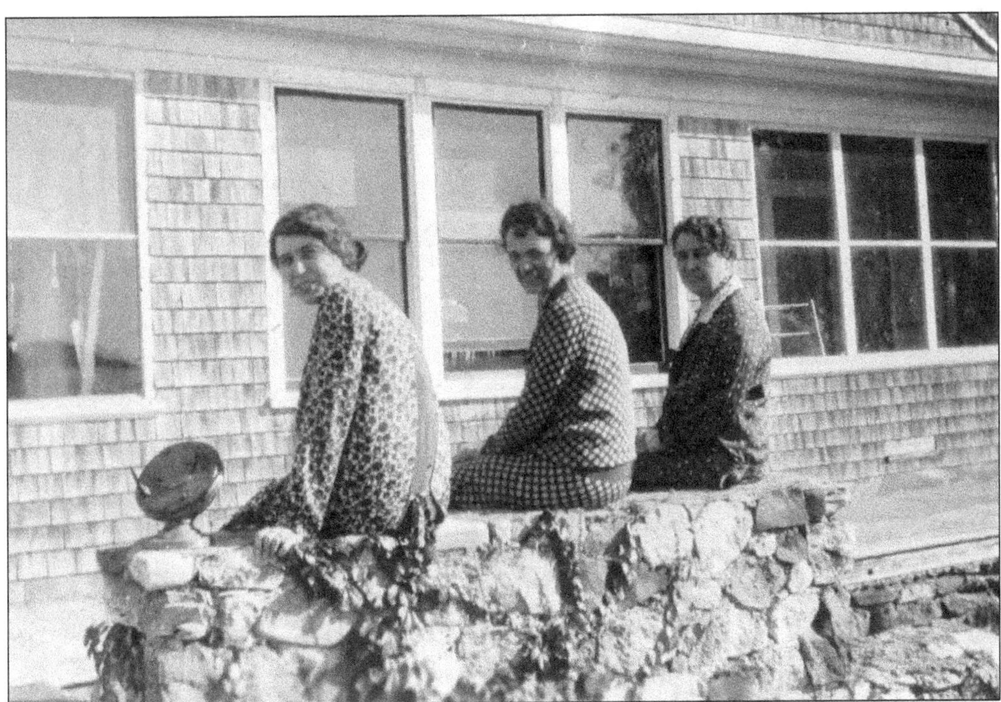

Marie (right) and her mother (left) were often entertaining visitors to Eagle Island. Here, they and an unidentified visitor are perched on part of the rock wall that edges the top of the west bastion where the Admiral had his library. (Courtesy of MAPUNE.)

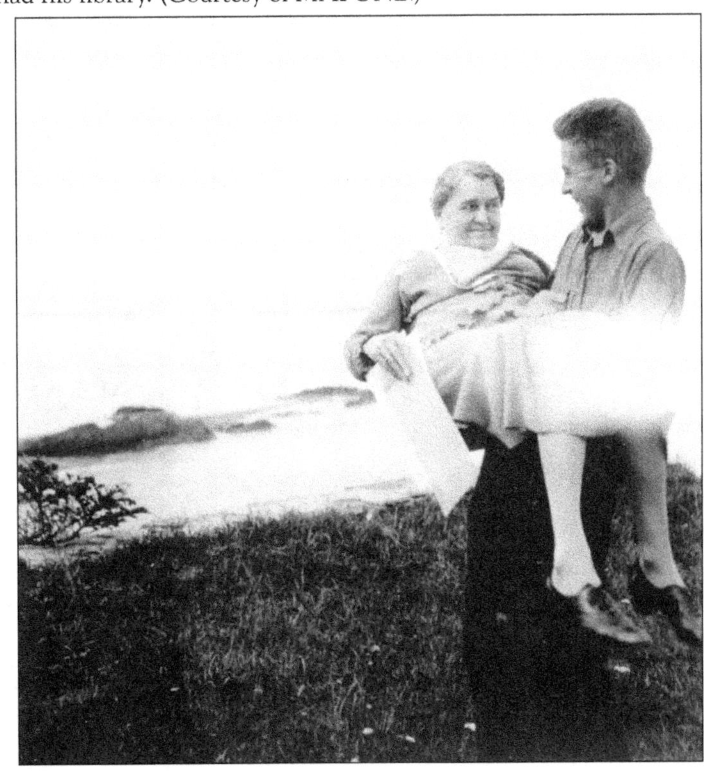

Josephine Peary was one tough woman. Here, however, she has given into letting her grandson Edward Stafford, Marie's eldest son, carry her. According to his note about this photograph, he was feeling all of his ripe young age of 18 or 19.

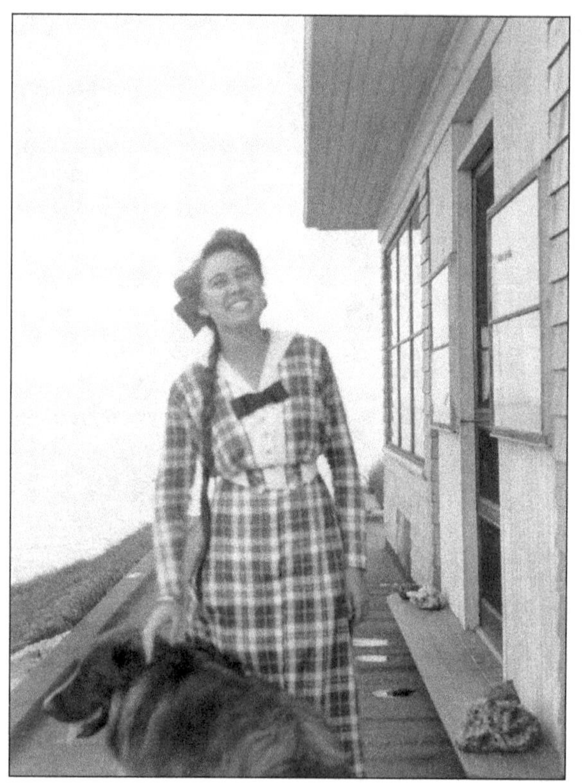

Never a bad day was had on Eagle Island. That has been the experience of many of the visitors and volunteers out on the island. Despite wind or weather, a day on an island in Maine is a good day. Here, Marie is clearly enjoying living on the island and hanging out with Rex. The house by this time had a formal front stone staircase to the north porch from the north lawn, evident at left.

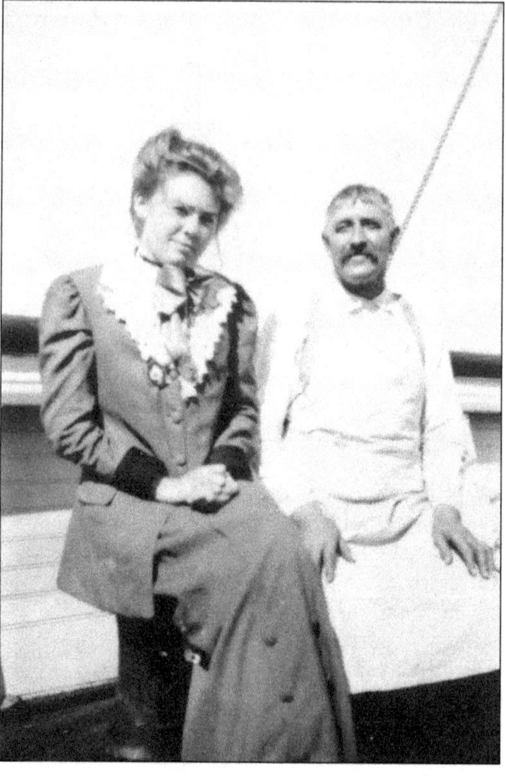

Marie is pictured here aboard the SS *Roosevelt* with the family caretaker, Charles Percy. Percy served as the steward for Peary on the SS *Roosevelt* during his last two voyages, and Charles and his wife, Martha, were caretakers of the island for many, many years. (Courtesy of PMAMBC.)

Taken around 1909, this is a nostalgic picture of Marie by the flagpole on the north lawn of Eagle Island. One can ponder whether she is looking for her father to return from his North Pole discovery or just relaxing and watching the ever-changing Atlantic Ocean.

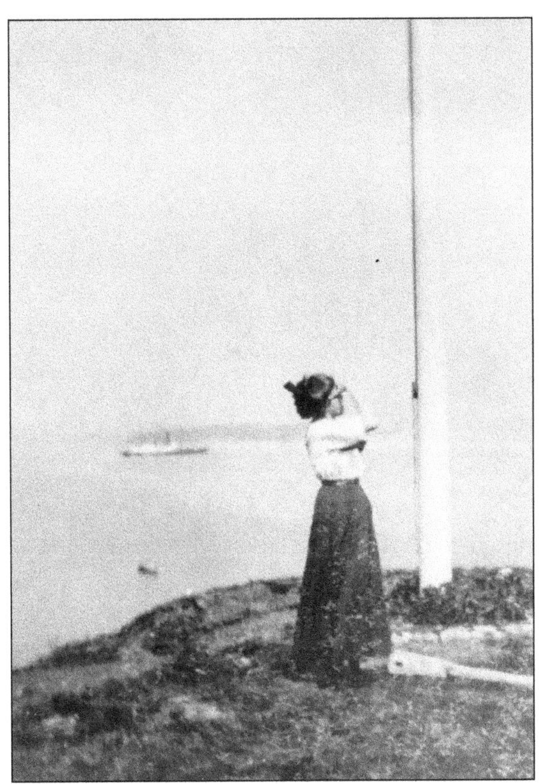

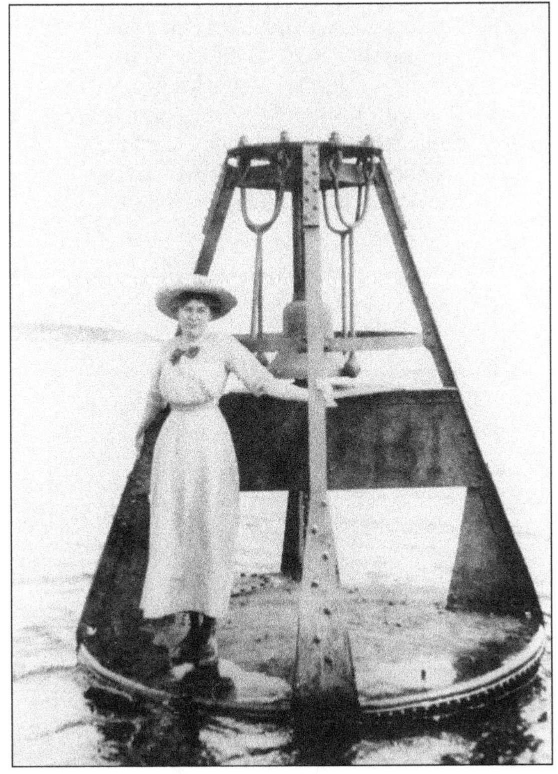

Around 1916, Marie is pictured on Bell Buoy No. B1, with Haskell Island in the background. This buoy was the Mark Island Ledge Buoy 1, so described in 1914 in the US Navy's *Indices of Notices to Mariners, 1–52*. It marked the Mark Island Passage and Mark Island Ledge. Mark Island and Haskell Island are northeast of Eagle Island and visible from the east side.

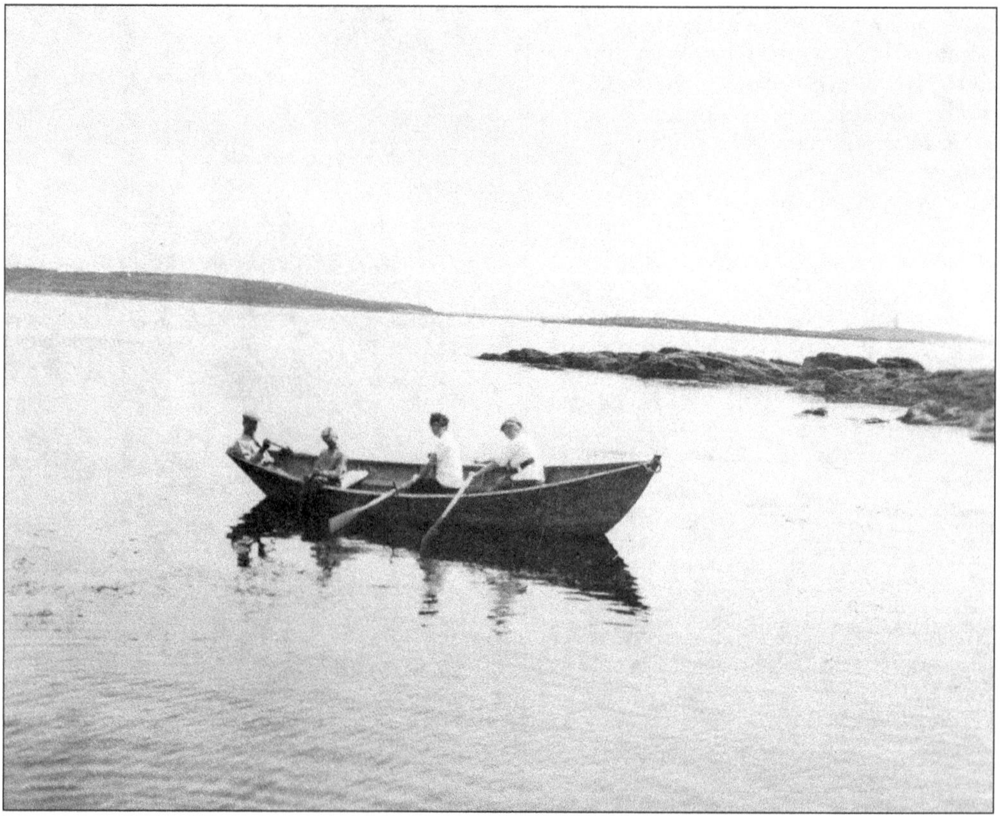

Letting the ladies do all the work, Admiral Peary is enjoying a boat ride with his family. Son Robert Jr., daughter Marie, and wife Josephine are shown sharing a summer day in the waters just off Eagle Island.

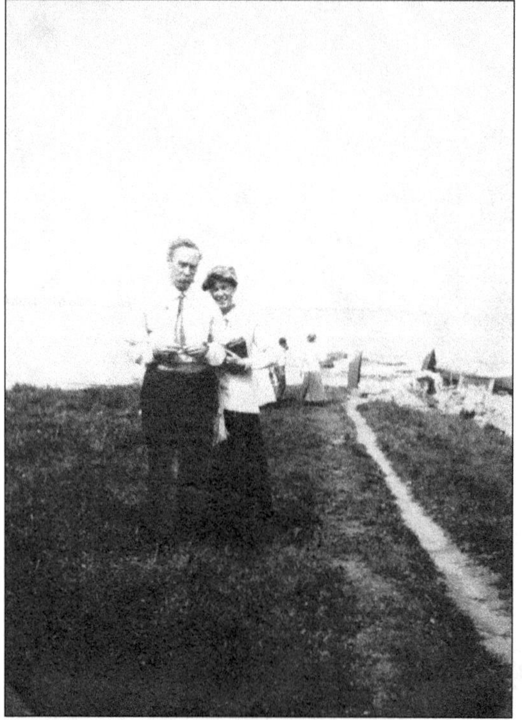

Marie is pictured here with her father. They are on the lawn west of the house, just below the west bastion and library. In the background is the sand beach that has a mixture of small, and occasionally large, stones rounded by the ever-present tides.

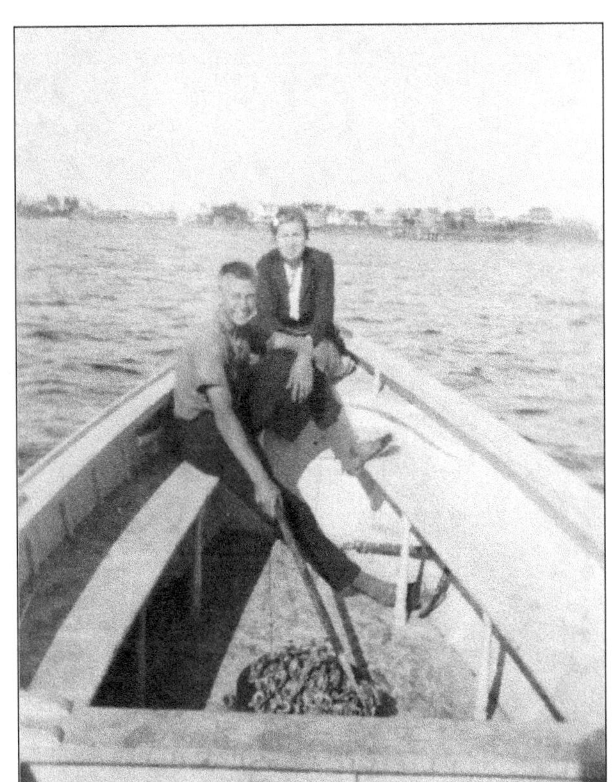

Marie and her brother, Bob, were always in boats due to the fact that they spent so much of each year on an island. The background is Potts Point, and the vessel they are sailing is the *Robert E.* Below, Bob and Marie are photographed exploring the island and taking pictures along the way.

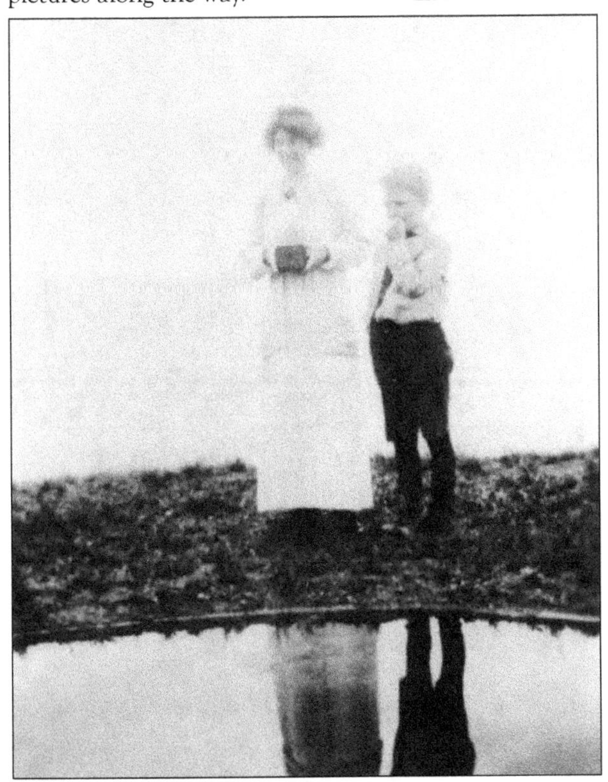

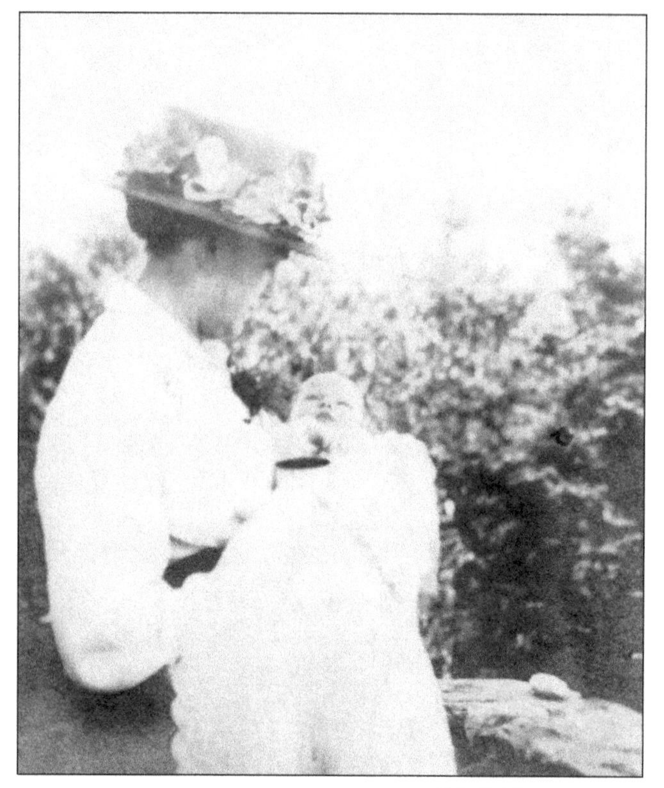

It is time for a new generation to make Eagle Island their home. These photographs poignantly show Josephine and the Admiral with their first grandchild, Edward Peary Stafford, born to Marie on July 16, 1918. Josephine is holding Ed, who at the tender age of seven weeks old is already a resident of Eagle Island. Almost a year later, the Admiral is offering Ed a ride in a baby carriage on the deck of the house. Josephine is decked out in a lovely boater with flowers on the brim, while the Admiral, "relaxed" on the island with his grandson, is still wearing a tie and spats. The Admiral passed away in February 1920. This was his last summer on Eagle Island.

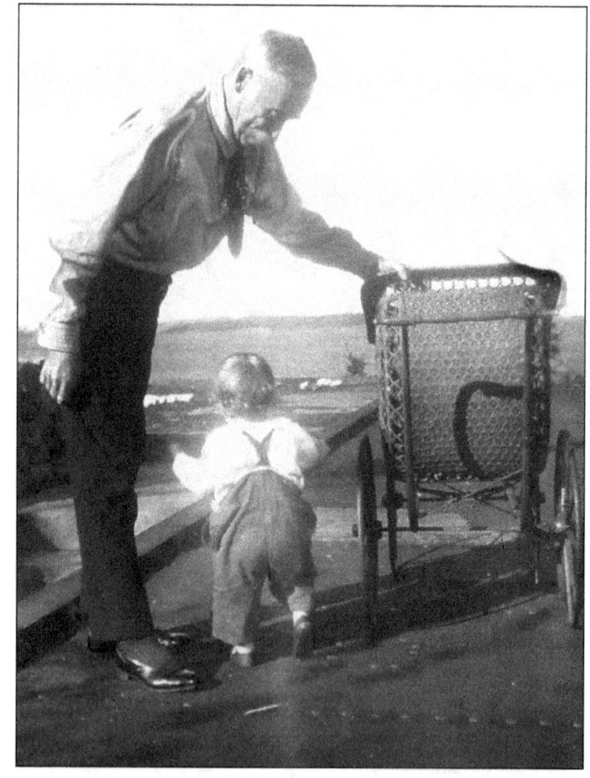

Six

The Next Generation

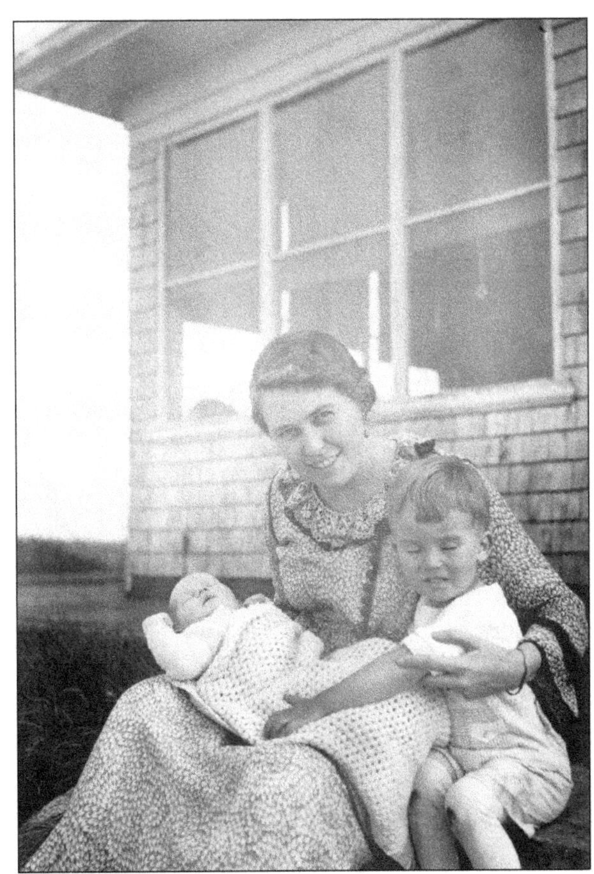

Marie has brought her children to Eagle Island. Both boys were born in July (Ed in 1918 and Bud in 1920). Ed, the elder, is already protecting his younger brother, who is wrapped up cozily and being held by his mother on the porch of the house. The boys' father was Edward Stafford, the elder son's namesake. He and Marie married in 1917 when she was 24 years old.

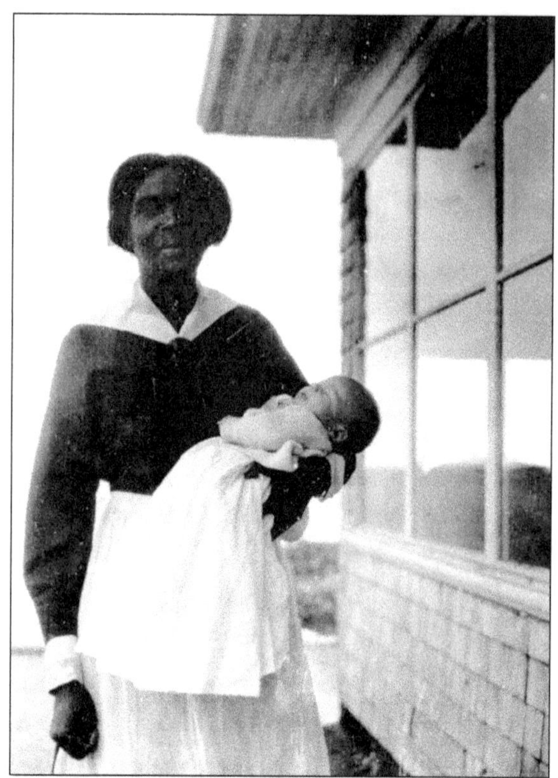

Mary Carr, shown at left, was one of the staff, and here, she is tending to the first grandson, Edward Peary Stafford, called "Ed." During the years on Eagle Island, there were many caretakers of the family and the island. Below, Marie proudly coddles her new son, Peary Diebitsch Stafford, also known as "Bud," with her firstborn, Ed, by her side.

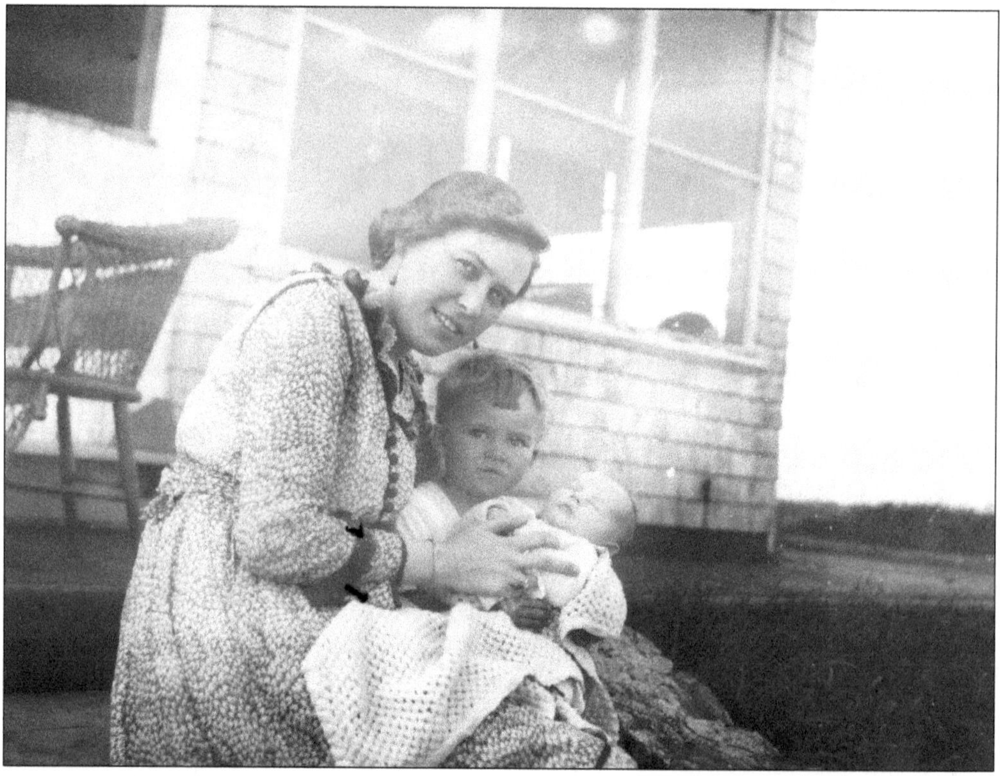

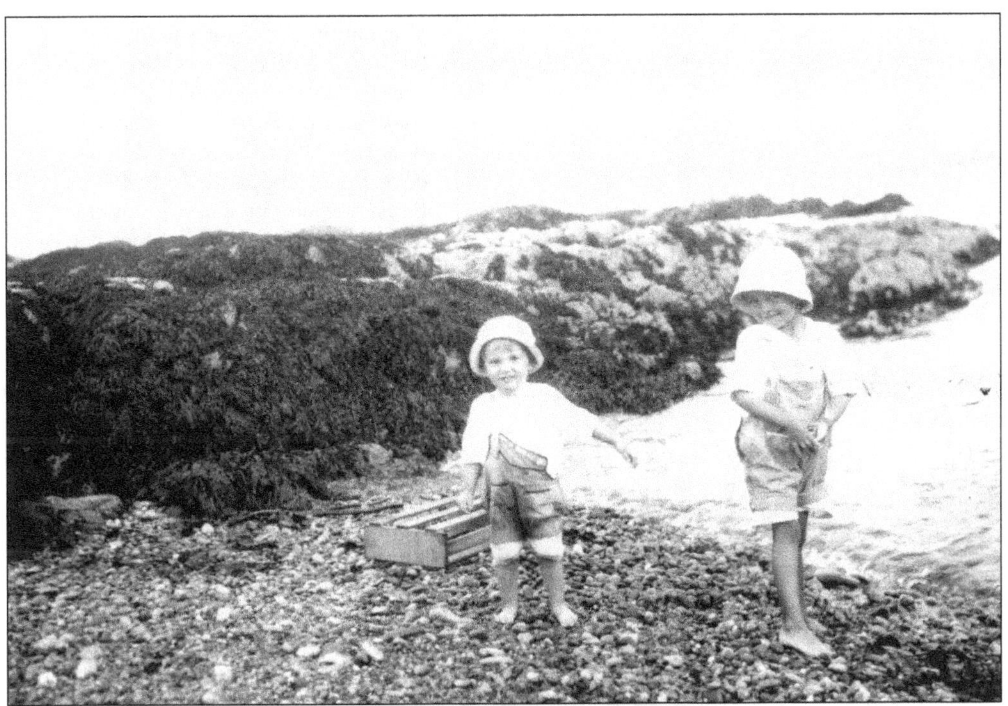

Ed (right) and Bud were very active children and delighted in all that Eagle Island had to offer. They played often in the front sandy cove of the island within eyesight of their mother, caretakers, and the house. Other times, both boys were found covered by and playing with the family's pet dogs. At right, Bud Stafford plays with Rex, the family Saint Bernard mix, while sitting on the eastern boardwalk near the east bastion.

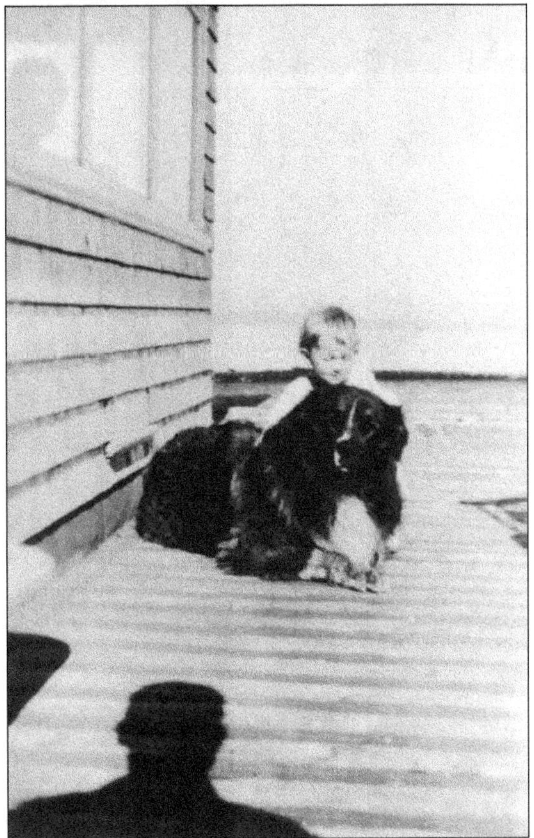

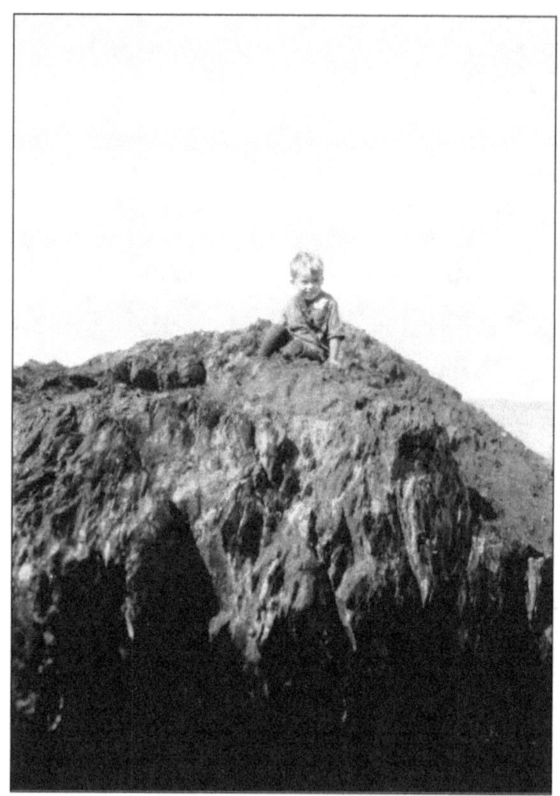

The family gave names to all the parts of the island. Fern Valley was the first path through the island that Admiral Peary bushwhacked (see page 119) this rock in the front cove, which they called "Turtle Rock" because its shape at low tide resembles a turtle's shell. Once the high tide rolls in, this rock is almost completely submerged underwater.

Like the Admiral and his children, Pearys' grandsons were in boats from almost the beginnings of their lives. Here, on a rainy day, Ed is waiting in his "dough trough" for high tide to row about in the front cove of the island.

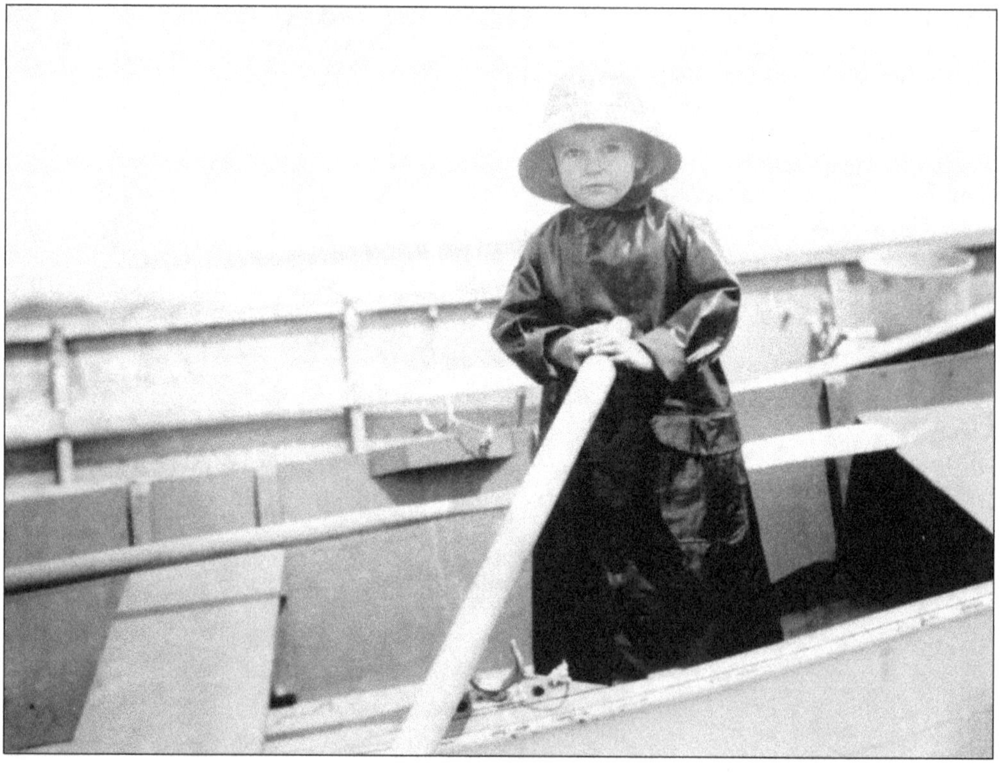

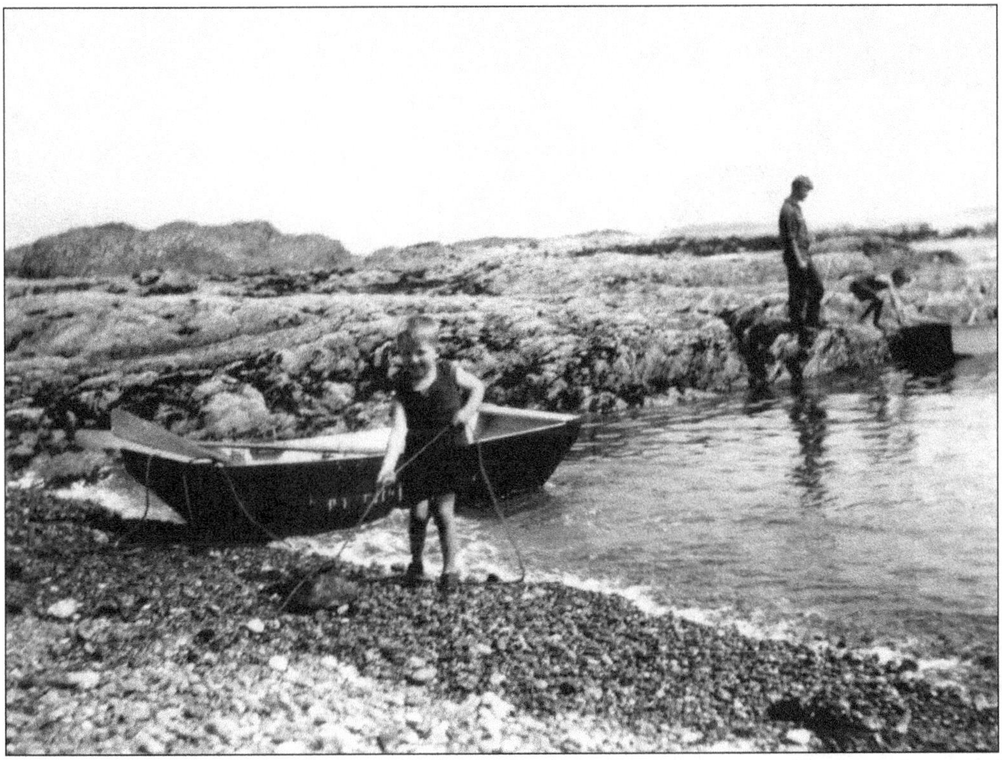

The caretakers on the island were with the family through generations and had a wide variety of responsibilities. In these photographs, Aaron Marden watches over the grandchildren, Ed and Bud, as they row around in their own boats and fish off the rocks and coves around the island. In the picture below, Marden has helped Ed, Marie's eldest, land a large sunfish. These sunfish (the common mola), which inhabit the waters off Maine and Massachusetts, can be as large as 6 to 10 feet and can weigh several hundred pounds. They scull their dorsal fin to move about and are called sunfish because they appear to be sunning themselves on the surface of the water as they float on their sides.

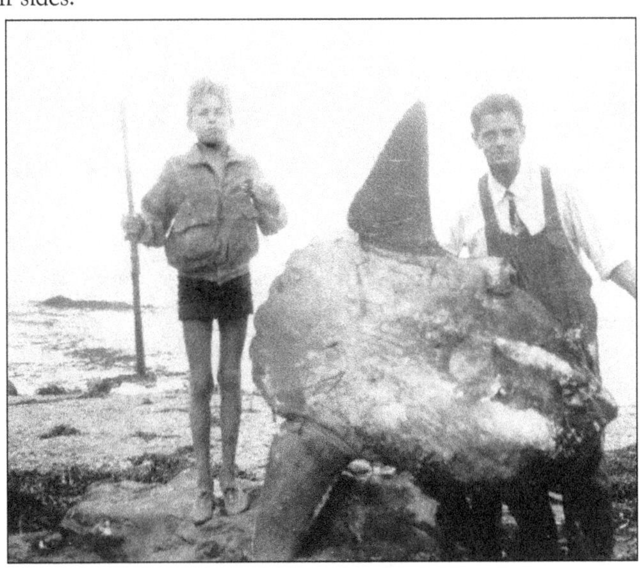

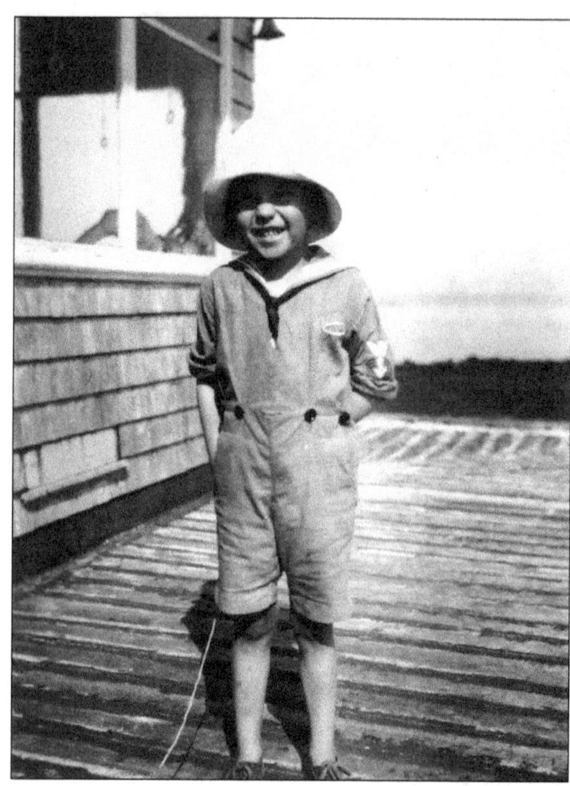

Ed Stafford is pictured at left in a Scout costume and in moccasins. Below, the swing set built with fallen trees was a source of much fun. Here, Ed (bottom) and Bud (top) Stafford play with a friend and do tricks.

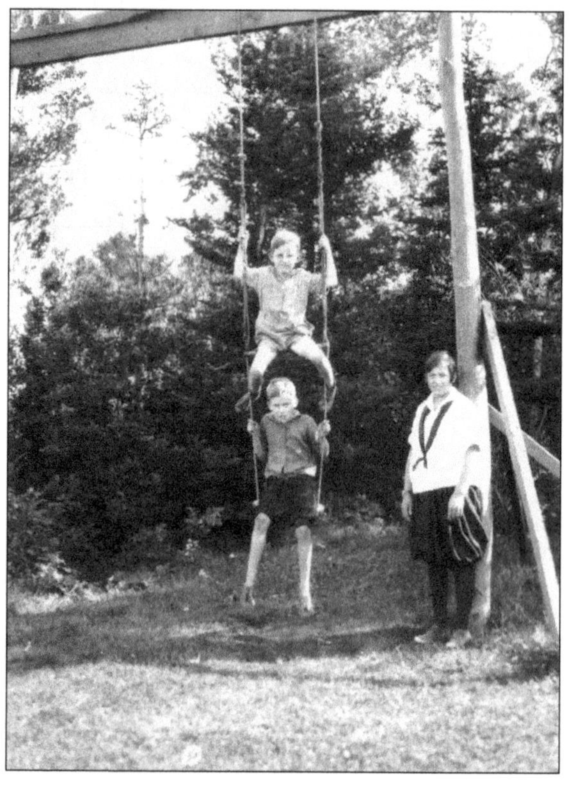

Boys will be boys, and the Peary grandsons were no different. What a place Eagle Island was for a child to play: a big lawn for a campsite and almost two acres of woods to hunt and run around in. The house behind the boys displays the large windows and screens that were installed on the two side porches to the rear of the house around 1912. With screens, the windows could be kept open and the sunlight was still able to pour in to heat the house and provide natural light. Below, Ed is dressed in a costume for Halloween, indicating that at least some of the family stayed on the island as late in the season as possible.

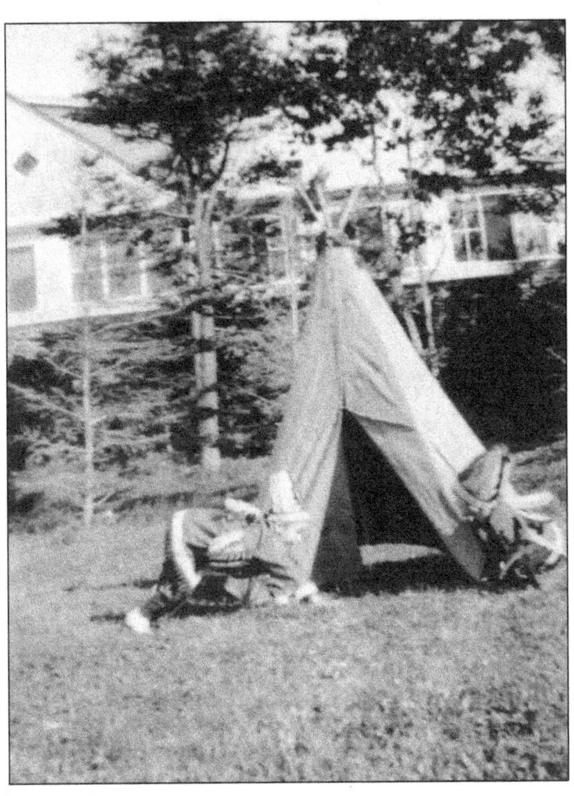

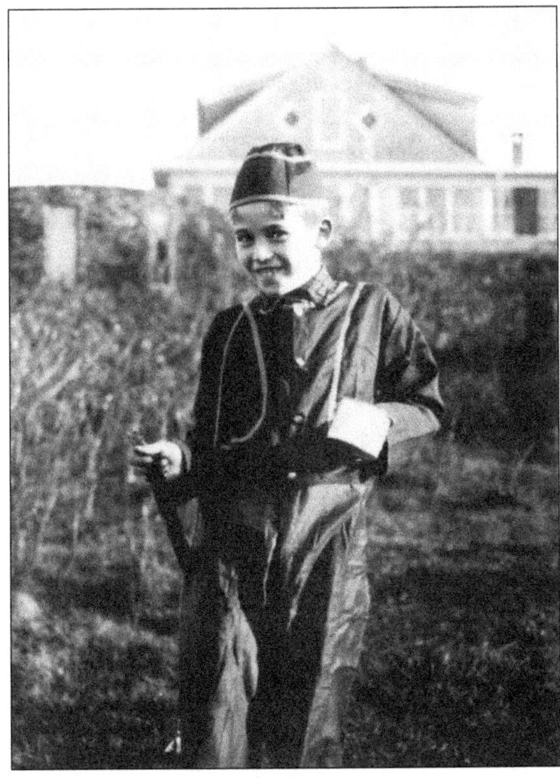

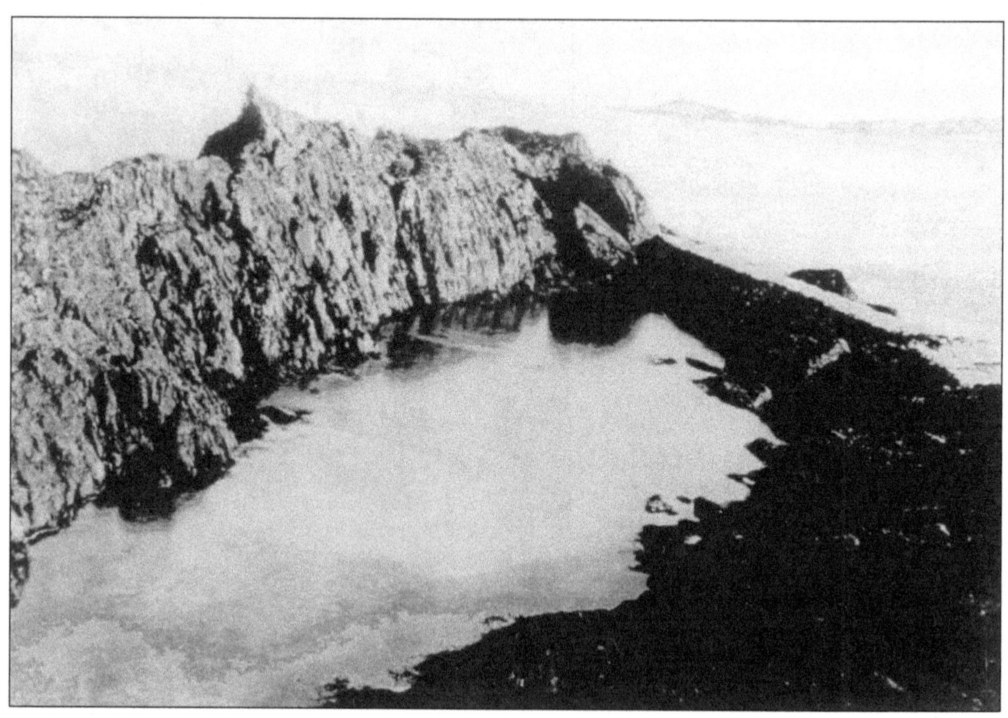

Admiral Peary read many books and journals about building with cement, stone, brick, and so forth, in ocean environments. With this knowledge, Peary constructed what the family called the "solar pool." He built a stone wall at the edge of this partially opened pool, which is visible in the photograph above, and the tides brought the water in to be warmed by the sun during the morning hours. The water was warm enough for the Stafford boys to swim in the pool.

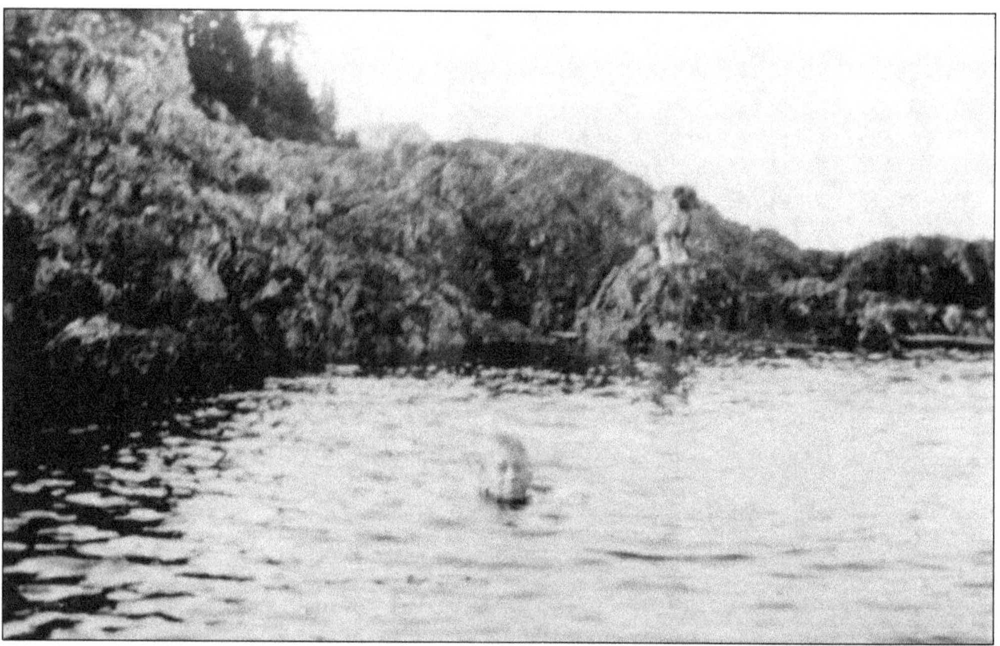

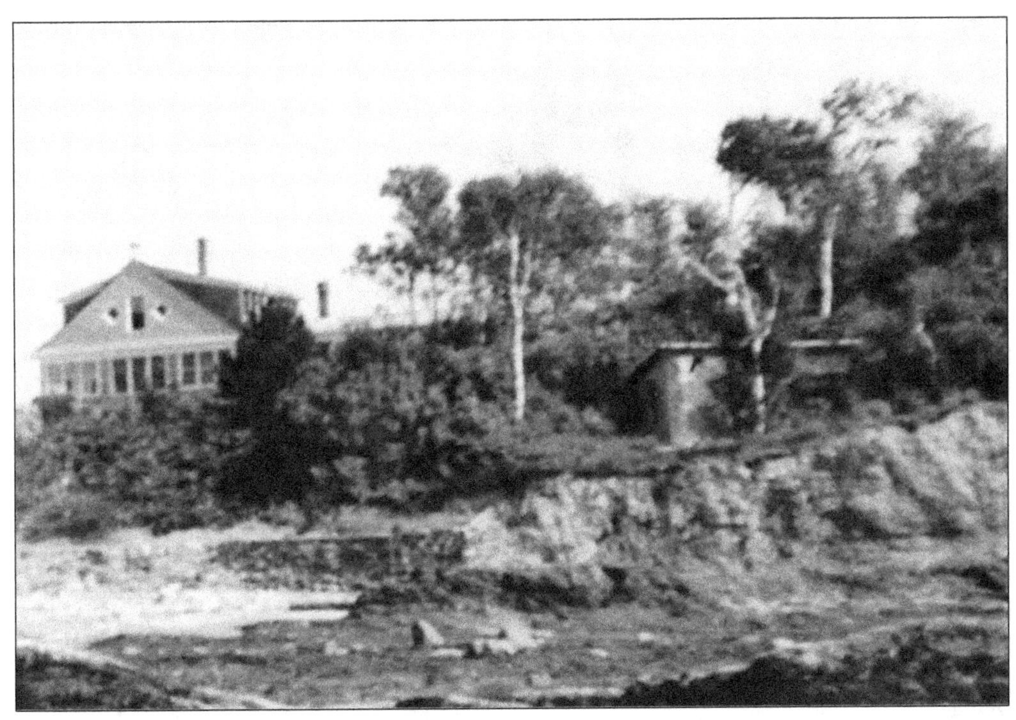

By the time Ed Stafford and his brother, Bud, were young lads about eight and nine years old, their grandfather's cottage had grown to become a proper house. Here, it is pictured from a vantage point of rocks on the west shore between the house and the caretaker's cottage. Seen on the edge of the rock ledge is Bob's workshop, which he built under his father's supervision in 1918. It was here that Bob constructed his sloop *Molly* (see page 77), as well as the boat in the foreground of the image below.

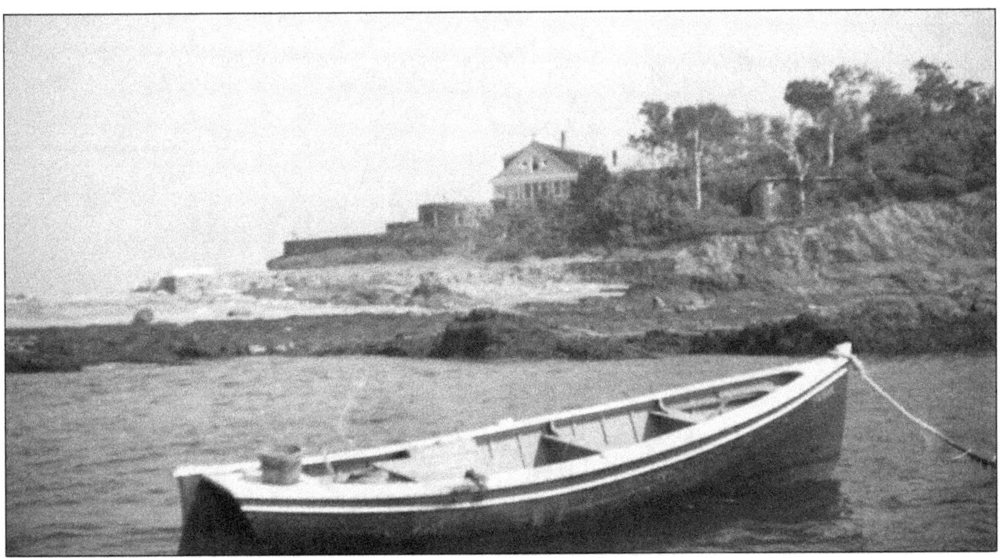

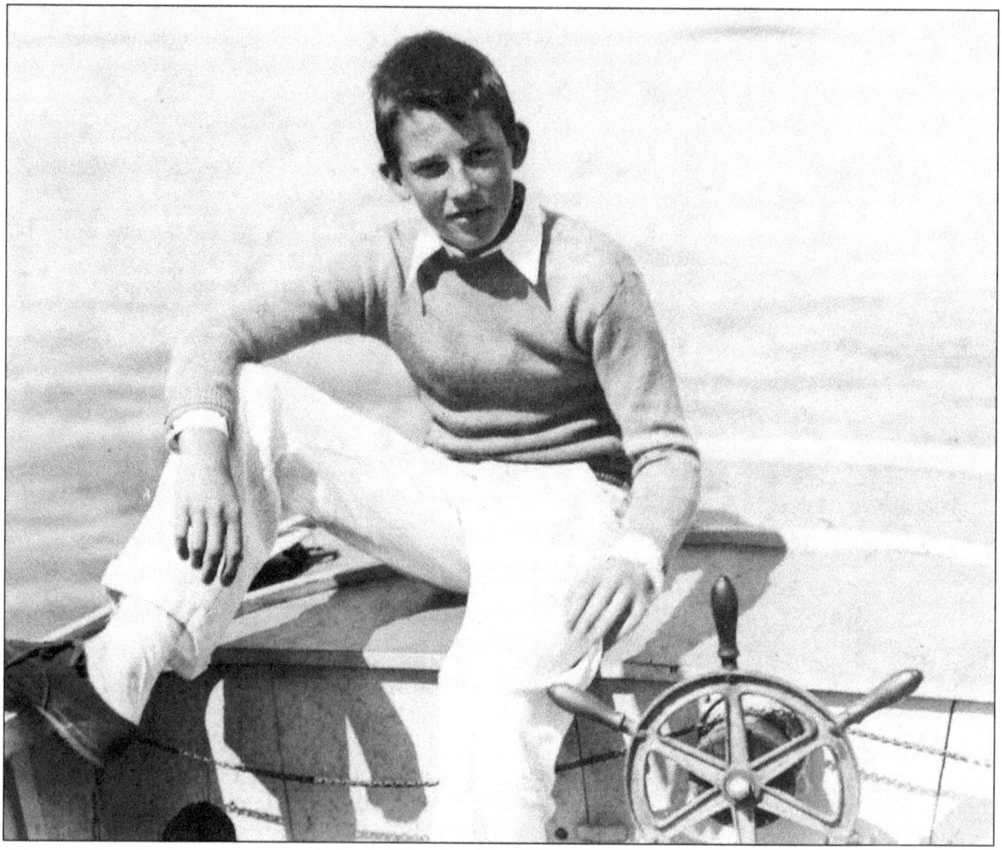

Above, Bob sits in the stern of the *Molly*. Gaff rigged with a clubfoot jib, this 28-foot sloop was often sailed by Bob alone. In the background of the photograph below, the house is just off his port quarter bow and his workshop is just starboard to the bow, while reflecting the setting sun.

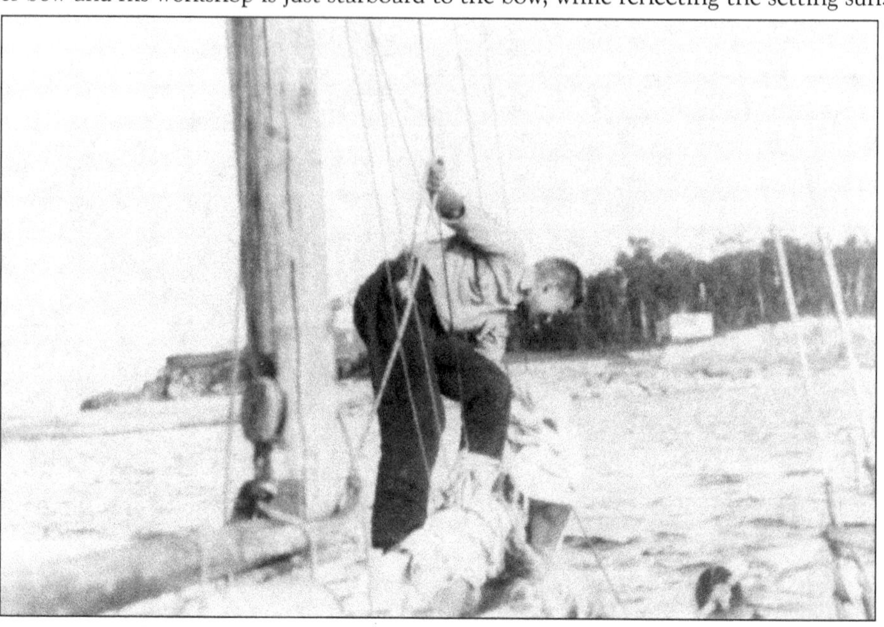

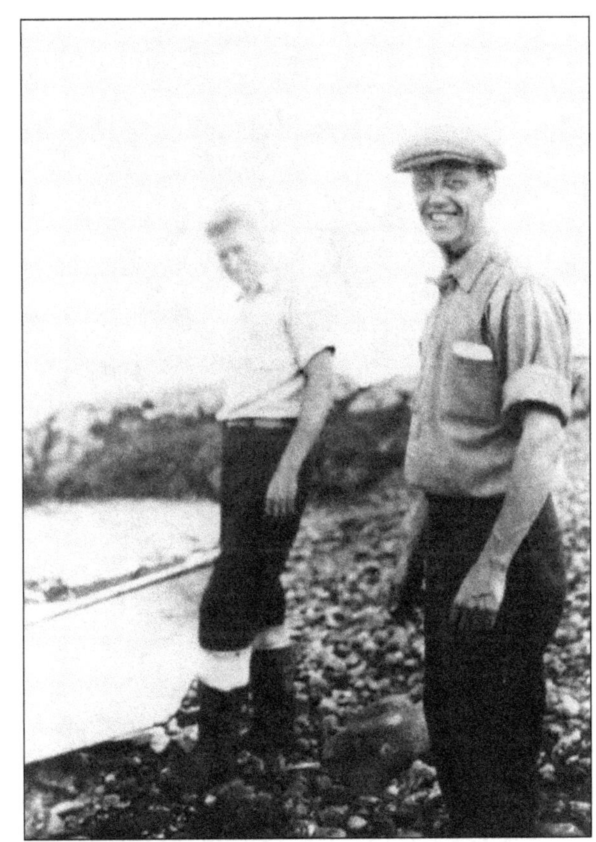

At right, Bob (right) his seen here with Gene Chase in 1926 ready to shove off and, by the looks of their clothes and boots, go fishing. Below, in the *Peppy*, another small roundabout in the Peary fleet, Ed is rowing his mother and brother, Bud, in the calm seas around Eagle Island. Normally swells of three to five feet and a breeze coming in off the open Atlantic did not allow for such lovely summer boating.

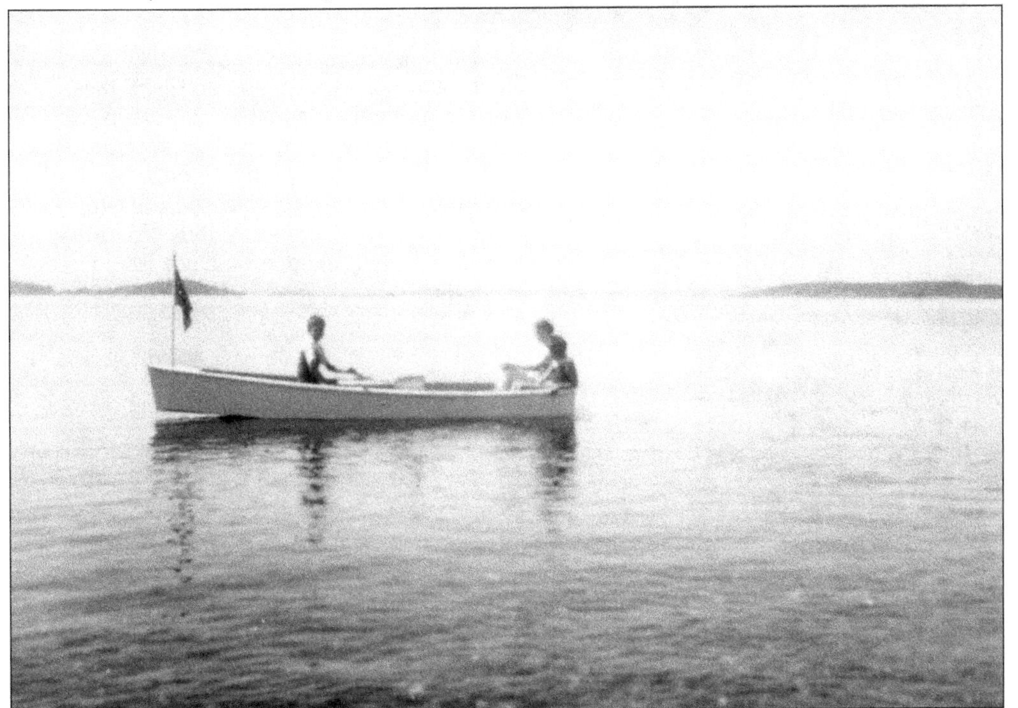

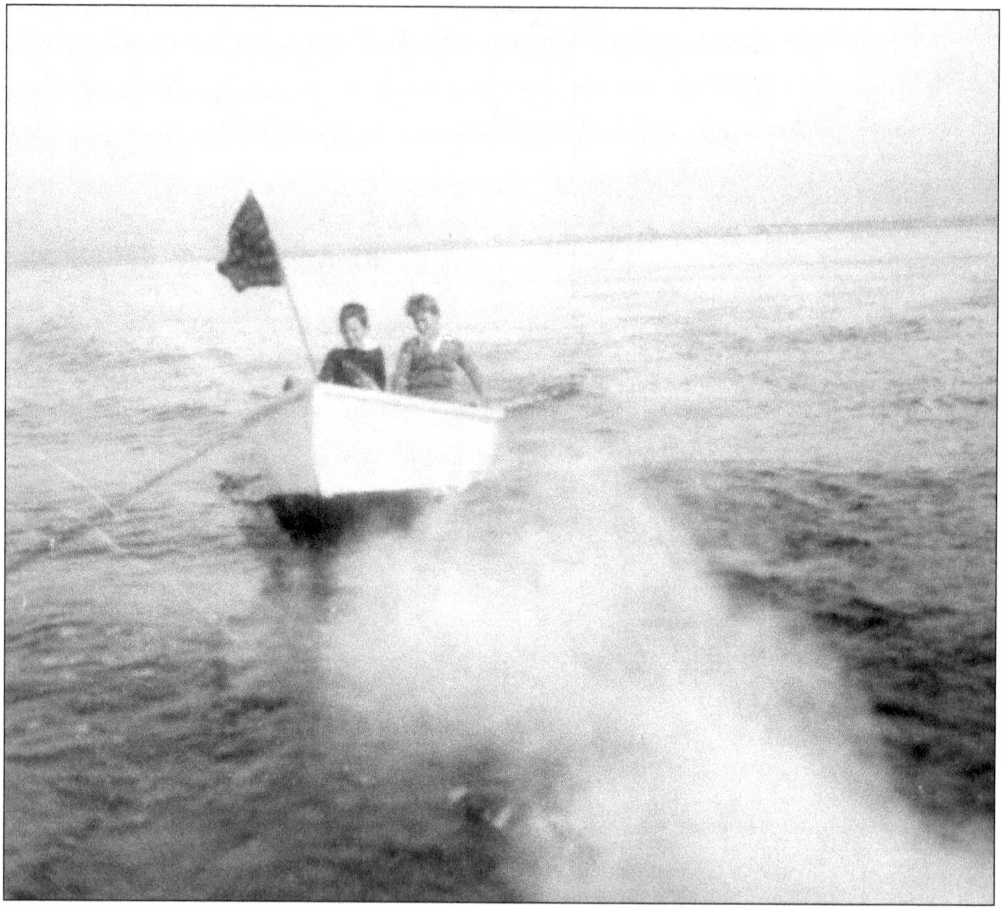

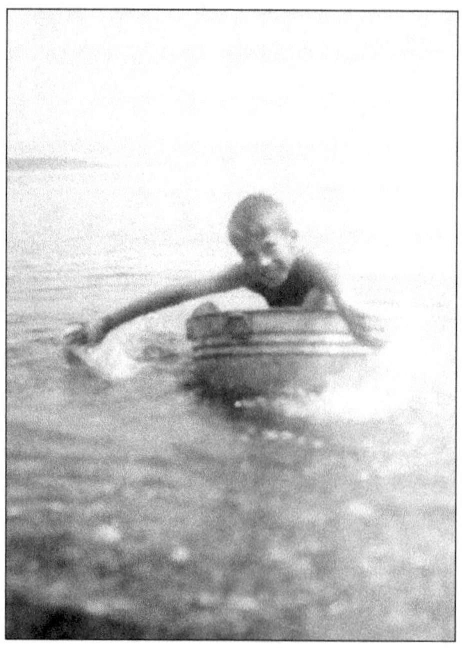

Boats of all sorts were found on the island, both traditional—Ed (right) and Bud in the *Peppy* being towed—and the not so traditional, such as the galvanized tub that Ed is "rowing." Boating and water sports were a large part of the daily life of Peary's grandchildren. No wonder they loved their summers on Eagle Island.

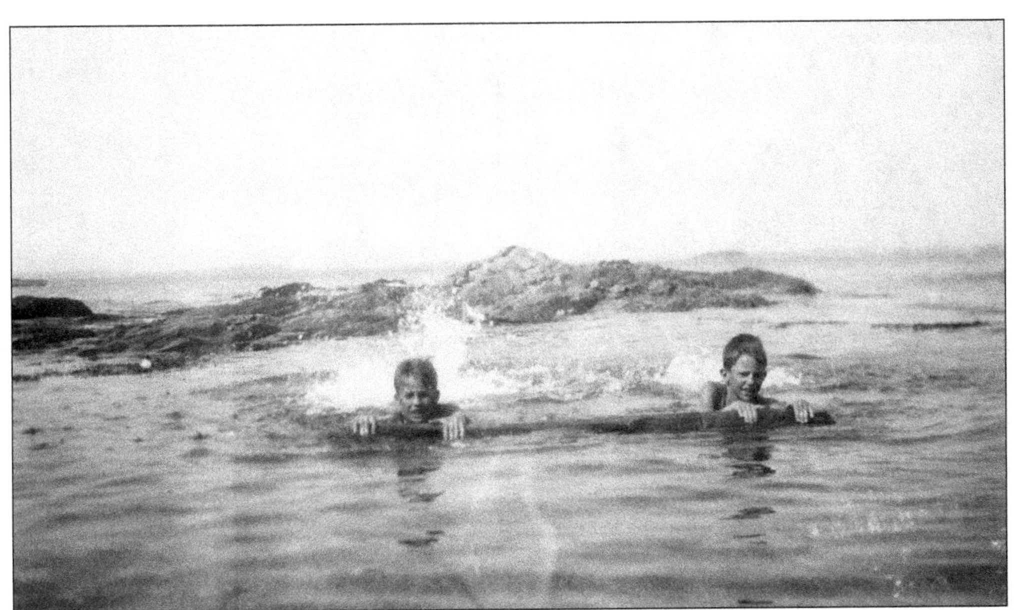

Along the coast of Maine in the summer months, the average ocean water temperatures reach the low 60s. Swimming in the ocean off the Maine coast requires courage just for the ability to claim, "I went in." The Peary children and grandchildren were born with such courage and had use of an island of coves and beaches in which to test it. Above, Ed and Bud use driftwood for flotation, and at right, Bob is relaxing in the sandy cove with his nephew Ed.

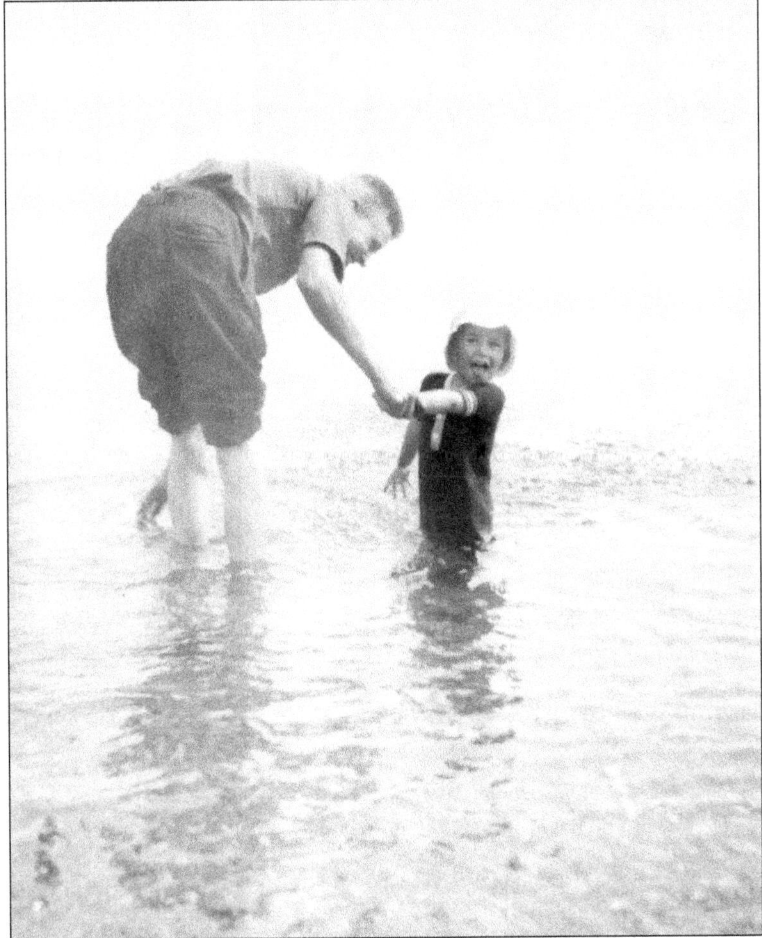

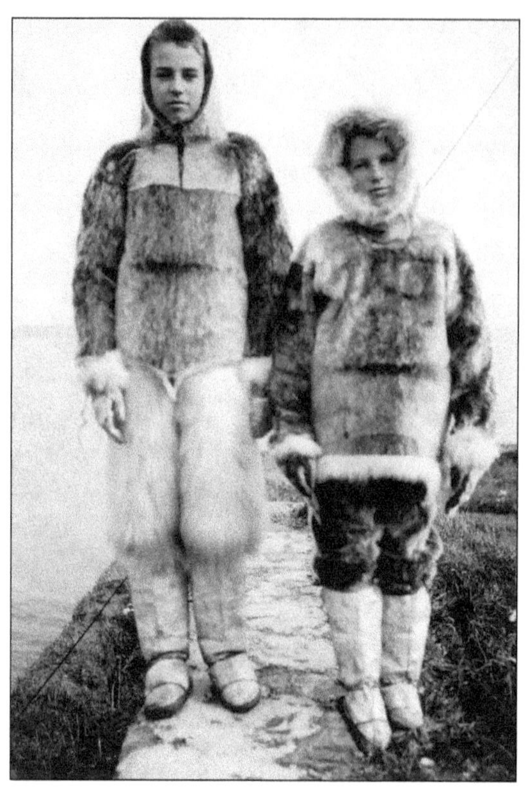

As discussed earlier (see page 33), traditional Inuit clothing was worn by Admiral Peary and his crew when they took forays from the SS *Roosevelt* in Greenland. Pictured at left in 1933, Ed and Bud Stafford display their Inuit clothing. The year prior, Marie Peary Stafford and her sons and other family members returned to Greenland to raise a monument to honor her father. The boys wore Inuit clothing such as this during that trip north. Below, Bob is standing in front of one of the sledges that his father would have used during his Arctic explorations. (Left, courtesy of Maine Bureau of Parks and Lands; below, courtesy of PMAMBC.)

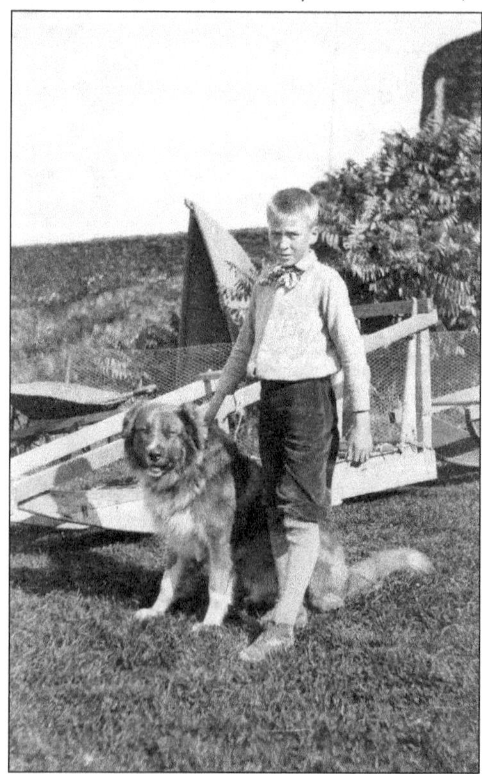

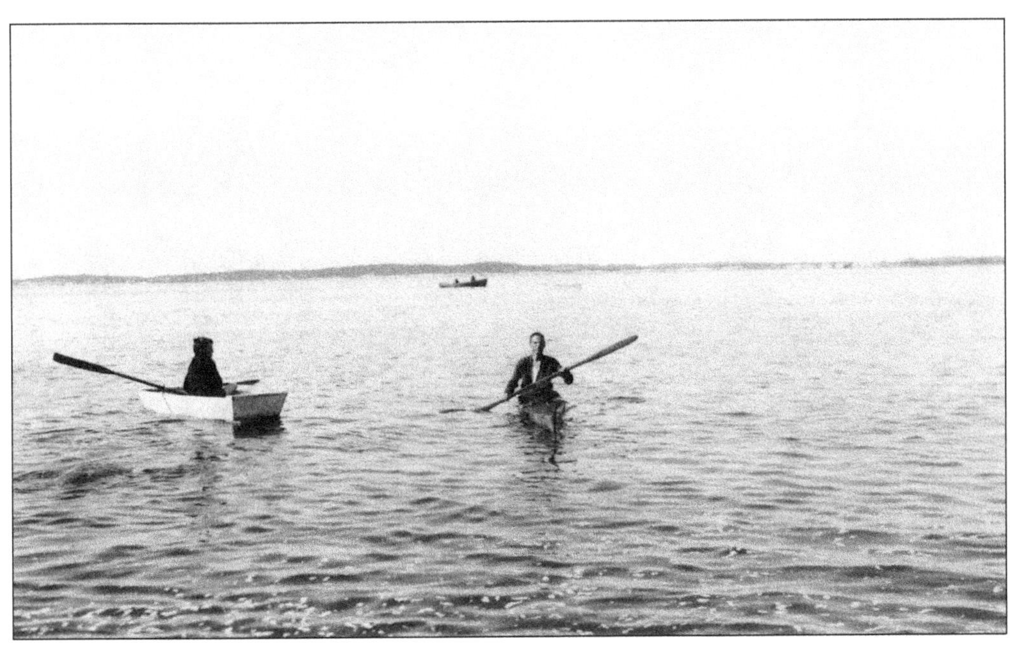

In addition to Inuit clothing, many of the Peary family members learned to use an umiak (Inuit kayak). Above, Ed Stafford Sr. (Marie's husband) is paddling in the front cove off Eagle Island, while Ed Jr. is in his dough trough. In the background, fishermen are tending to their work. Below, Ed Jr., at an older age, is trying out the umiak for himself.

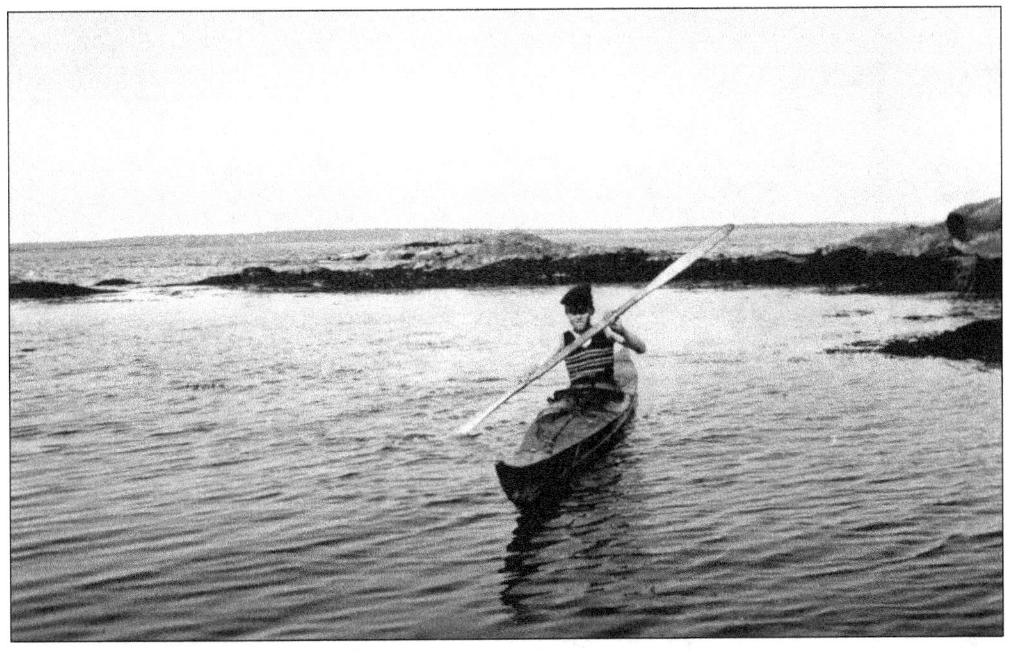

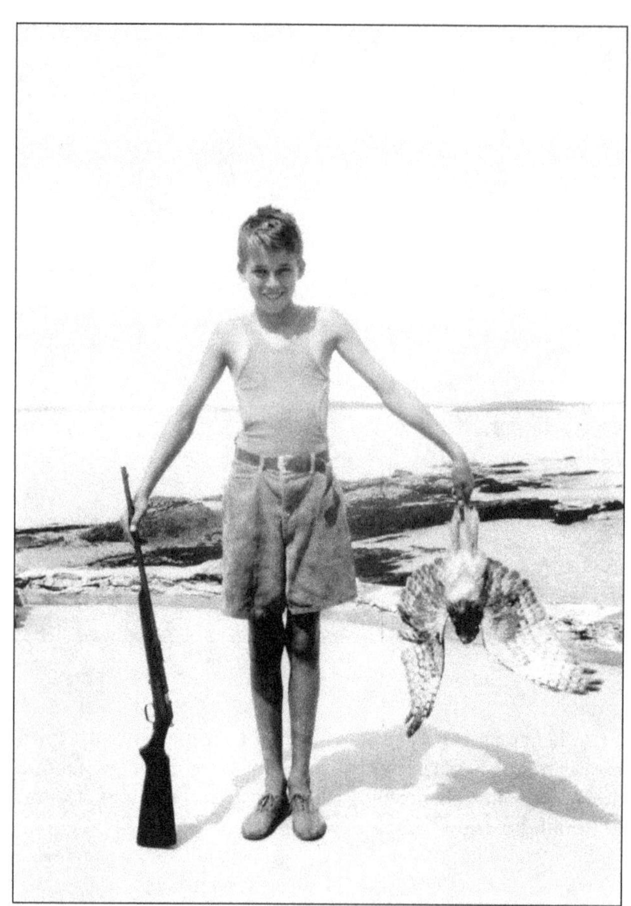

Hunting for food and sport were traditions of the Peary family. Here, Ed Stafford has shot his first hawk with a rifle his grandmother Josephine Peary gave him on his 12th birthday. Below, Stafford is showing off a seal he shot while grandmother looks over at his prize. Josephine herself was quite the markswoman.

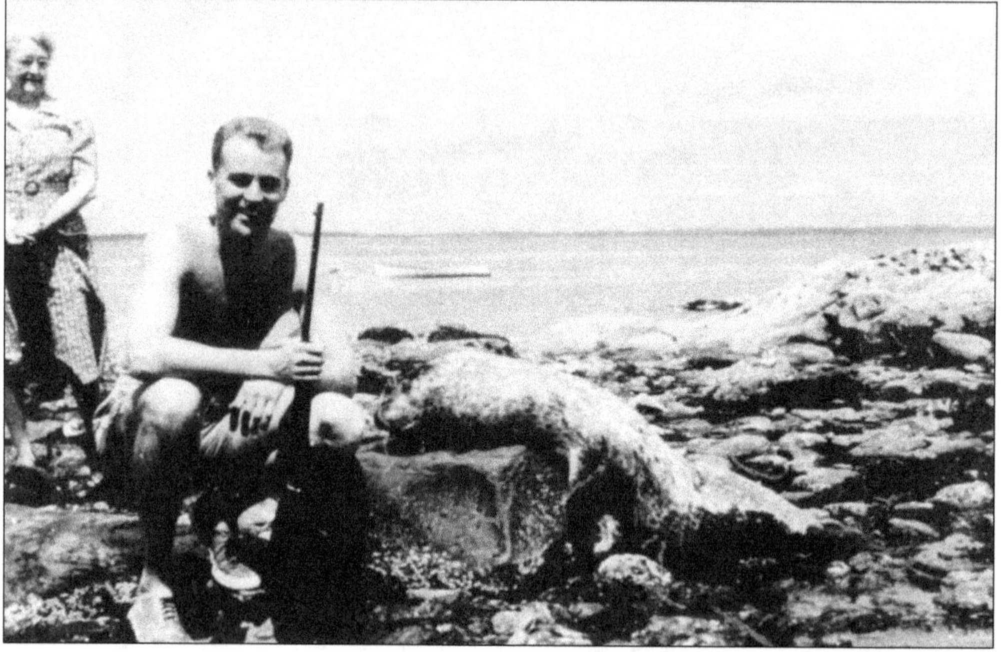

Fishing for the day's catch for meals was a favorite pastime. At right, Ed (right) is pictured with his friend Lawrence Frizzell, "Brute" to his friends, with their haul; and below, Ed, with an unidentified friend, shows the day's catch.

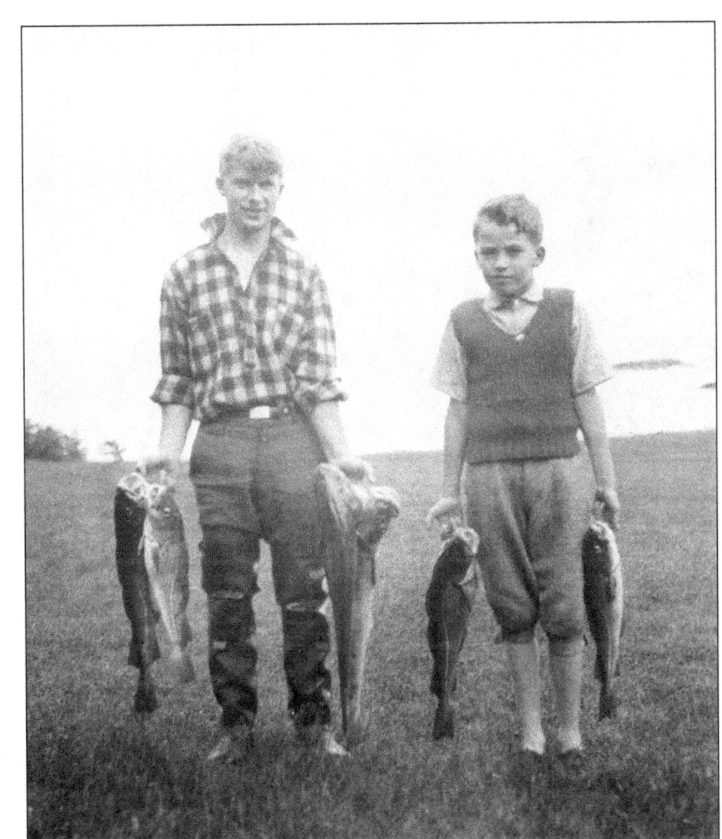

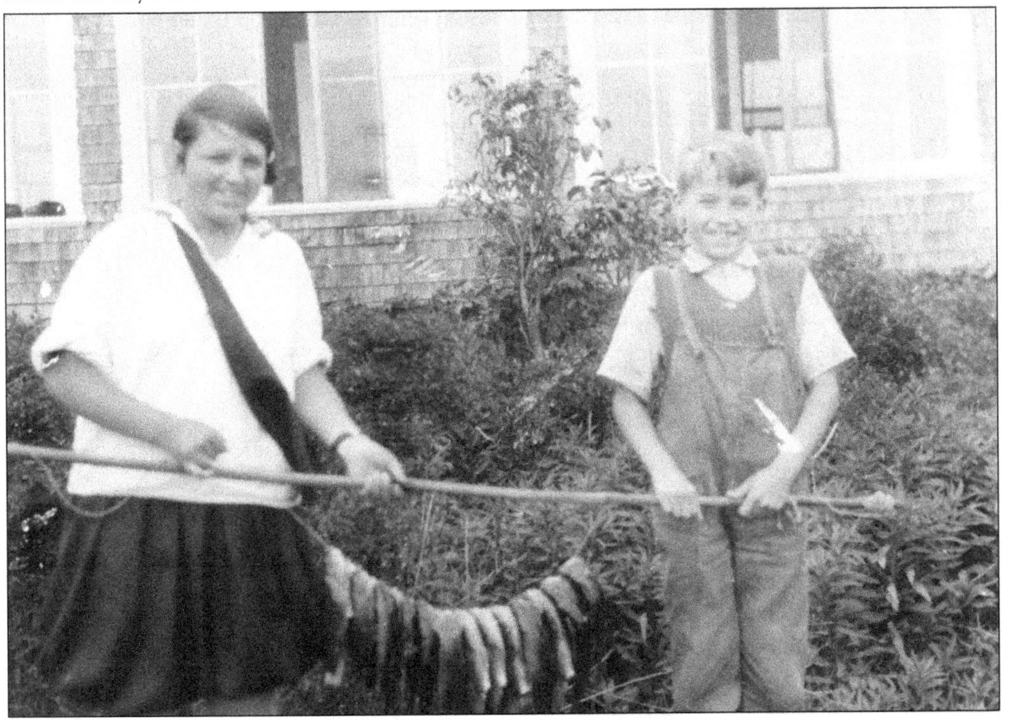

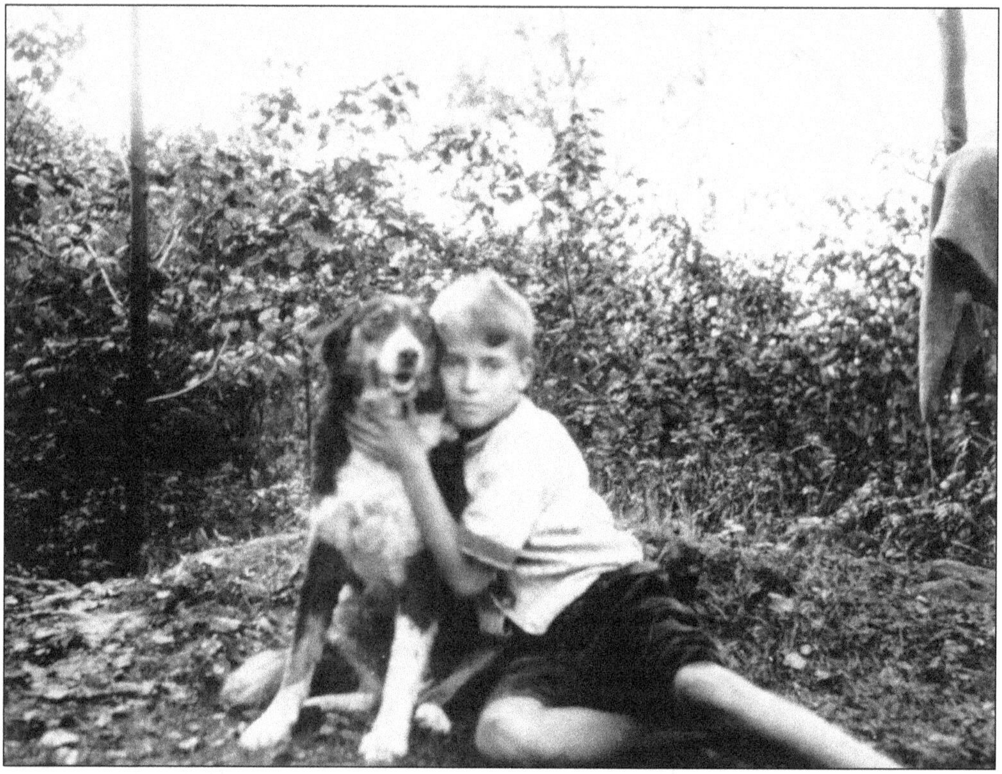

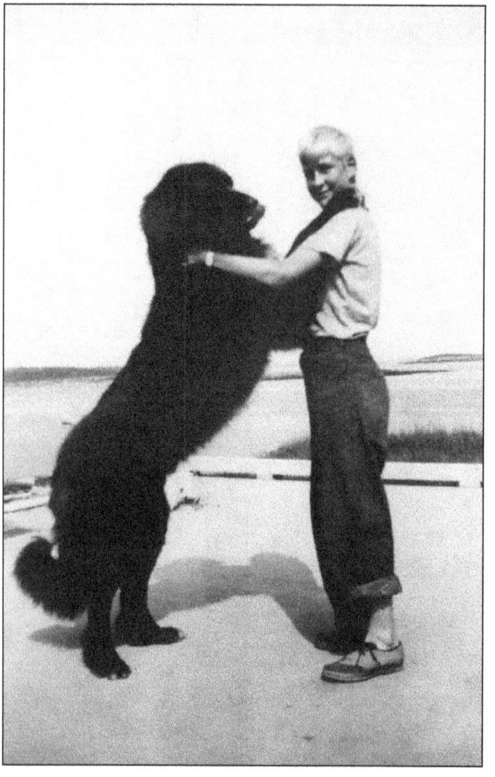

Dogs were a central part of the Peary family. Here, Mike the dog, a Saint Bernard mix, is cuddled up with Ed. Ed's brother Bud is matching his size against the family's Newfoundland mix, Brutus.

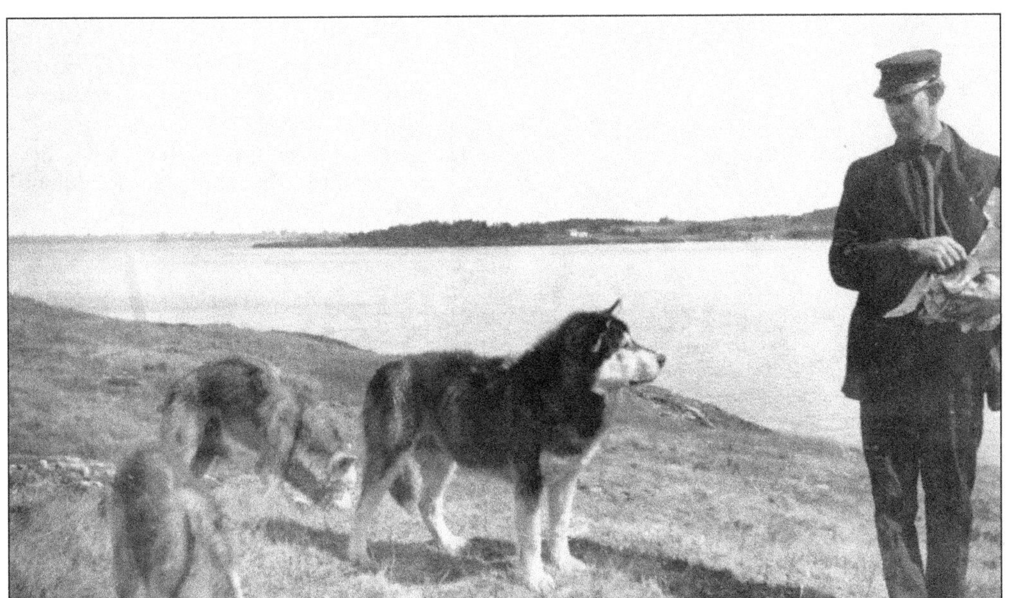

It is feeding time for the Inuit sled dogs that Admiral Peary kept on Upper Flag Island across a small channel from Eagle Island. They were pretty rough and wild dogs, and feeding was usually done from the safety of boats. There are stories of the dogs hearing local sheep on coastal farms that populated the peninsulas nearby and swimming over to have a meal of mutton. In one instance, a farmer actually sent Admiral Peary a bill for the sheep the dogs killed, and Peary is said to have paid up. (Courtesy of GJMBC.)

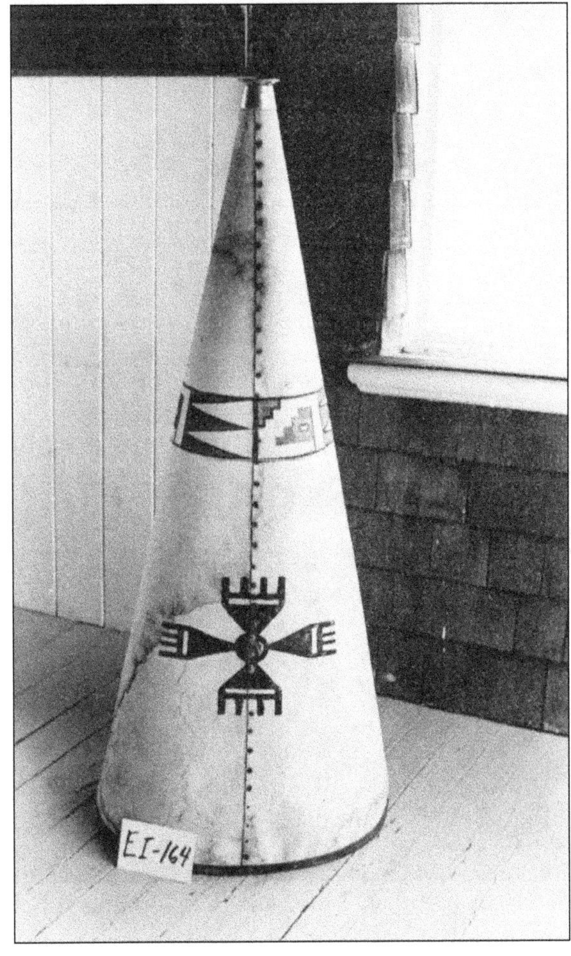

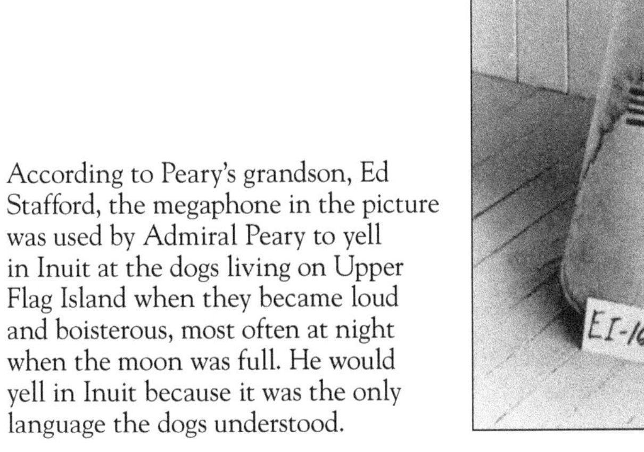

According to Peary's grandson, Ed Stafford, the megaphone in the picture was used by Admiral Peary to yell in Inuit at the dogs living on Upper Flag Island when they became loud and boisterous, most often at night when the moon was full. He would yell in Inuit because it was the only language the dogs understood.

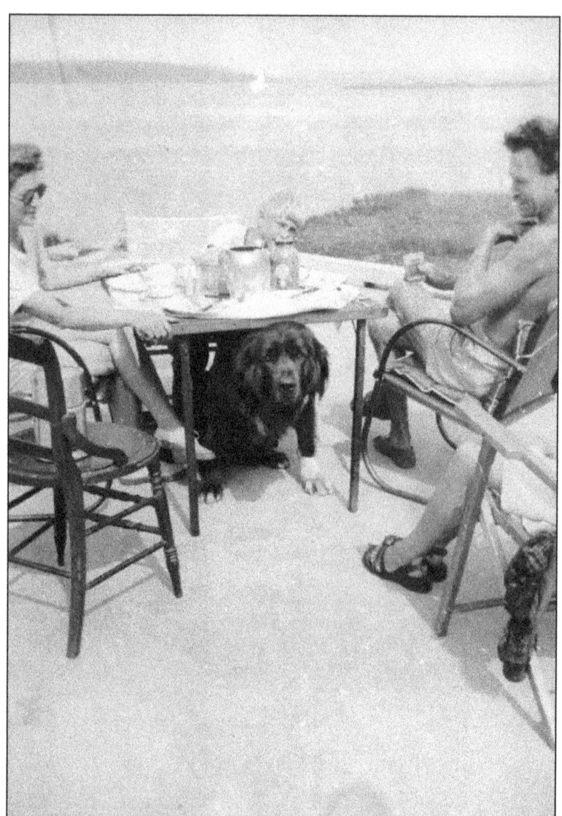

By the 1940s, Bob Peary, the Admiral's son, and his family spent a great deal of time on the island during the summers. Bob was an engineer, like his father. Here, he is pictured with his wife, Inez, with Brutus, the family Newfoundland mix, barely fitting under that table.

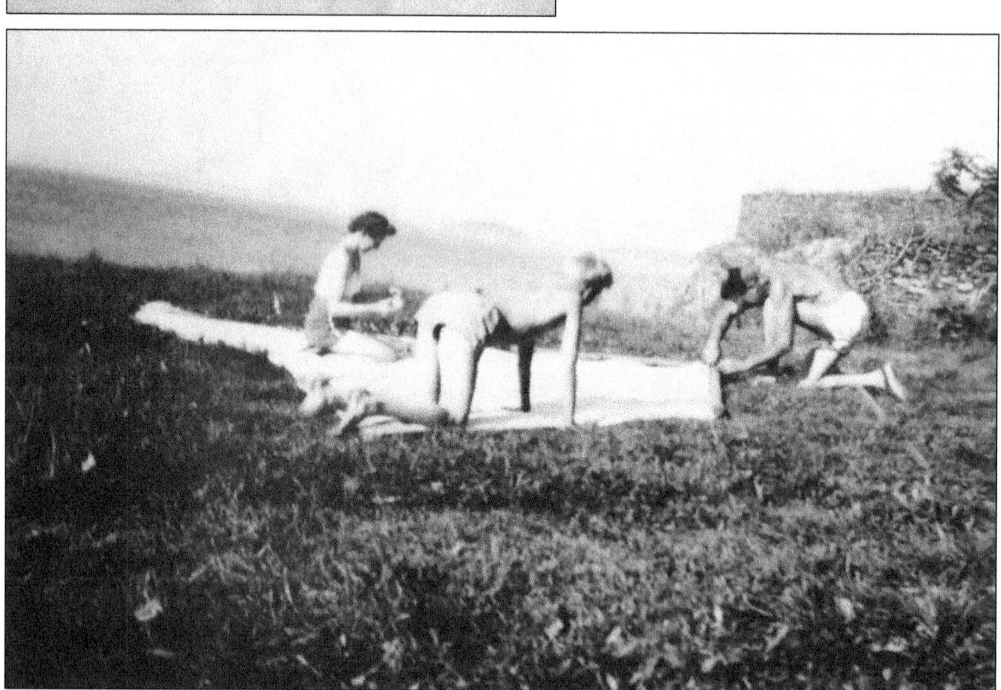

Bob Peary (right), wife Inez, and their son Robert E. Peary III ("Bert") are pictured fixing a sail for one of their boats.

In the 1940s, Bob Peary's family made a go of living on Eagle Island year-round. Jody and Bert are pictured with Angora rabbits that the family attempted to raise on Eagle Island as a business venture. However, just as they were starting their business, the Angora rabbit fur business fell into a decline due to the development of man-made fabrics for everyday wear. Below, Jody is pictured with a goat named Cleopatra. One could assume that the goat was a source of milk and possibly cheese.

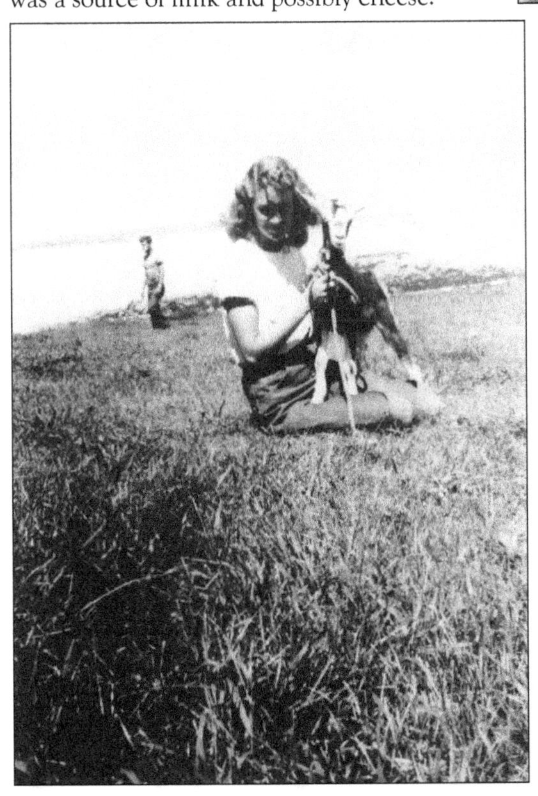

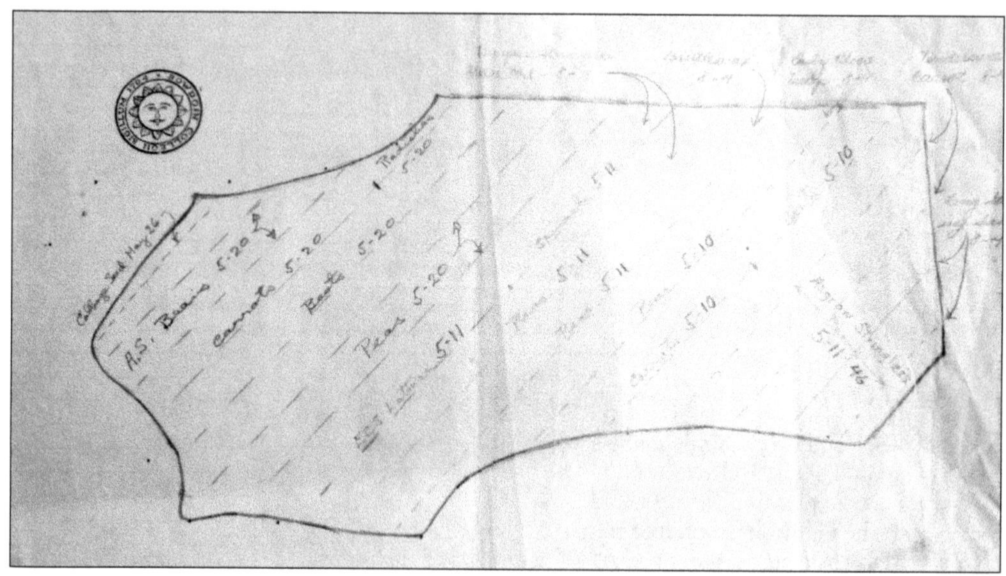

During their years on Eagle Island, the vegetable gardens were large and very well maintained. These drawings are the plans for the gardens and indicate the incredible variety of vegetables they planted and that could grow on the island. Meticulous records were also kept as to when the plantings were done and when the vegetables blossomed, produced food, and were harvested. Fresh vegetables popular on the Peary family's menu included peas, carrots, spinach, lettuce, Swiss chard, onions, radishes, and cauliflower. (Both, courtesy of GJMBC.)

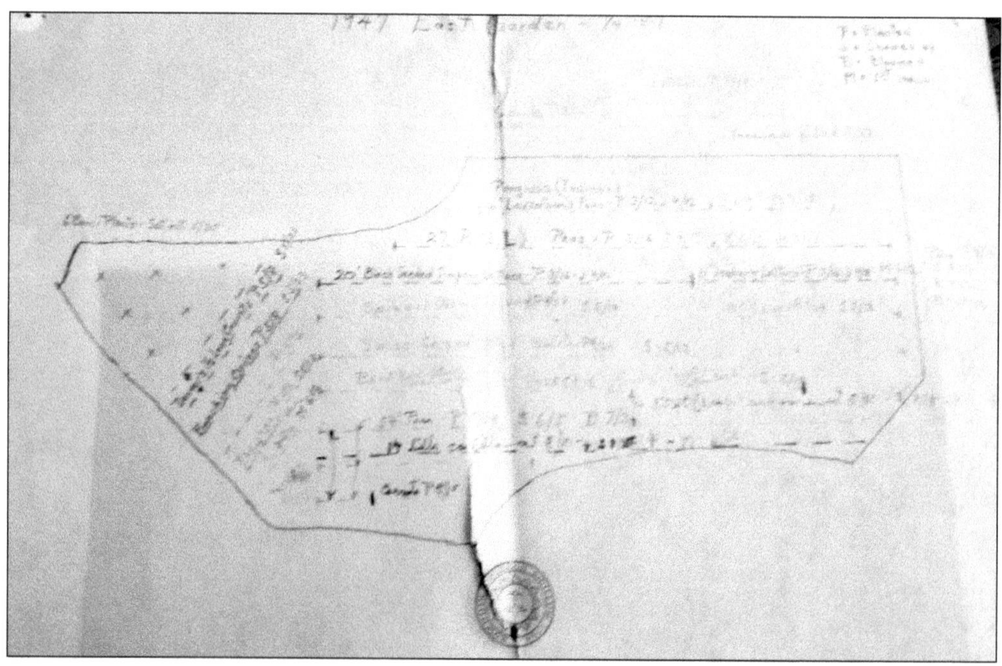

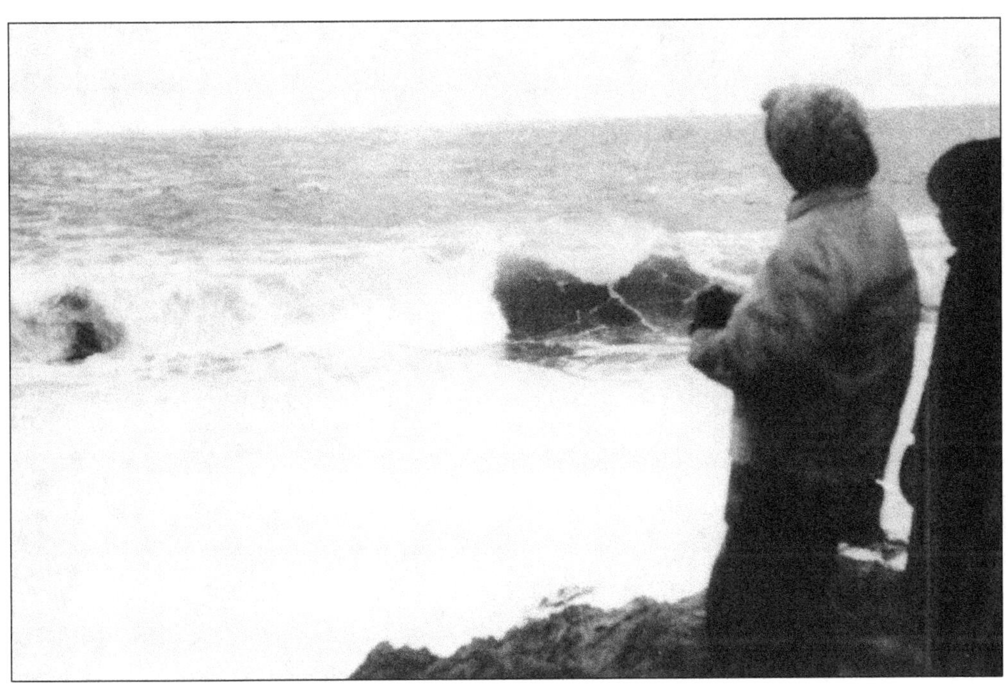

Living on the edge of the Atlantic Ocean with winds and weather howling would have been a very cold existence at times. The "ice-cream" surf off south beach is an example of the pummeling the island took during the winter. Though the beauty of the season is evident in these photographs, wintering on Eagle Island would have been an adventure not for the faint of heart.

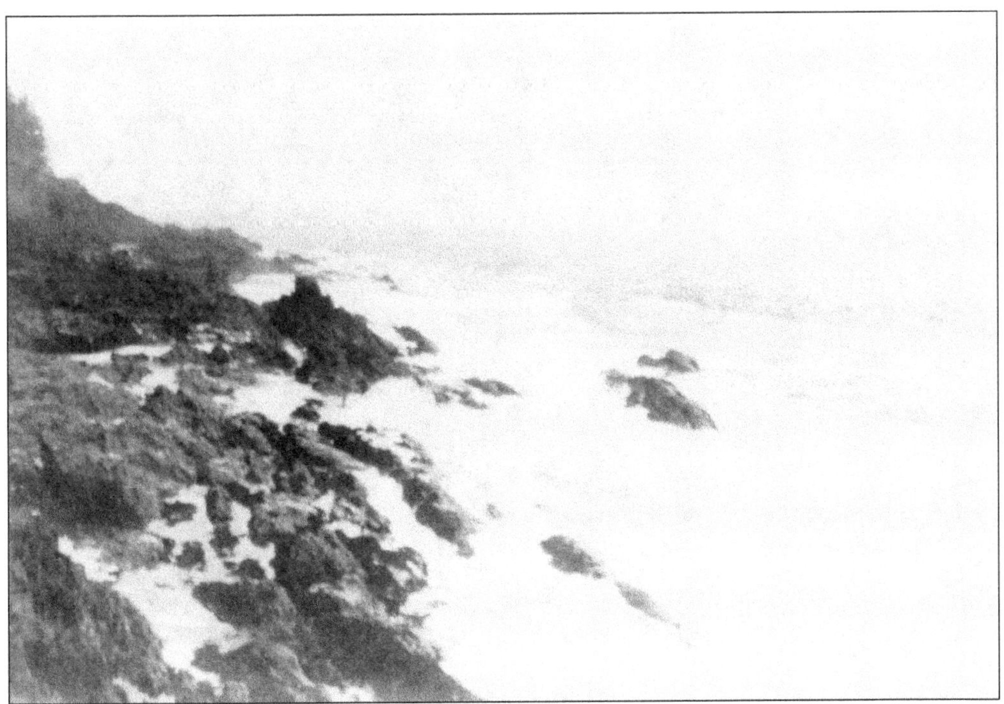

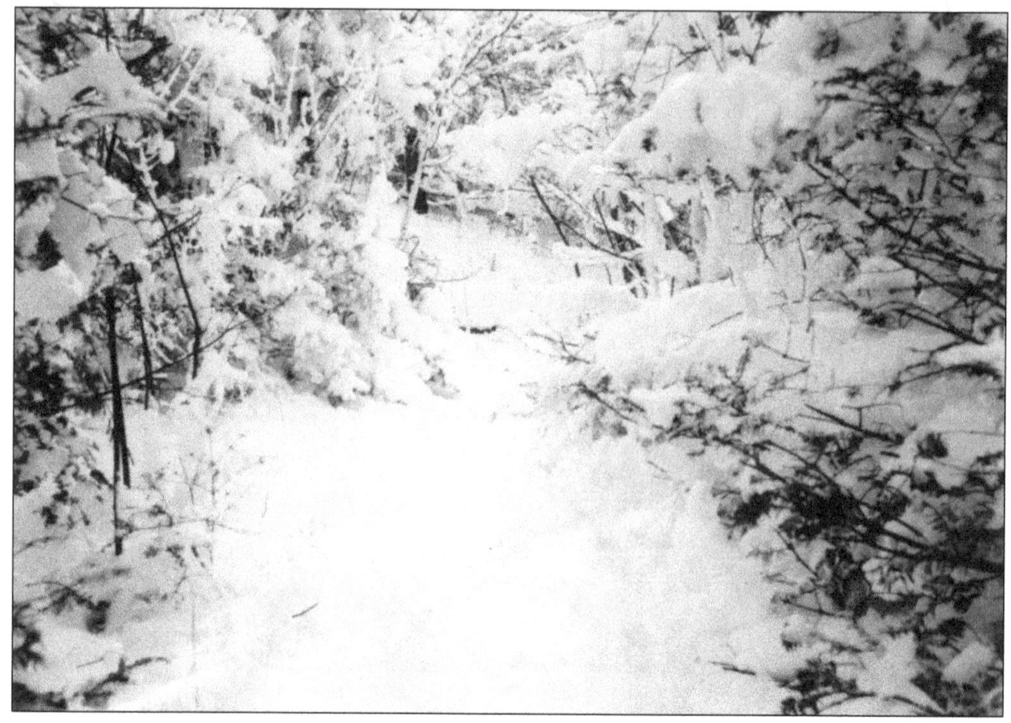

The two photographs here show the snowfall on the interior of the island and the trails deep with powder, giving the island a winter wonderland appearance that belies the cold and harsh weather. Ice and snow create problems for trees and shrubs. Coated with weighty ice and snow, many break and do not survive the season. One can almost feel the cold.

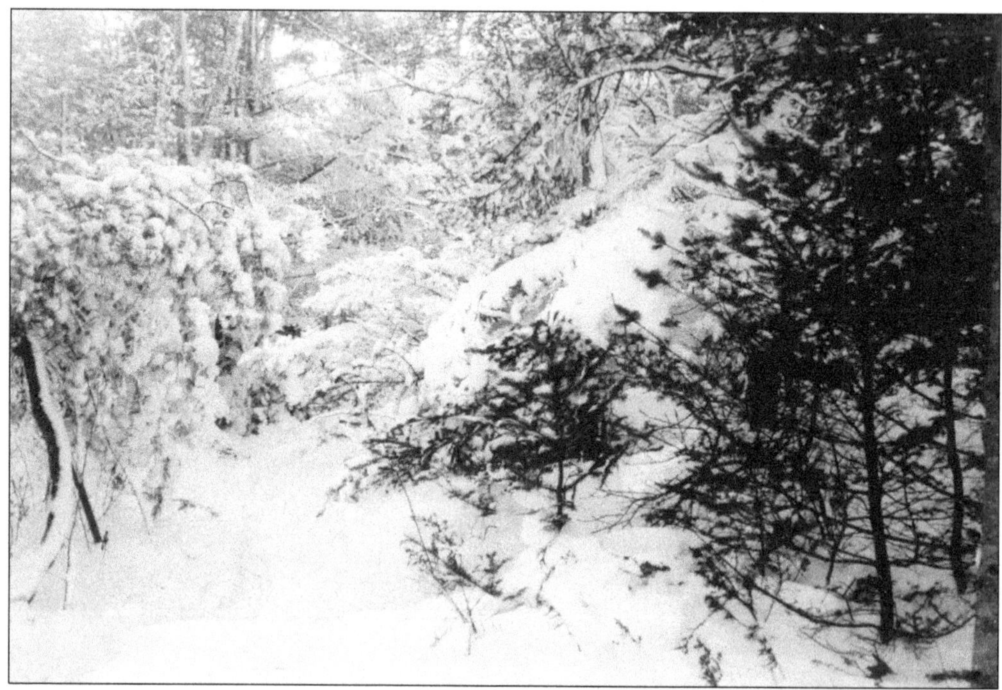

Seven

The State of Maine and the Friends of Peary's Eagle Island

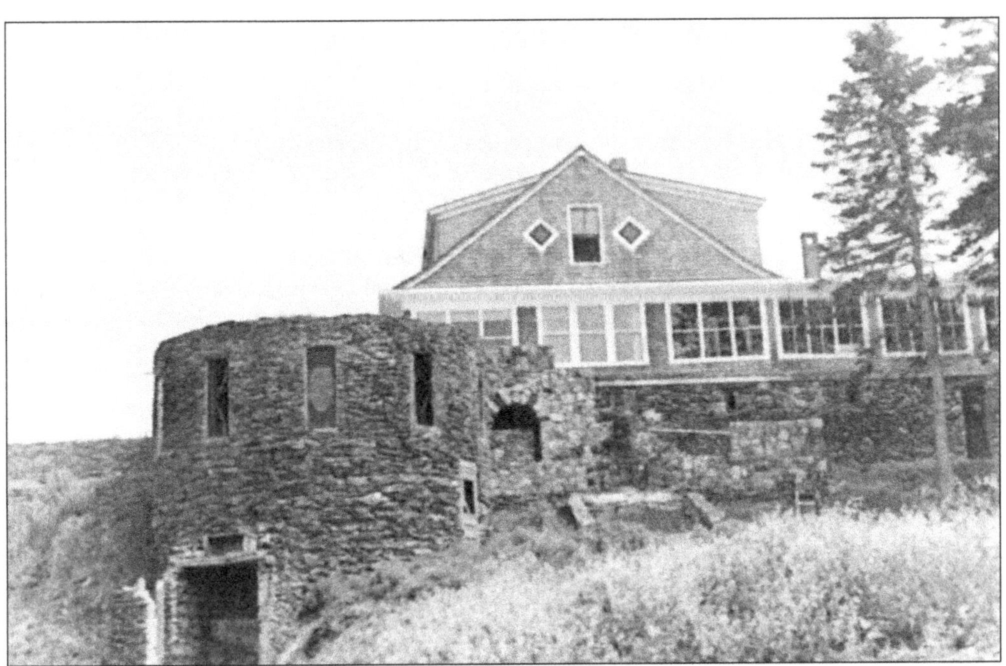

Management and care of the island became the responsibility of the Bureau of Parks and Lands (now part of Maine's Department of Agriculture, Conservation and Forestry). In 1967, the state assumed ownership of the island. The buildings had not been lived in for many years and had fallen into a state of disrepair. The photograph is from an aerial survey of the island done in the 1960s.

Know All Men by These Presents,

11266 805

That I, Marie Peary Kuhne, of Brunswick, County of Cumberland, State of Maine, being desirous of making a gift to the State of Maine in memory of my parents, Admiral and Mrs. Robert E. Peary, ~~in consideration of~~

~~paid by~~

~~the receipt whereof do hereby acknowledge,~~ **do hereby give, grant, bargain, sell and convey unto the said** STATE OF MAINE, its successors

~~heirs~~ **and assigns forever, a certain lot or parcel of land** with the buildings thereon, situated in Harpswell, in said County and State, bounded and described as follows:

The island known as Eagle Island, consisting of 17 acres, more or less, lying about 2 1/2 miles from South Harpswell.

Said property shall be used by the State as a historic site for the purpose of recreation and nature study by the people of Maine and their guests in such manner that its essential beauty shall not be unduly disturbed; and so long as my brother, Robert E Peary, Jr. and I are living, the State shall not make any substantial changes to the island without securing our prior consent. After our deaths it is requested that the State consult with our descendants prior to making any substantial changes.

The State, upon acceptance of this gift, shall keep the buildings and property in an adequate state of repair and protect and preserve them so far as reasonably possible.

In 1967, Marie Peary Kuhne (she married William W. Kuhne in 1967) conveyed Eagle Island, the house, the caretaker's cottage, and all their possessions on the island to the State of Maine. This is the deed to Eagle Island from Marie Peary Kuhne. In it, she and her brother, Robert Jr., stated that Eagle Island was to be preserved and maintained as a museum for "the people of Maine and their guests."

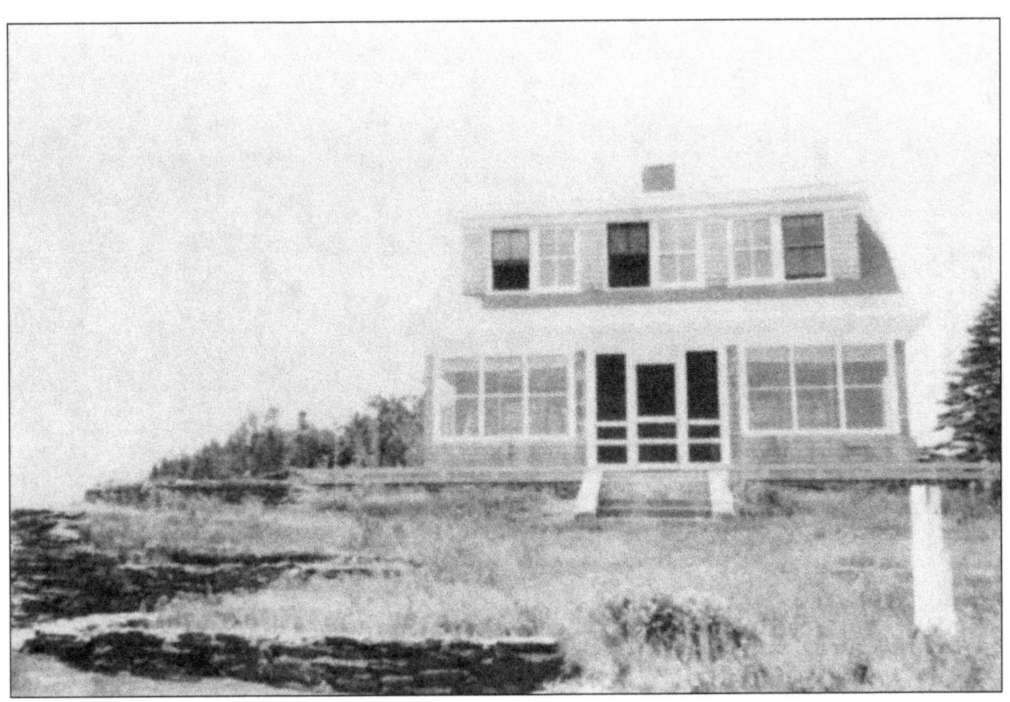

In the late 1960s, the State of Maine began repairs to Peary's cottage. Every effort is made to maintain historical accuracy when making repairs. The cottage Peary envisioned remains basically unchanged from the last expansion in 1912–1913.

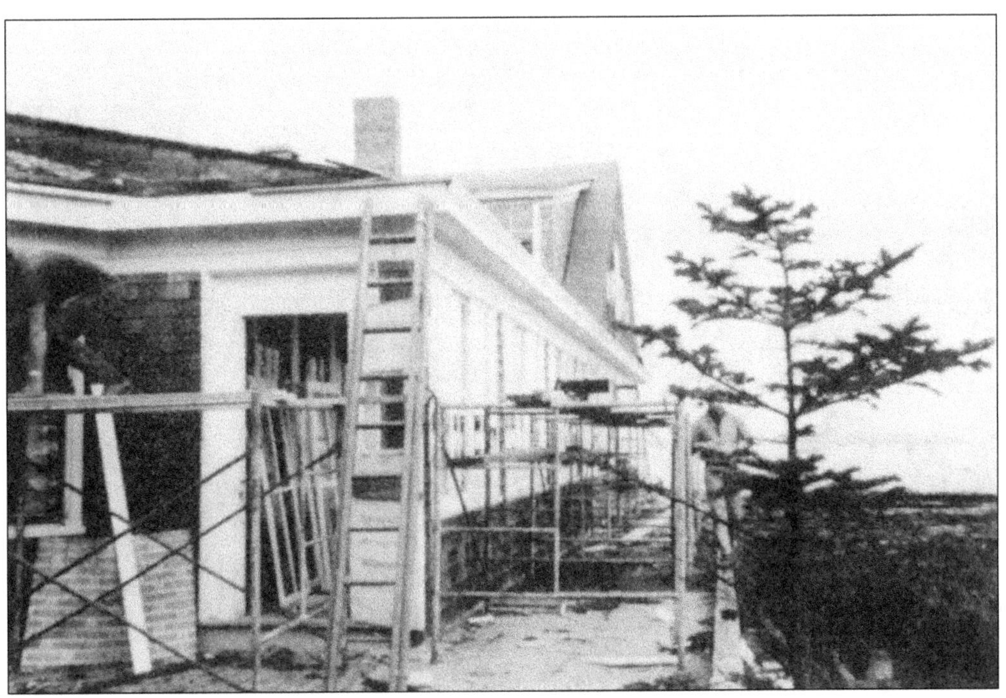

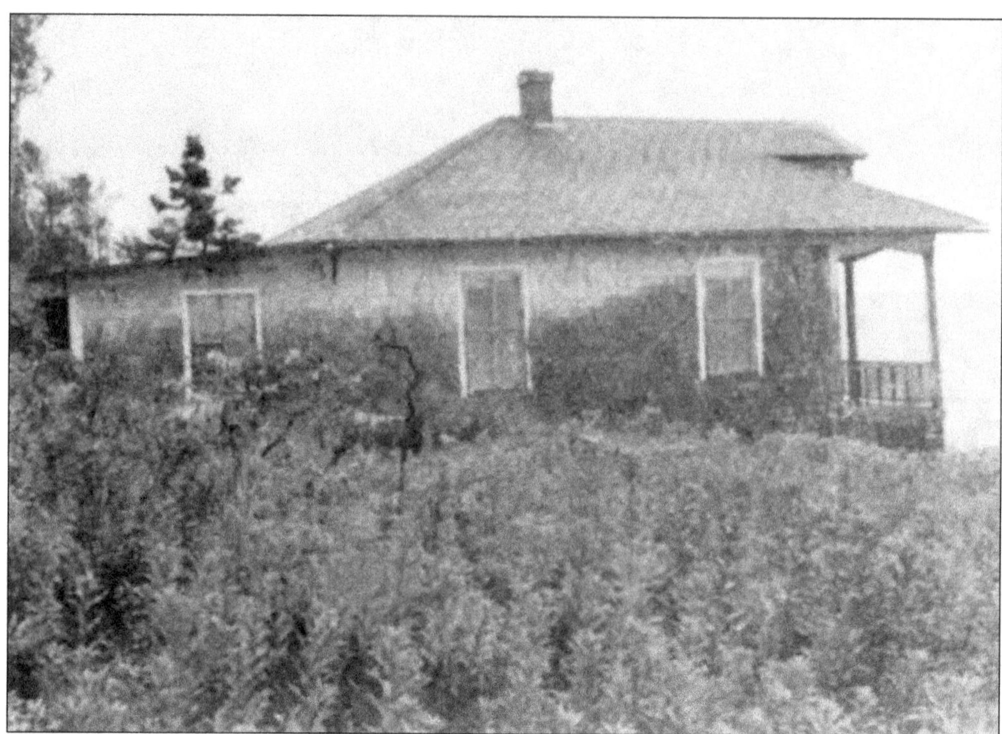

The caretaker's cottage, originally built in 1904, has seen very little change from the original plans. The stairway that faced the west side of the house is gone. The porch has a railing across the front, and the only entrance into the cottage now is in the back. It too had no electricity or running water in the conventional sense. In 2013, the state added solar panels on the top of the new welcome center, which help to provide electricity to the caretaker's cottage.

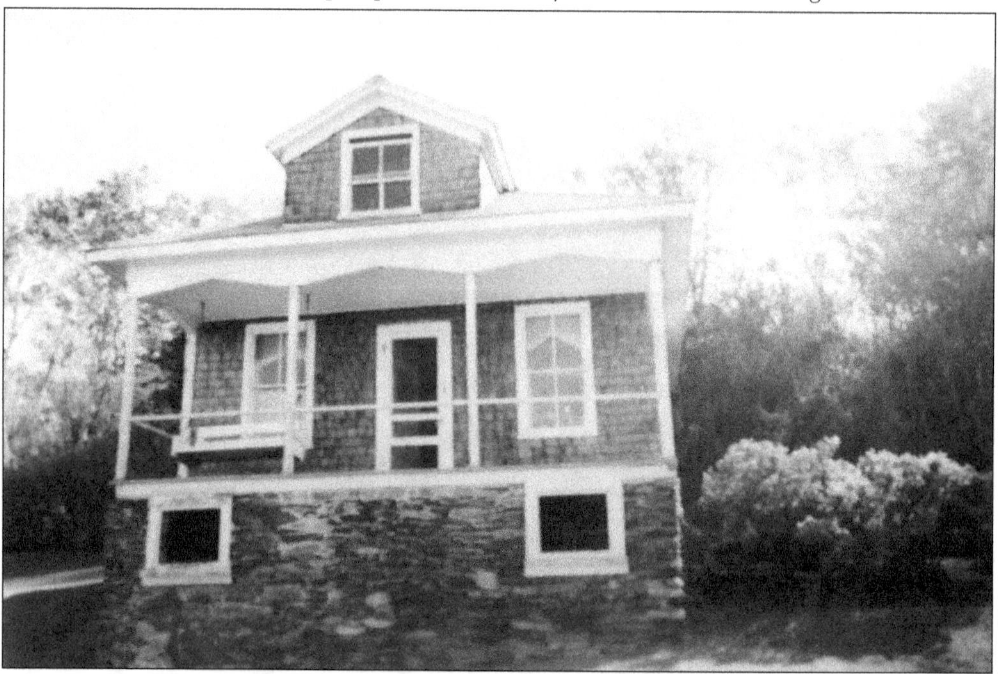

This aerial view of the main house and of the caretaker's cottage shows them nestled in the snow. The caretaker's cottage (right) is as much of a historic structure as the main house. It sits on a stone foundation that is almost a full story high due to the grade and slope of the land. It remains the summer home to the state's staff who manage Eagle Island. The main home looks cold and lonely with boarded-up windows. One can get a sense of the size of the foundation and the west bastion and what an effort it was to raise the house an entire story to put in a foundation.

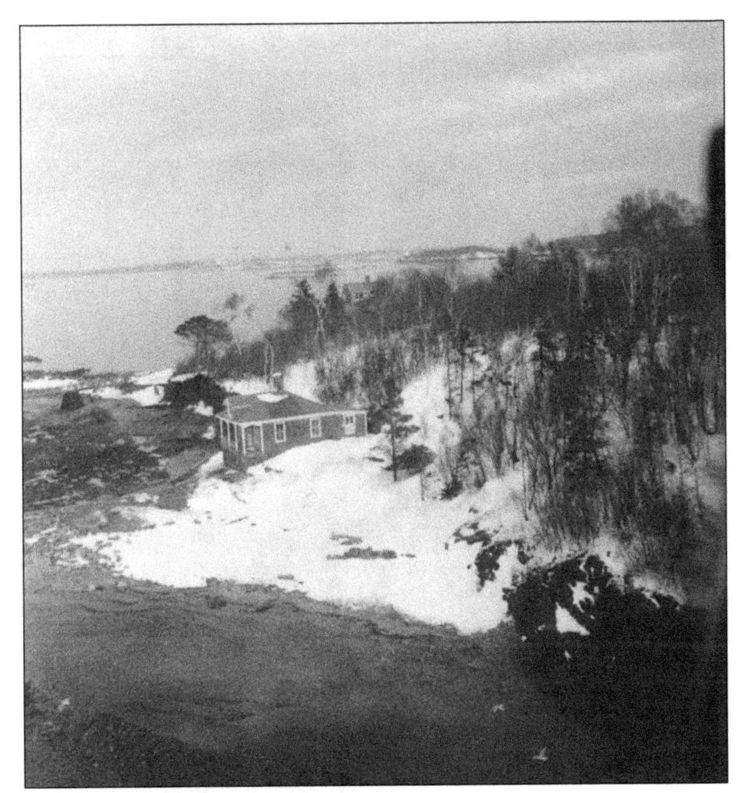

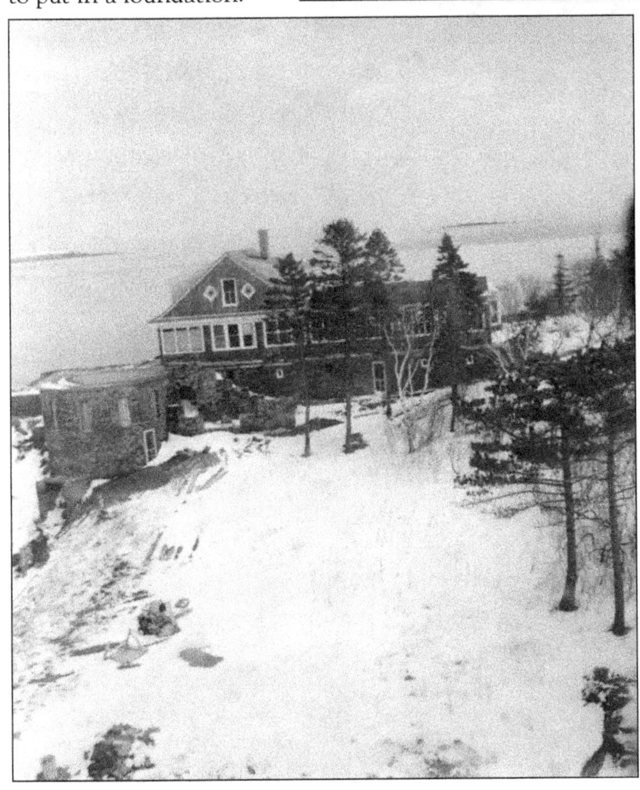

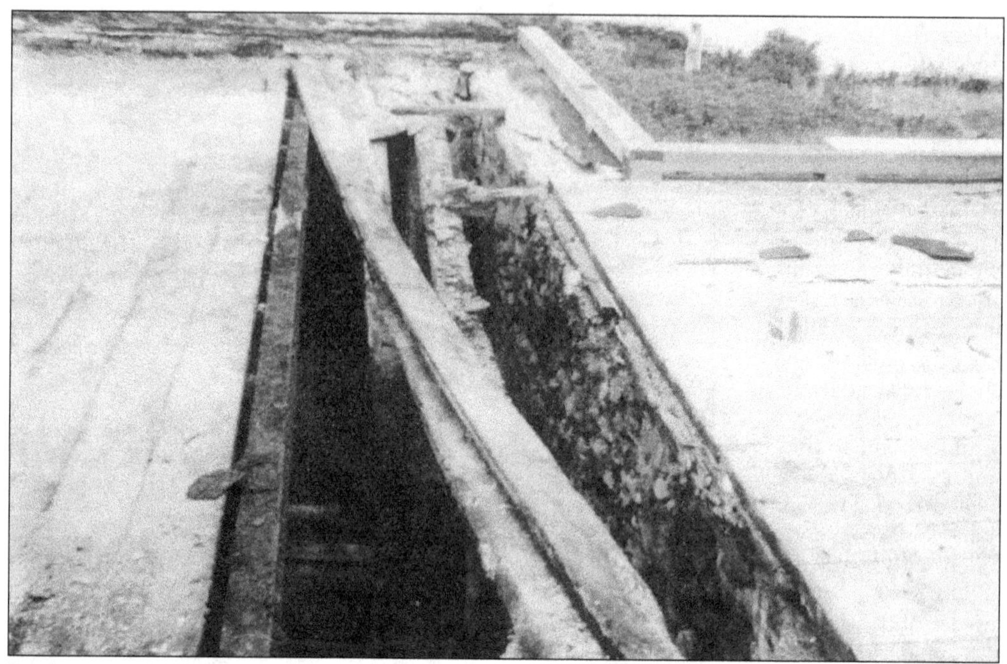

By the time the state came to own Eagle Island, the sod roof of the east bastion had caved in, revealing steel I-beams that supported the roof. Only the walls survive today. By the 1990s, the roof of the west bastion failed and led to damage inside the library.

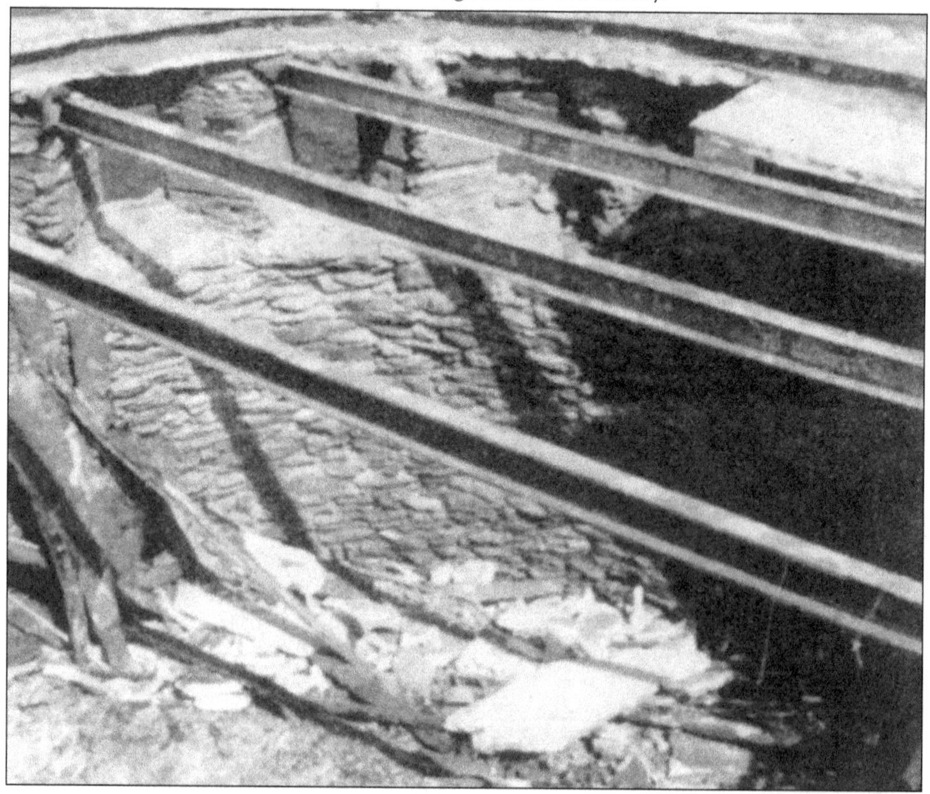

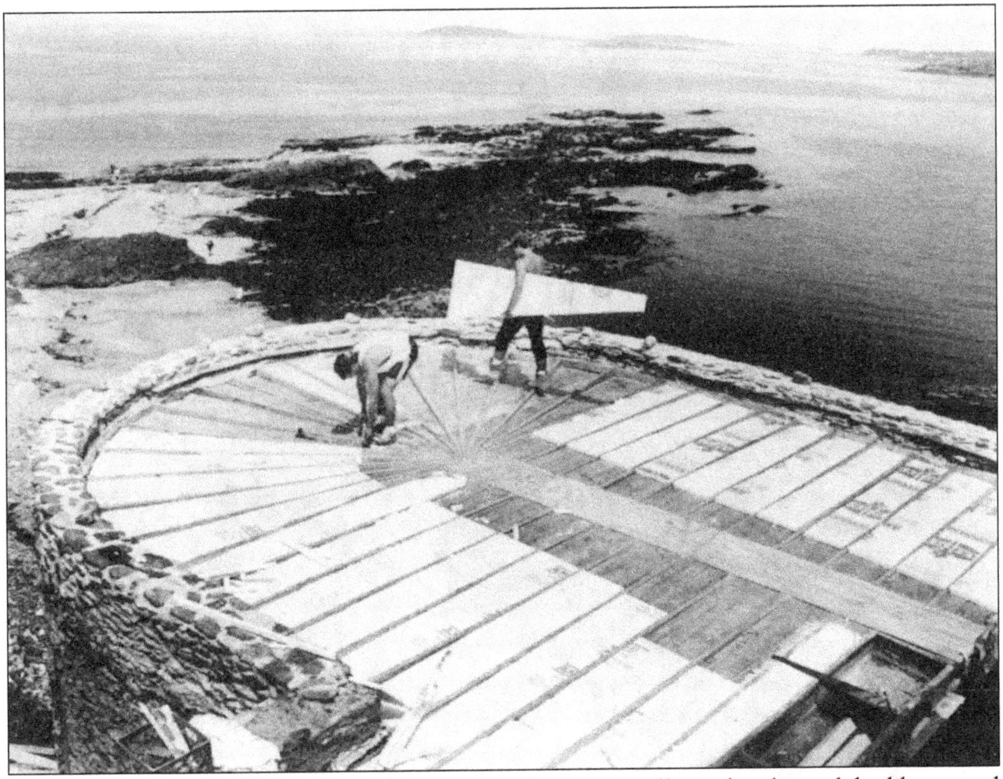

The State of Maine had to remove the entire roof, interior walls, and ceiling of the library and replace them all with the same yellow southern pine that was originally used in this room and the rest of the house. The exterior roof now has a synthetic membrane to prevent water damage. The library today looks the same as it did when Peary used this room as his study (see photograph on page 123).

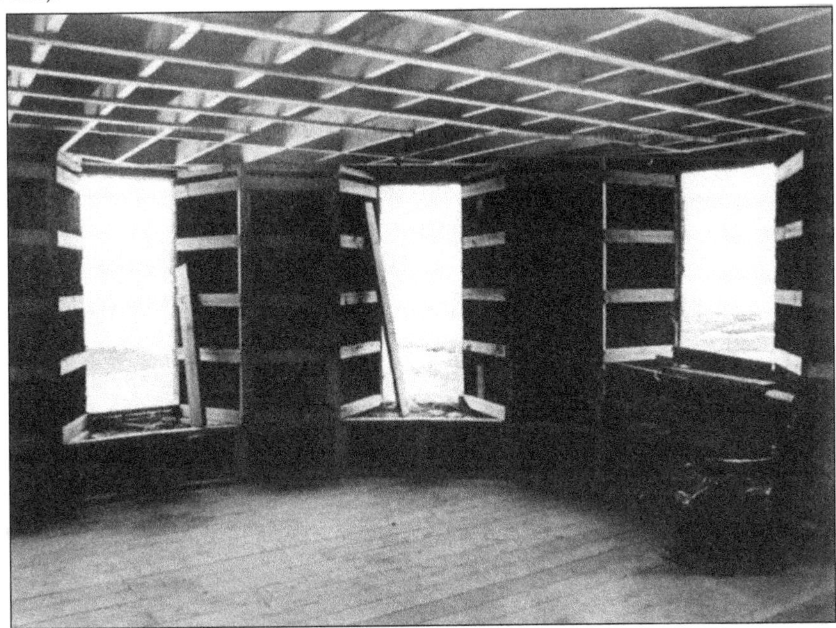

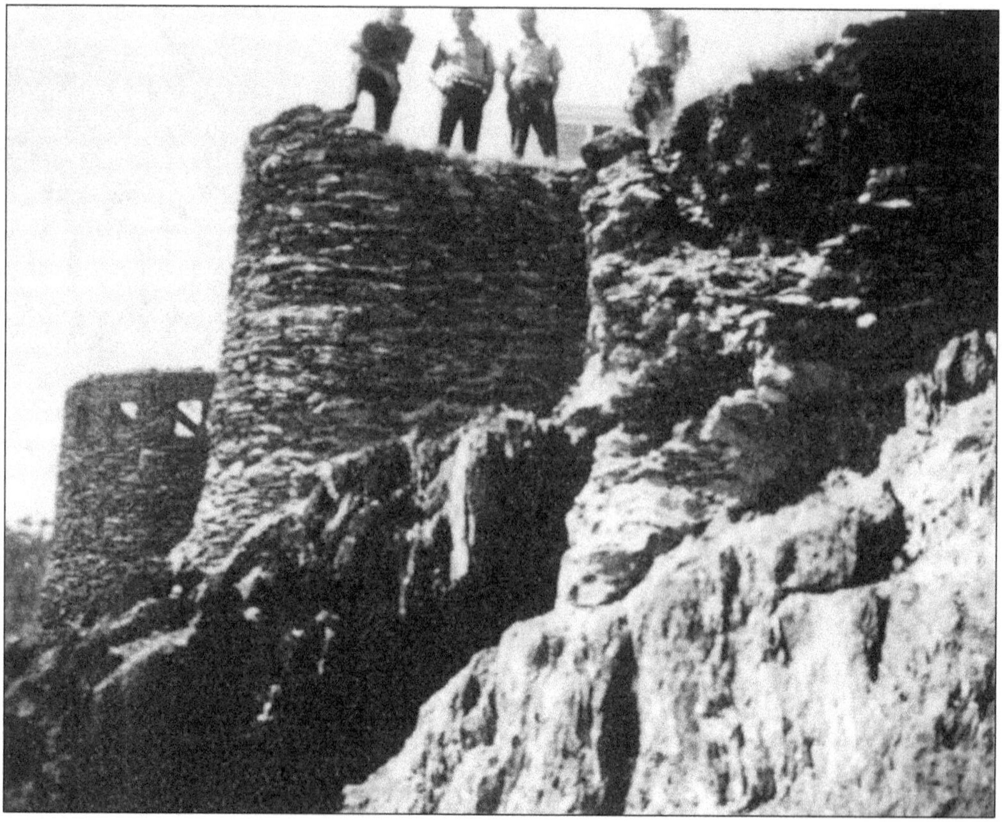

The northern end of Eagle Island has an impressive seawall system. The wall had started to tilt outward and eventually would have toppled into the sea. To repair this, the wall was shored up with anchored cables, which pulled it back into alignment.

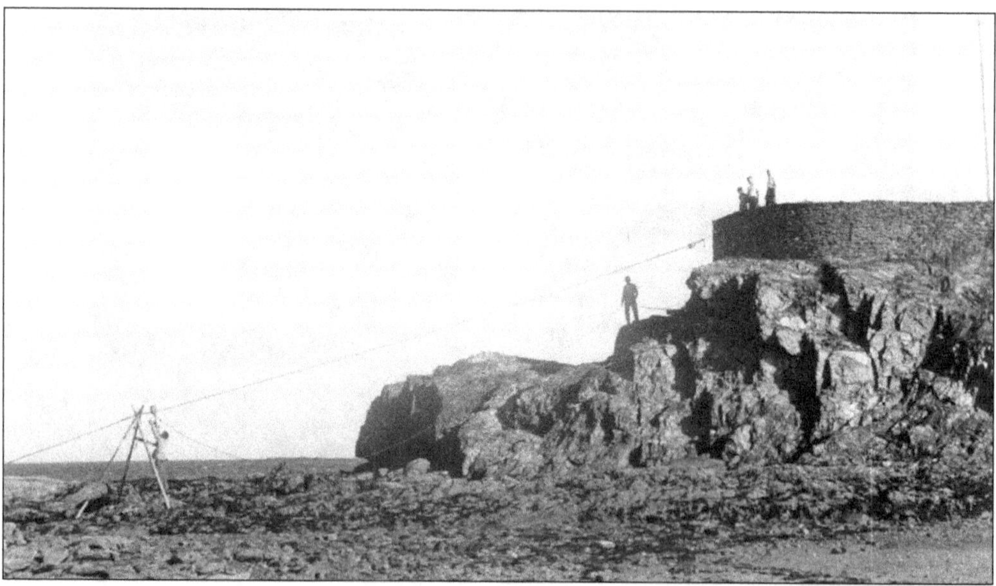

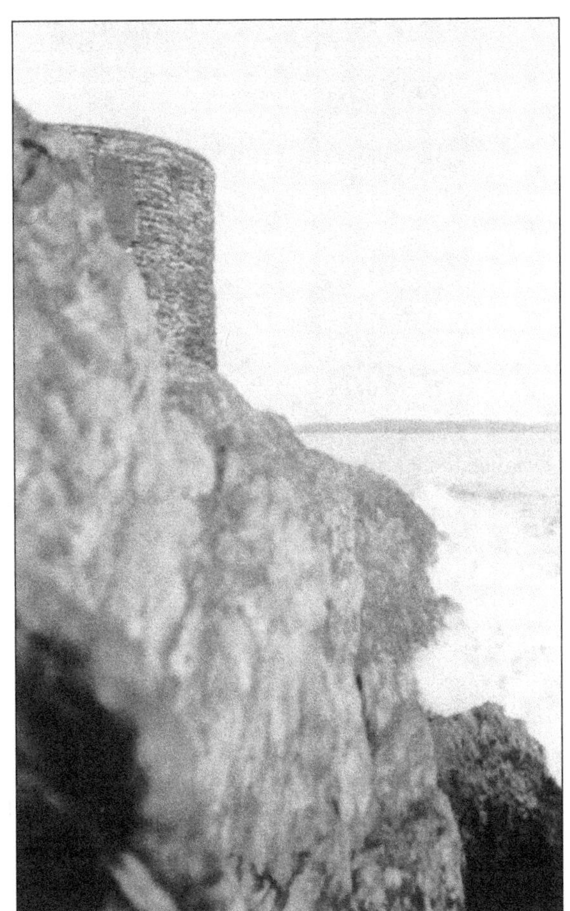

The ocean's power and a century of waves beating on the seawall systems that Admiral Peary built around the island left the bastions and seawalls in need of restoration. At right, the east bastion is being slammed by waves from the Atlantic. Below, the roof of the bastion, with the remnants of a skylight, show the evidence of decades of weather and sun.

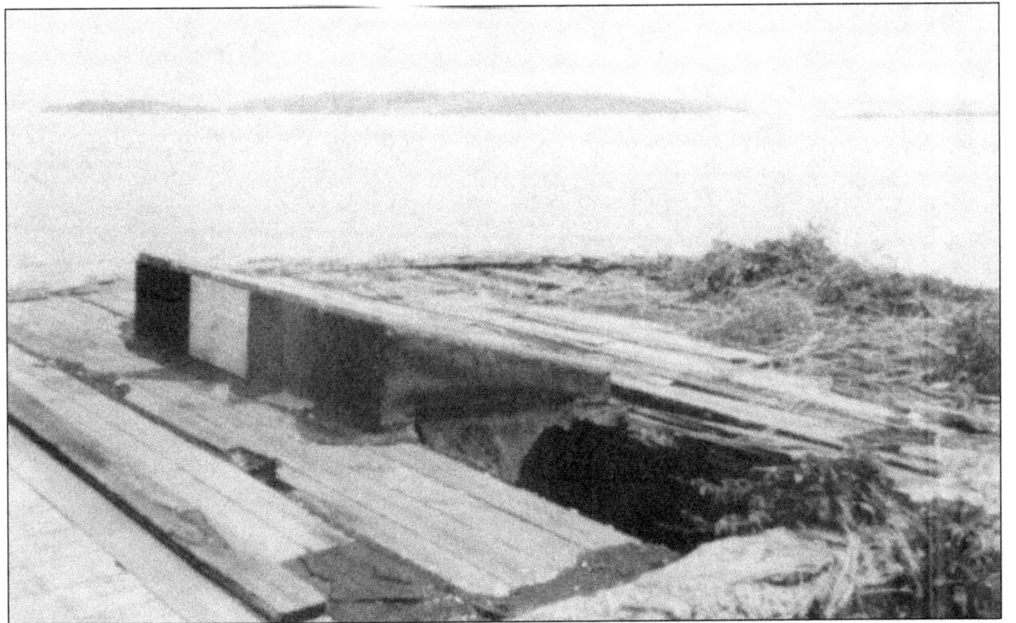

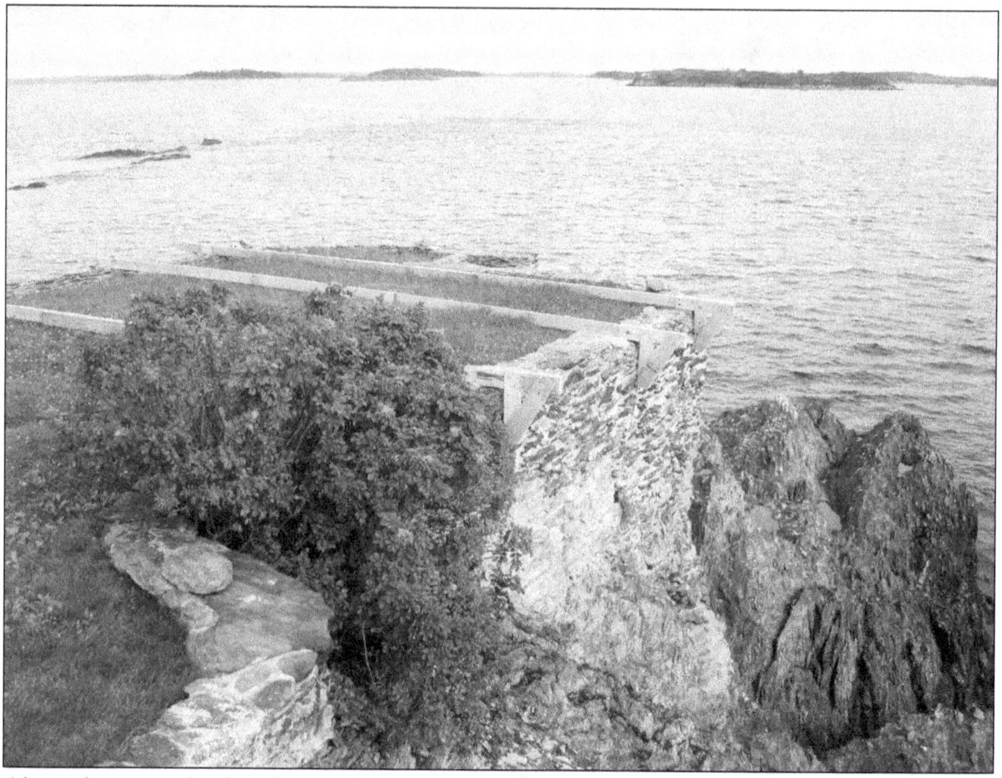

Above, large wooden handmade clamps were used to hold the bastion and the new stonework in place while it set. Below, rocks and mortar are thoughtfully being built "back into" the eastern wall of the north bastion.

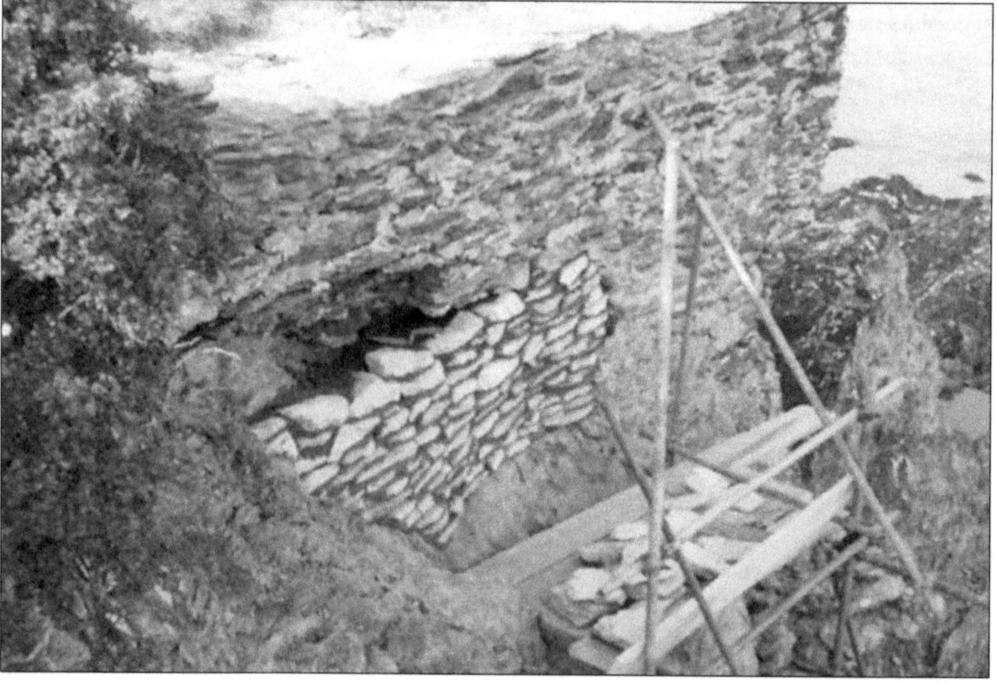

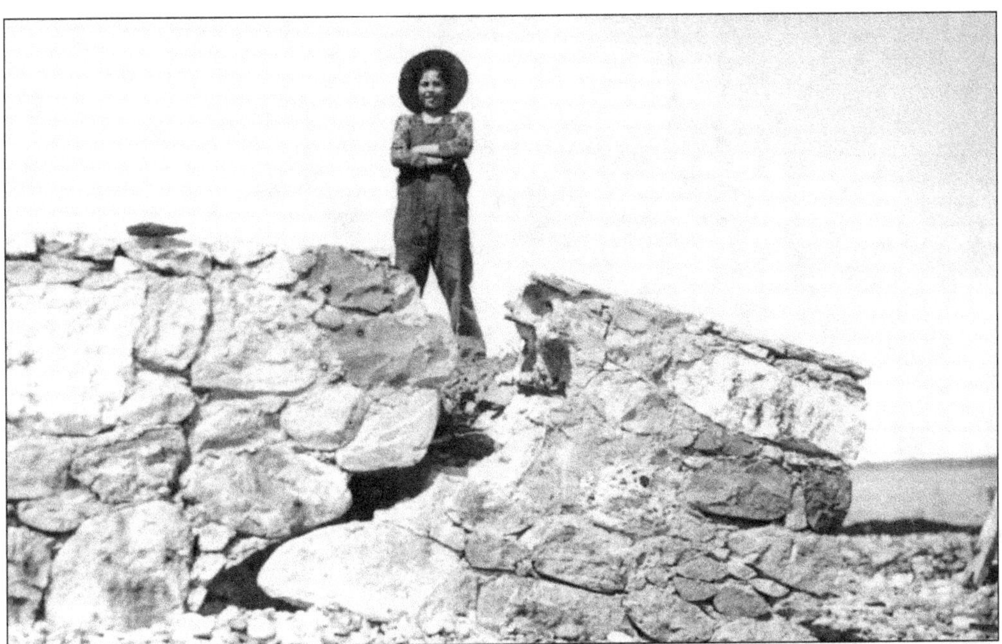

Ed Stafford, dressed here in overalls, perhaps ready to work, surveys the seawall damage between the large front lawn and the sandy cove beach to the west of the house. Clearly, the seawalls take a beating from ocean storms and high tides. At right, the seawall here is the pump house, and the damage by constant waves from tidal action is evident. Not only were the tides a significant factor in seawall damage, but fluctuations in ocean water temperature affected them as well.

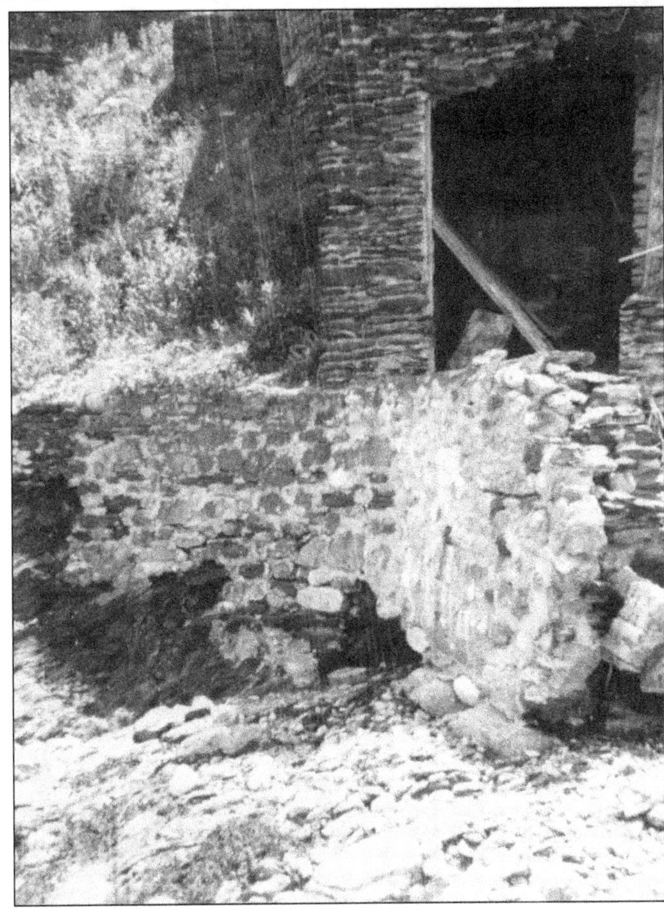

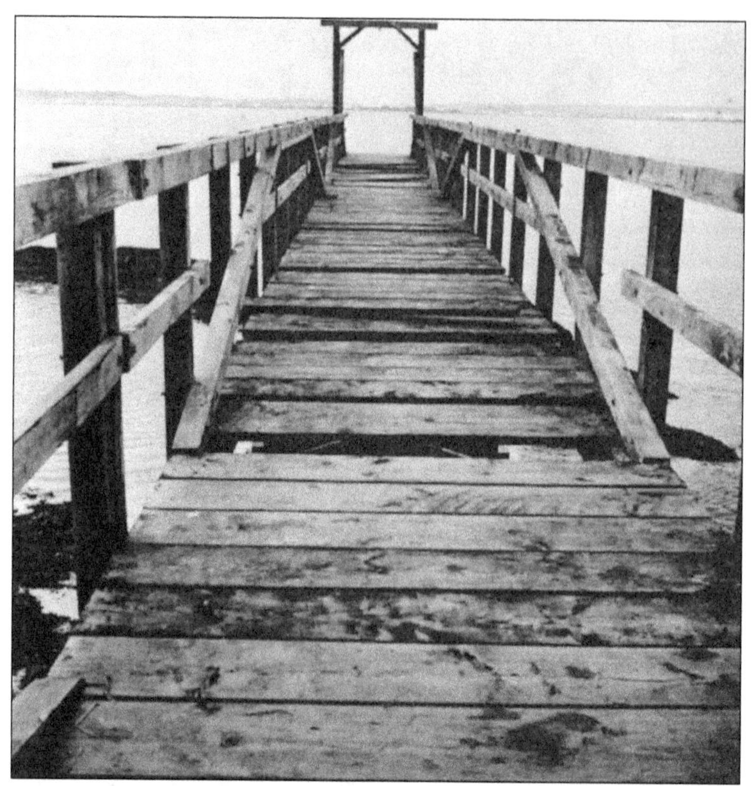

By the 1970s, the pier onto the island was also a casualty of weather and neglect. The current pier is situated about halfway between the main house and the caretaker's cottage in a cove on the west side of the island. The pier serves as an obvious access to the island for visitors who, unlike the original owners, are not equipped to land onshore.

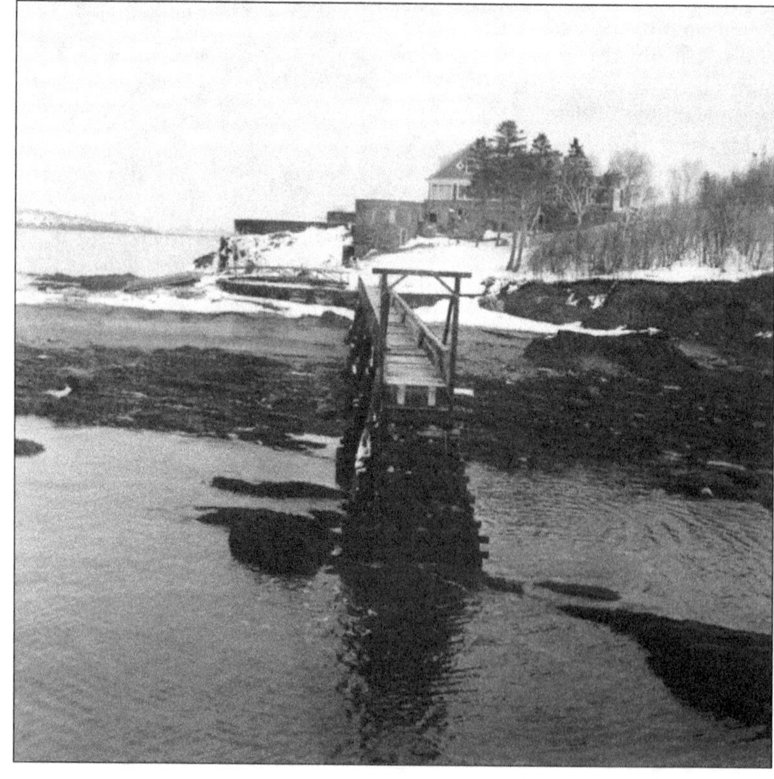

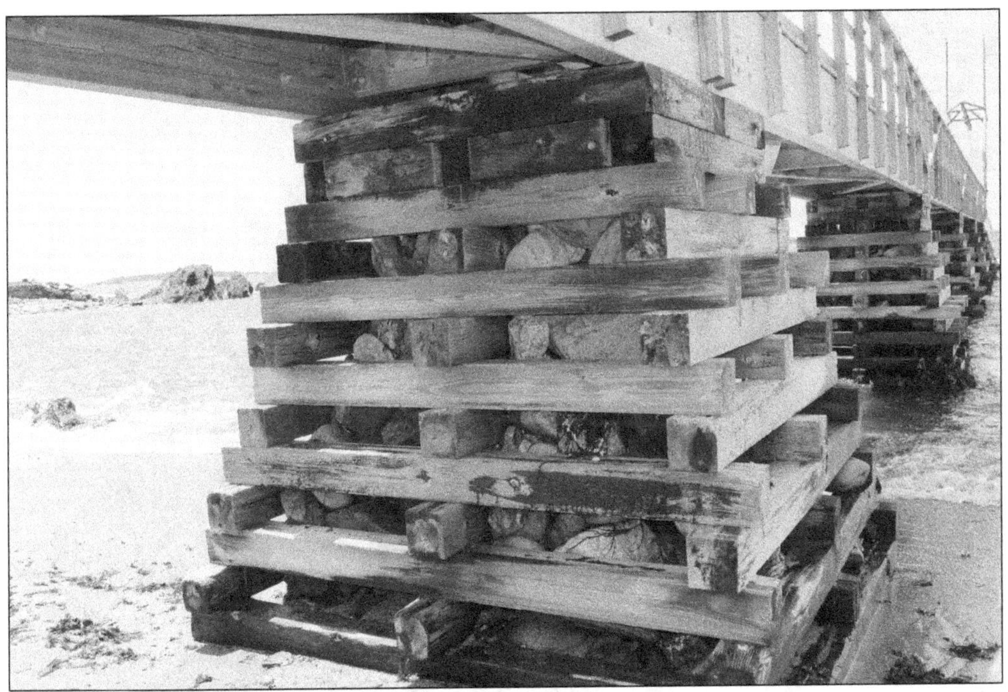

This crib-type structure can sufficiently withstand heavy winds and waters. To prevent constant slamming of waves and tide against a solid structure, this open cribbing allows the tides to ebb and flow while providing solid footing for the pier above. The pier and the footings are made of wood. Below, state workers are installing the gantry, which raises the ramp.

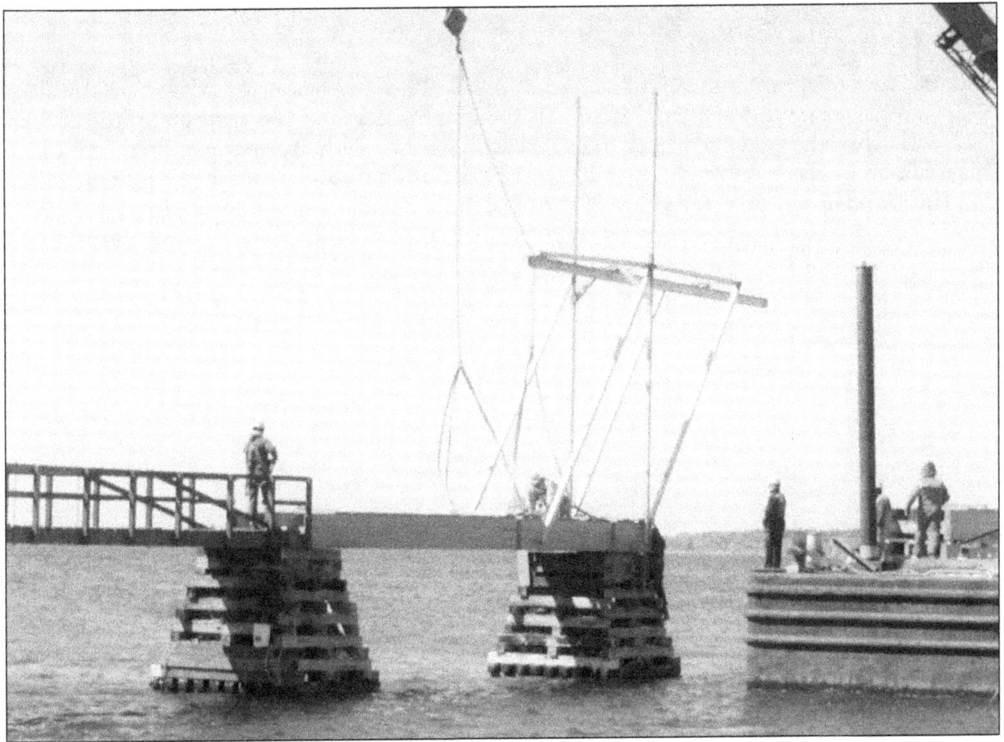

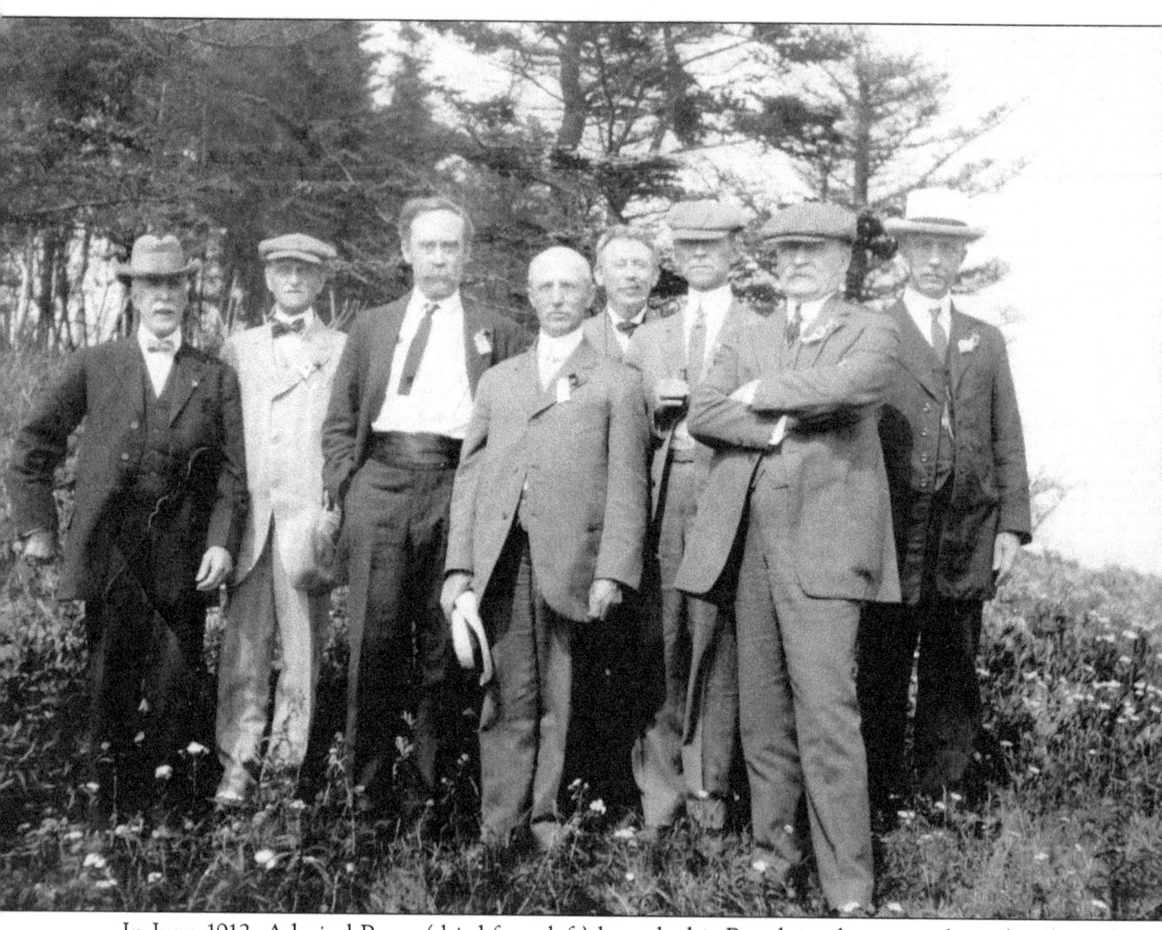

In June 1912, Admiral Peary (third from left) brought his Bowdoin classmates from the class of 1877, with whom he graduated, back to Eagle Island for their 35th class reunion. In recent years, this tradition has been reintroduced and members of Bowdoin's 50th reunion class are invited to visit the island. Many take advantage of the opportunity. (Courtesy of GJMBC.)

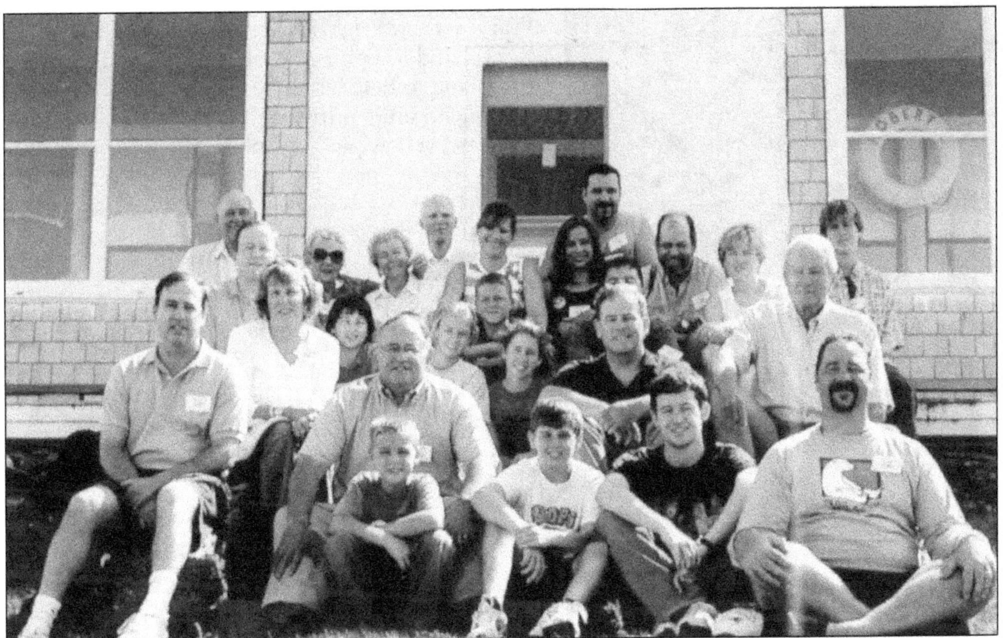

The Peary family returned often and held many family reunions on Eagle Island. Here, a group of Peary descendants is resting on the stairs heading to the north porch door and on into the living room.

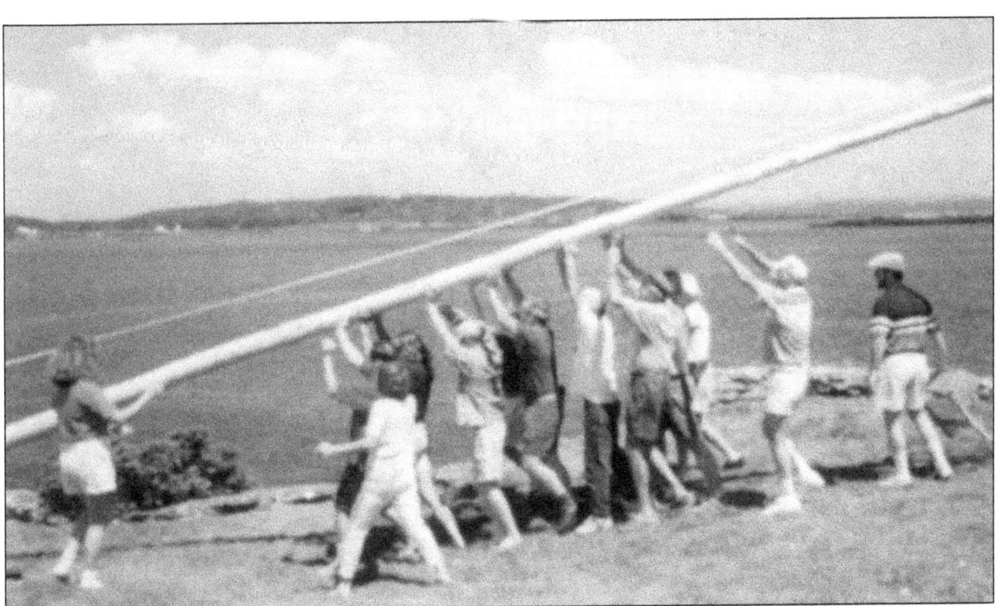

Descendants of Admiral Peary are seen here raising the flagpole on the north lawn—described by someone as "the Pearys at the Pole."

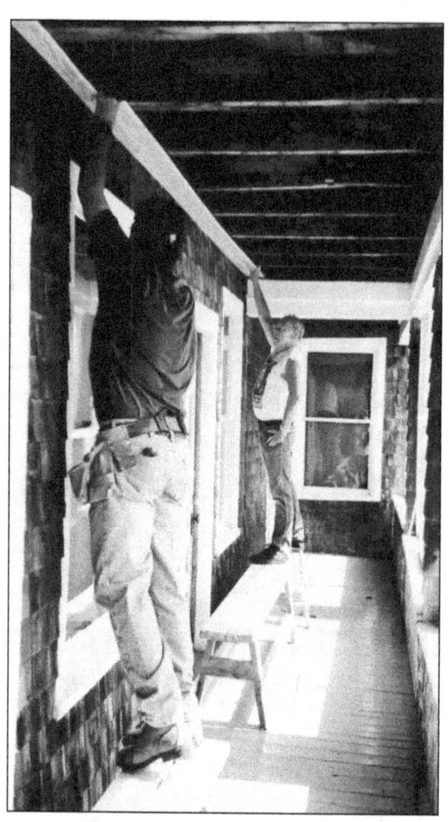

Peary Stafford (right), a great-grandson of Robert and Josephine Peary, has returned to the island to help with needed repairs. He is helping an unidentified volunteer replace the southern yellow pine ceiling on the east porch.

Robert Peary Jr. (left), Robert E. Peary III (center), and Ed Stafford are seen here outside the Admiral's library. The event was the rededication of the library in 1992 following repairs to the roof and ceiling. Stafford provided guided tours for visitors to Eagle Island, relating stories of his childhood there.

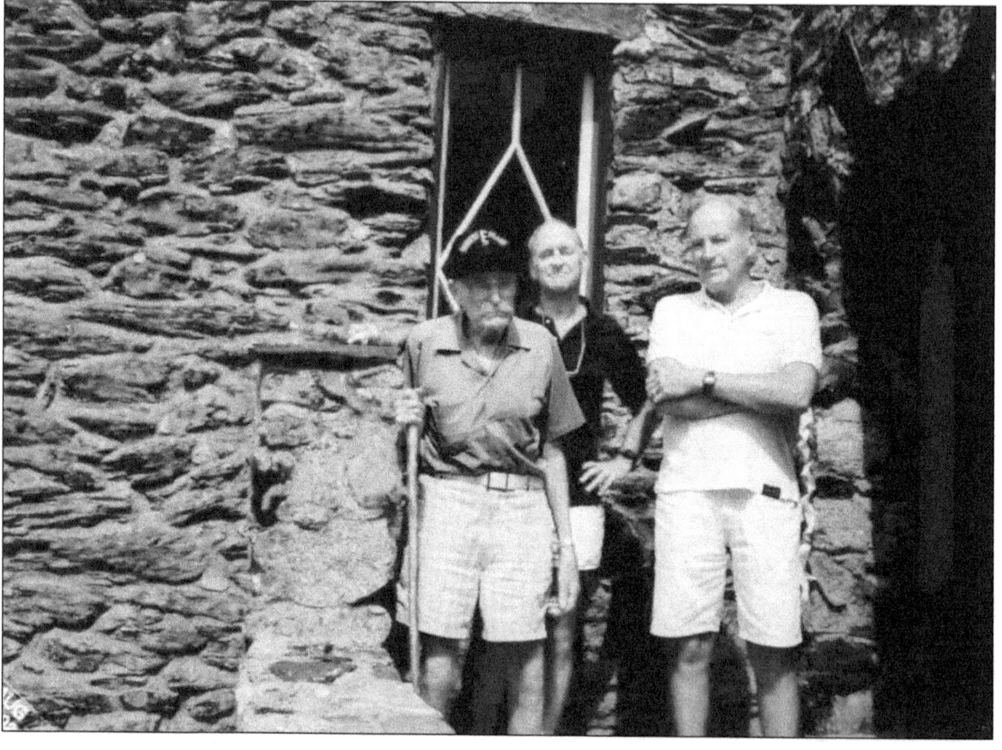

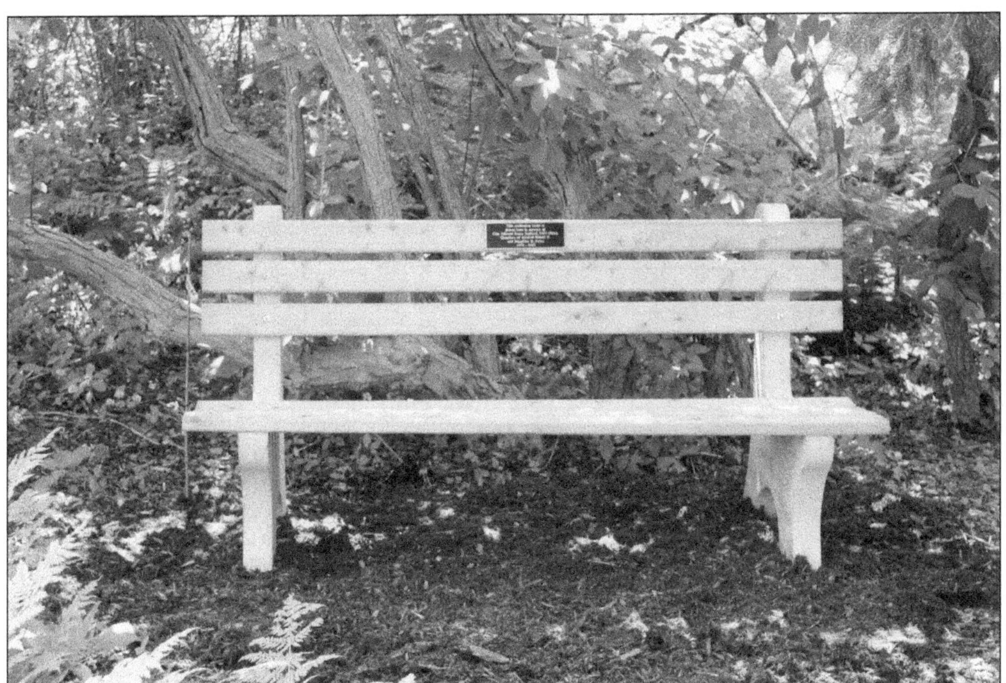

Ed Stafford passed away in 2014. He did so much to welcome visitors to the island. The Friends of Peary's Eagle Island donated this meditation bench in his memory and honor. This bench can be found beneath a large white hydrangea tree that Josephine Peary had planted many years ago.

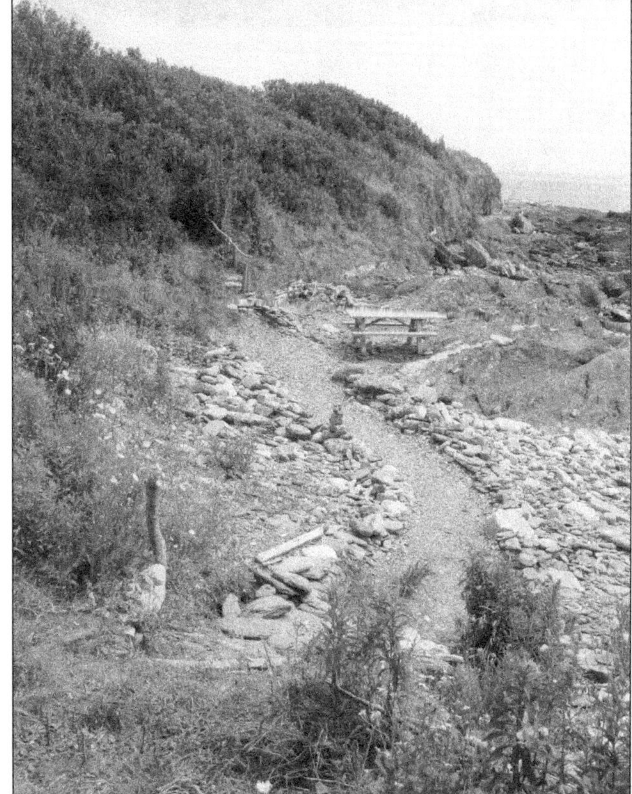

This is the trail across the south end of Eagle Island. Every year, winter storms demolish this section of the trail. It must be re-created each summer during a Trail Day conducted by the Friends of Peary's Eagle Island. Volunteers clean trails, spread mulch, and install water bars on the trails.

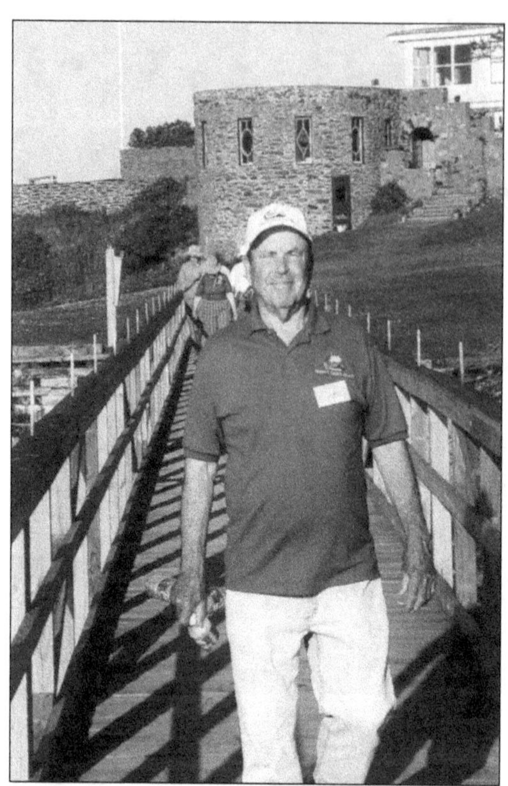

With approval from the Town of Harpswell, the Friends of Peary's Eagle Island volunteers, led by Adm. Harry Rich (USN Ret.) and in cooperation with workers from the State of Maine's Bureau of Parks and Lands, built a welcome center. The building was constructed largely with hand tools and pure determination. It is a wooden structure, 18 feet by 22 feet, with a shed roof, cedar shingle siding, and six-over-six double-hung sash windows. It is tucked away in an area very near where Bob's workshop once stood.

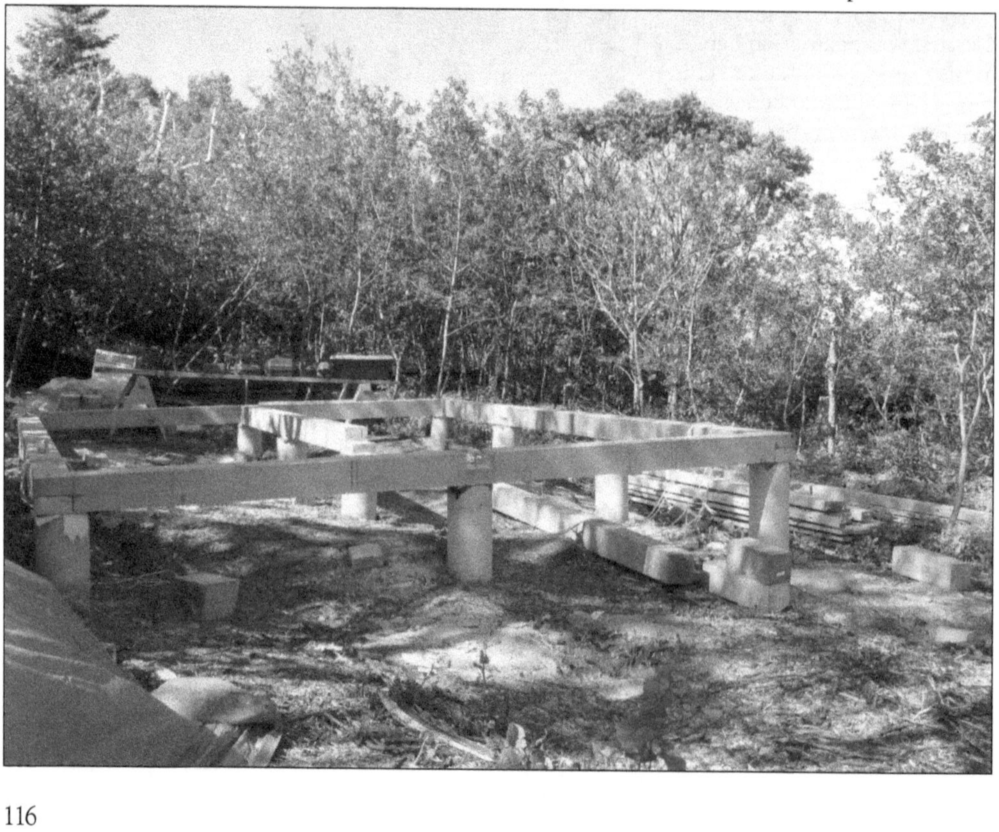

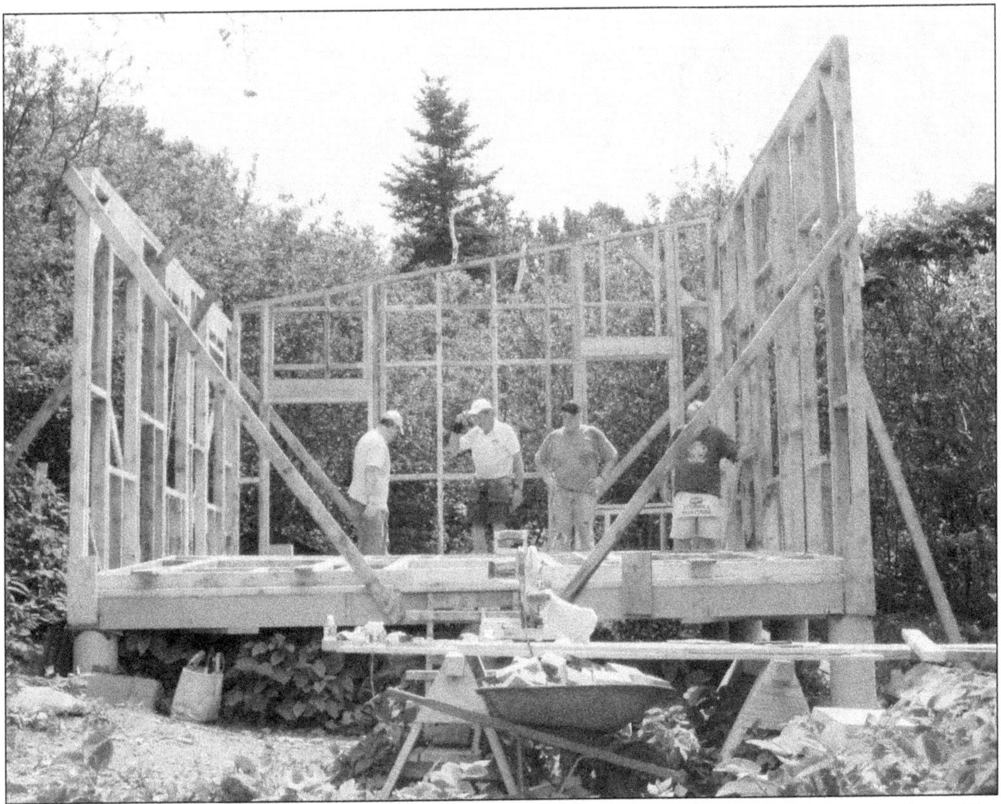

Under the supervision of the Friends of Peary's Eagle Island, the welcome center was built wall by wall. Above, with three walls up, the fourth and front wall was raised on Trail Day 2012, similar to an old-fashioned barn raising. Below is a photograph of the welcome center as it stands today. It was designed by Friends of Peary's Eagle Island board member Ned Dewey and closely resembles the original workshop Robert E. Peary Jr. had on the west side of the island (see page 83).

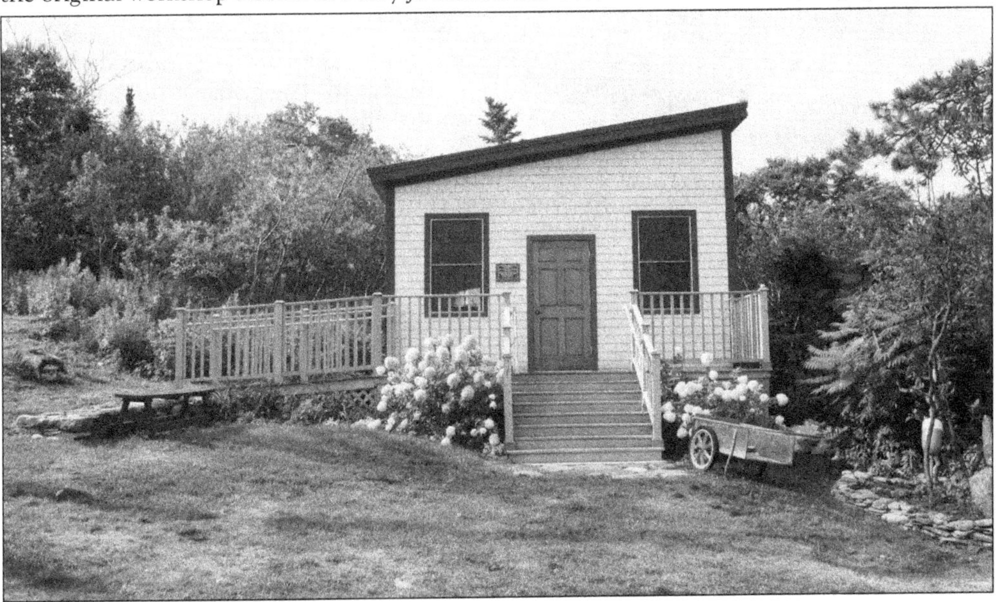

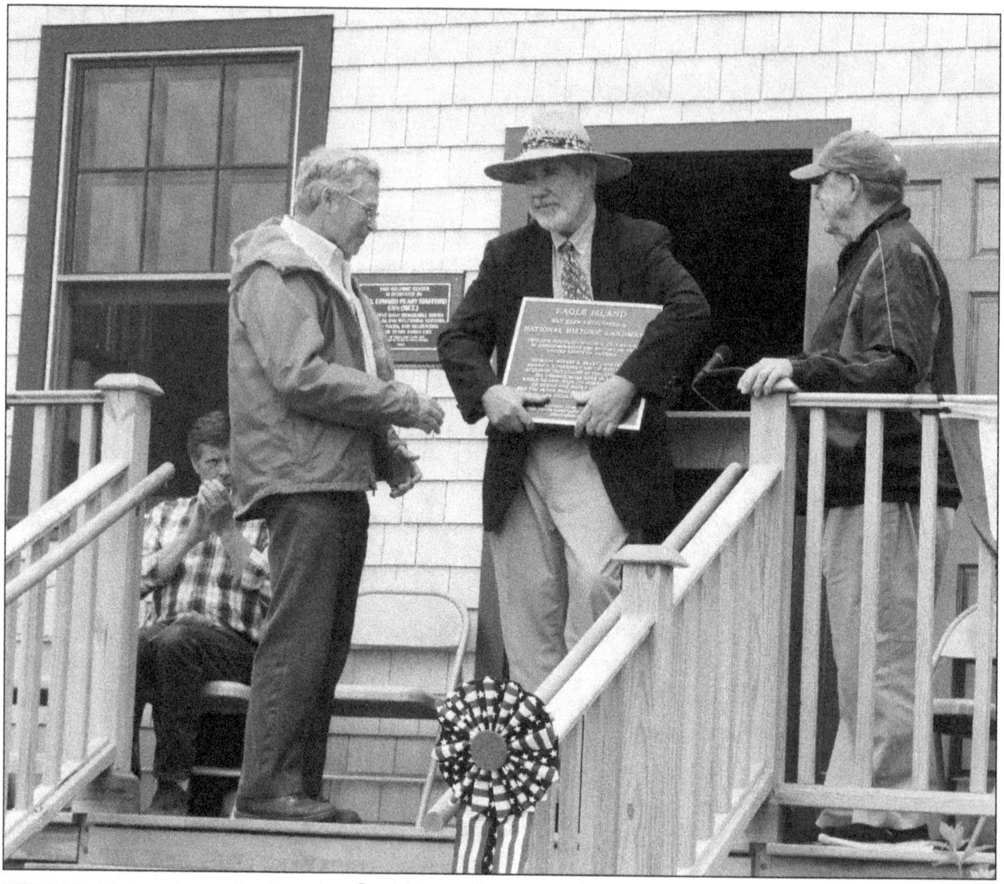

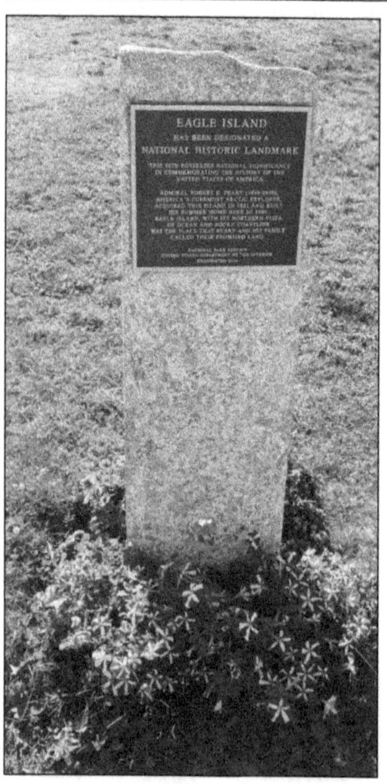

In 2014, Adm. Robert E. Peary's Eagle Island, a Maine Historic Site, was awarded National Historic Landmark designation. During the summer of 2015, that award was presented to the Maine Department of Agriculture, Conservation and Forestry's commissioner and to the Friends of Peary's Eagle Island. The plaque is now affixed to an old granite mooring that was found on the seabed near the pier. The park staff calculated the weight of the block of granite, floated it to the high tide mark on the beach using spare mooring balls for buoyancy, and then hauled it across the lawn using PVC rollers to its present location.

Eight

The Admiral, Josephine, and Their Cottage

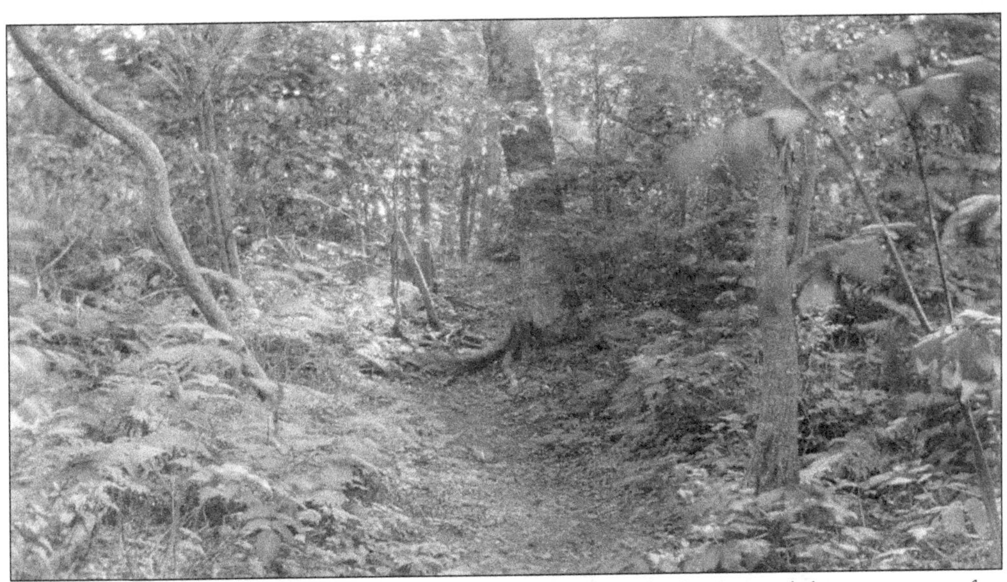

The interior of Eagle Island now has six or seven trails where birds nest, and these are open after birds have fledged their nests. The trail pictured here, once called "Fern Valley," is part of what is now known as Admiral's Way. It was the first trail carved out of the woods by Admiral Peary, thus the name. Eagle Island offers a wonderful blend of being in the Maine woods but open to vistas of Casco Bay and the wide-open Atlantic Ocean. This was part of the charm of Eagle Island when Admiral Peary and his school buddies landed here as young men. Eagle Island, every part of it, was home to Admiral Peary and eventually all his family.

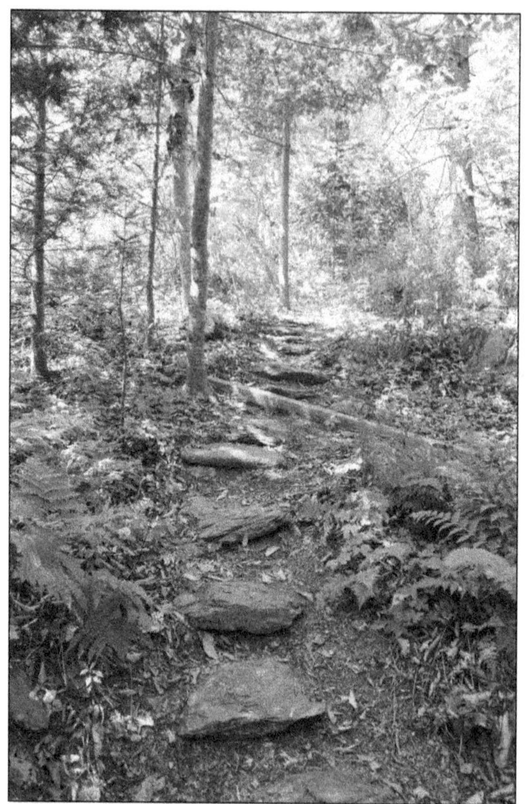

At left is a walking trail on Eagle Island that takes the hiker through a typical Maine woods scene—pine trees, birch trees, sparrows, and finches. Below is a view off the east coast of the island showing Mark Island, which is one of a dozen granite day markers (navigational aids) along the coast of Maine; it opened in 1827. It now has a light and is a lighted aid to navigation.

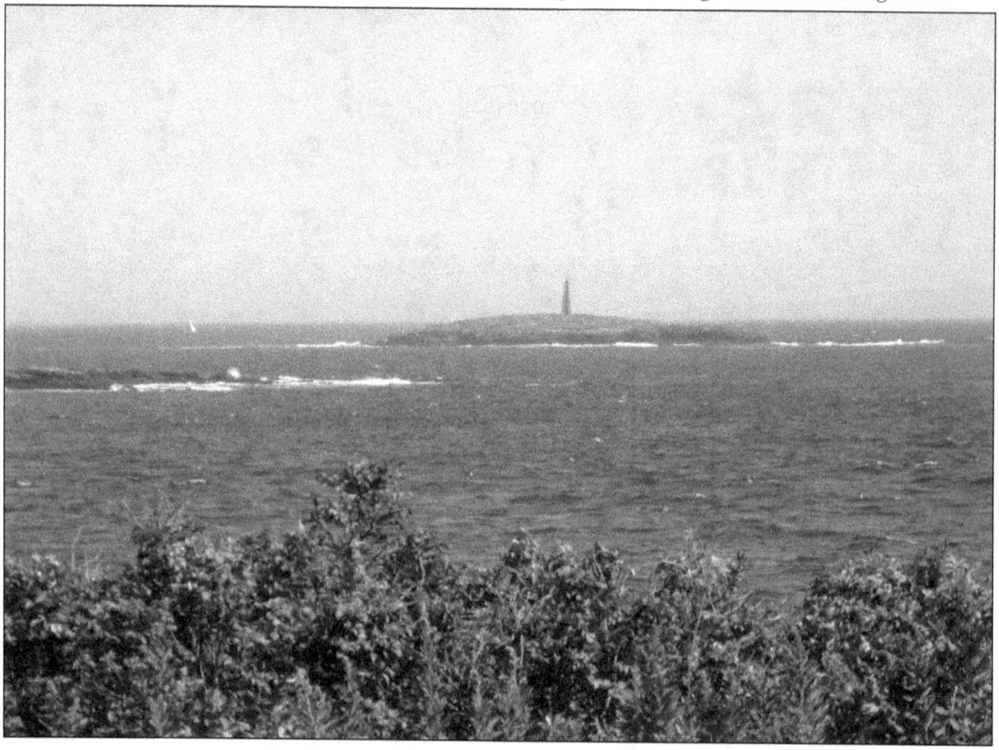

The weather vane pictured at right is a replica of the SS *Roosevelt*. Perched atop the roof on the west side of the house, the original weather vane has since been replaced due to age and a century of exposure to harsh ocean weather. It is on display in the house. Below is a compass rose Peary had painted on the floor of the north porch. The N points toward the North Pole so any visitor could look north from that point and remember what Peary achieved.

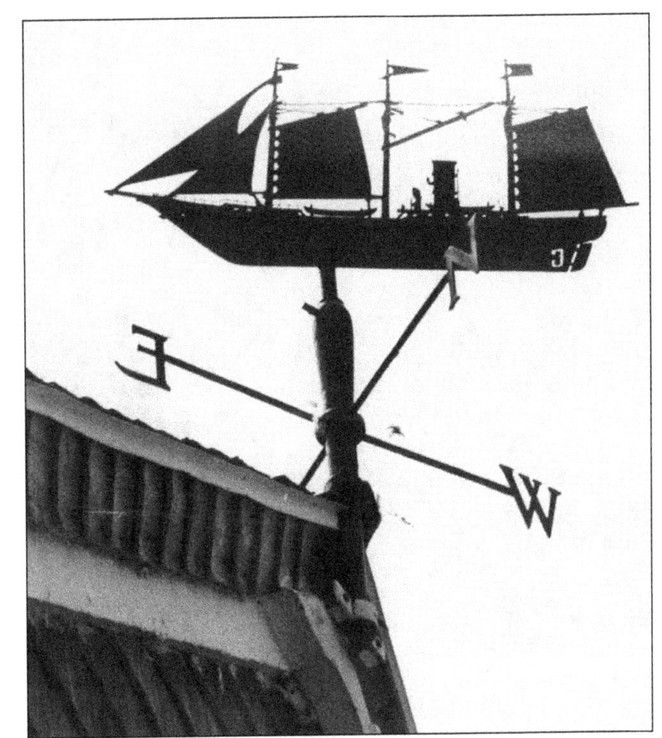

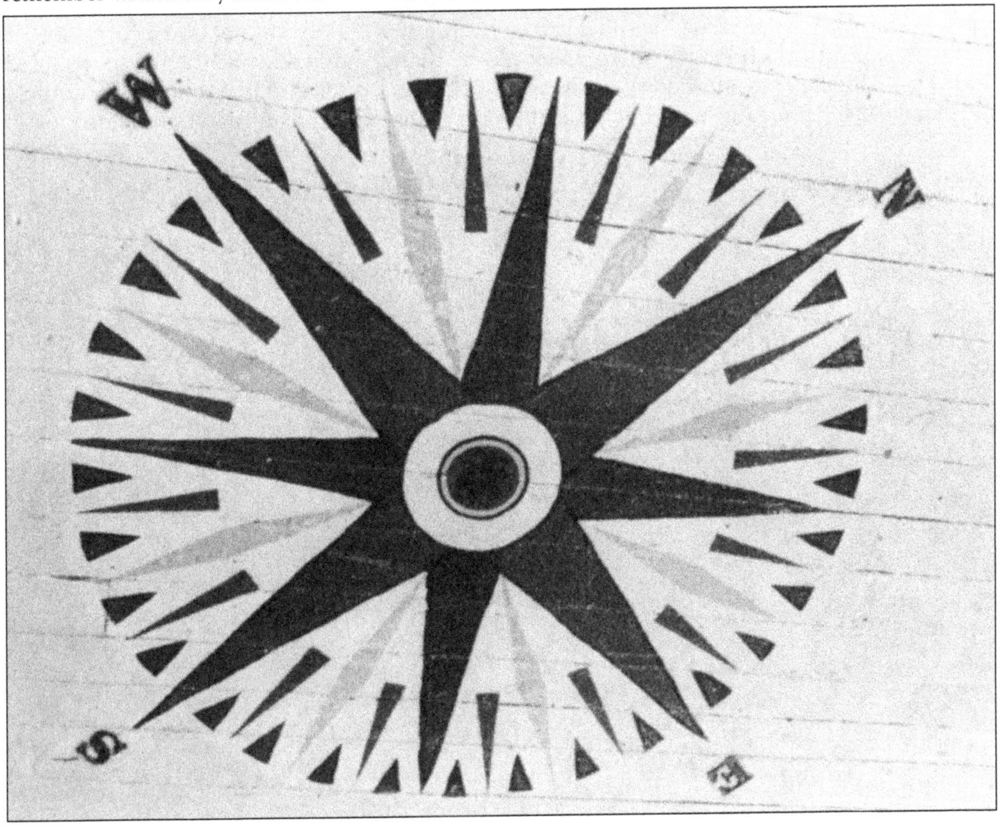

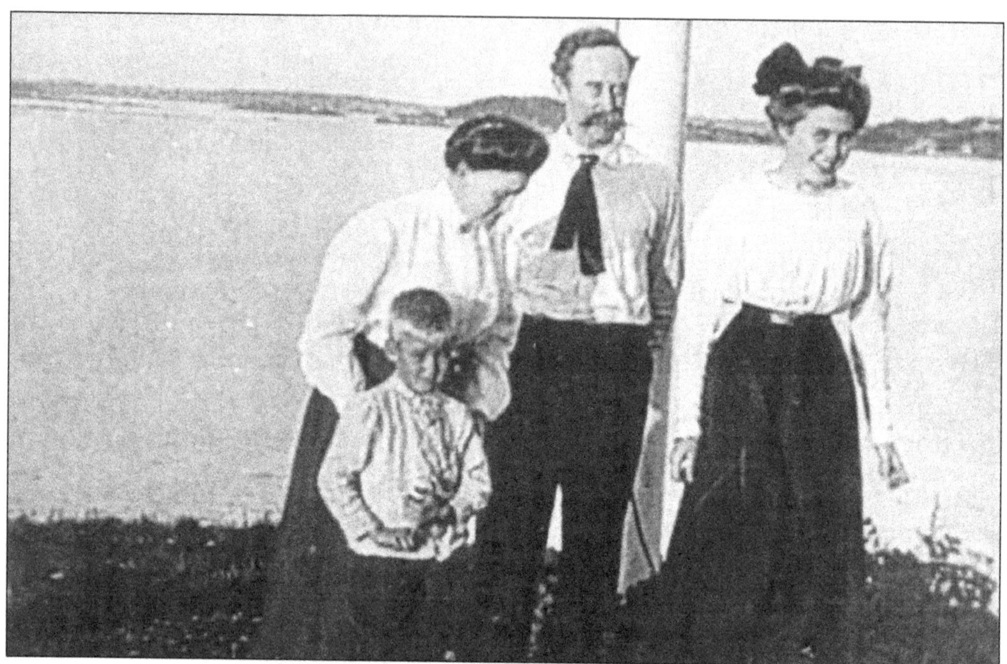

Here, Admiral Peary is grouped with his family—Jo, Marie, and Robert Jr.—on the north lawn, with Casco Bay in the background. The Peary family knew Eagle Island as their home away from all the noise of the world, especially after his achievement in 1909. Life was simple on the island, but it was all about family. The sons and daughter of Marie and Bob Stafford would carry on that tradition, as did their children. Walking around the island and looking at the house (pictured below on a late summer's afternoon), one can almost hear echoes of children yelling and running, the piano playing some rag, and the bustle of keeping up a house on an island in Maine.

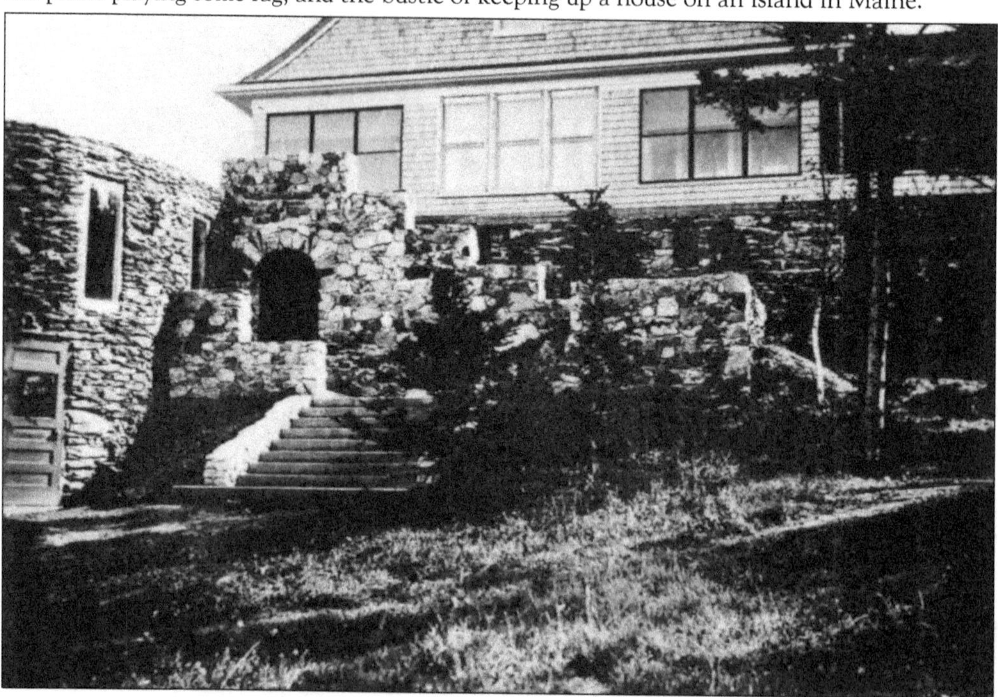

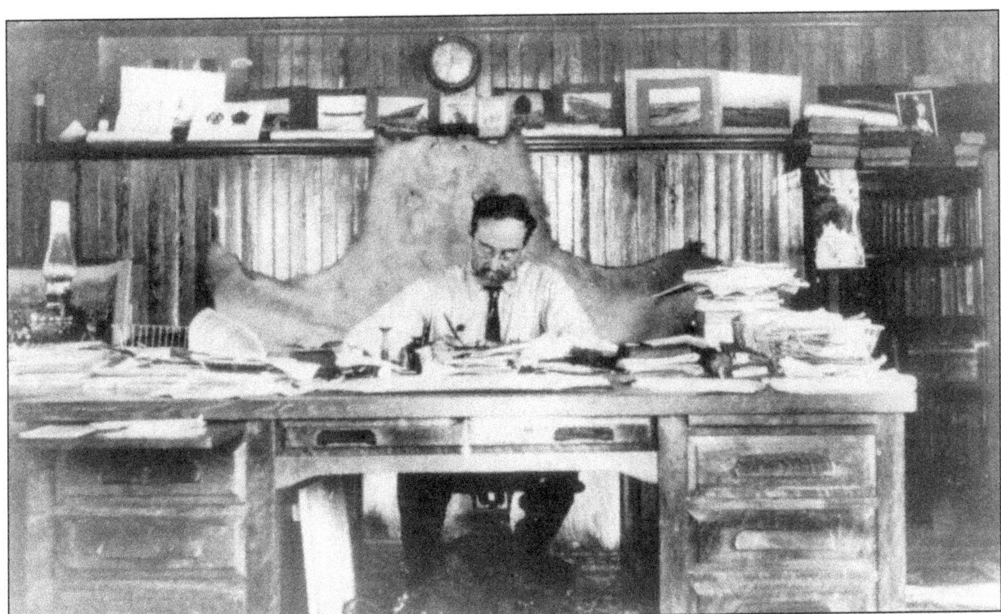

The Admiral is at his desk in his library, with a large polar bear fleece from the Arctic perched behind him. His success in being the first to reach the northernmost point on the globe was a singular achievement and was built upon his years of research, reading, experimentation, and understanding. Peary understood his success depended upon his team of men on the ship and on the ice. Many of those men were Inuit and knew the Arctic, sled dogs, and sledges better than the Admiral did. The Inuit became an integral part of Peary's team and, in many ways, his success. Marie, pictured at right, supported the Admiral in all his pursuits and joined in many of them herself.

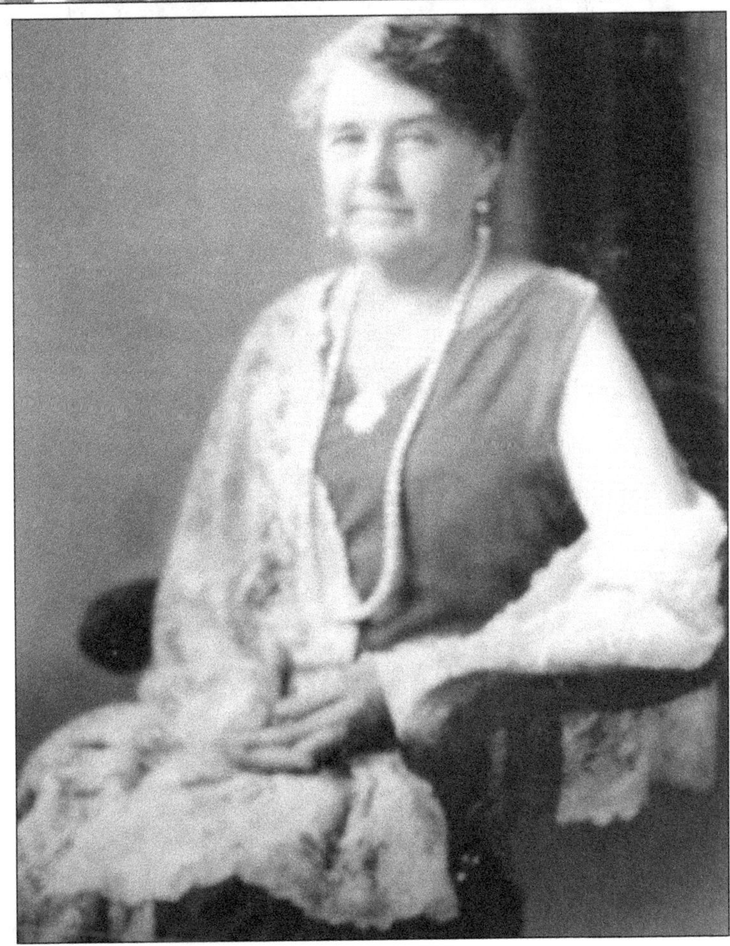

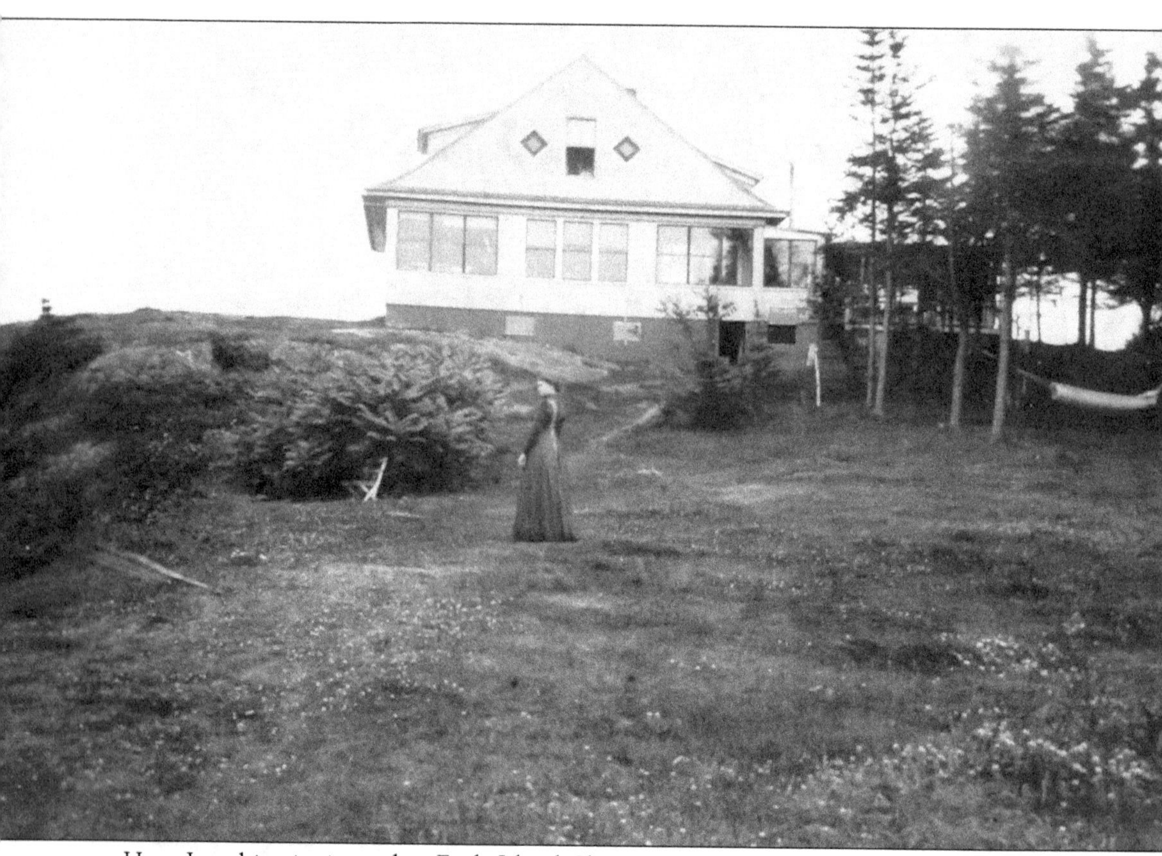

Here, Josephine is pictured on Eagle Island. She continued to visit and live for many summers on Eagle Island years after the Admiral passed away in February 1920. This simple cottage, where Josephine and Robert E. Peary, with their two children, Marie and Robert Jr., made their home away from home and their first permanent residence, remains the physical center of the Peary house today. Though enlarged two times to accommodate the growing Peary family, their home remained for the Pearys their little "cottage" on an island in Maine—Eagle Island. (Courtesy of JDPUNE.)

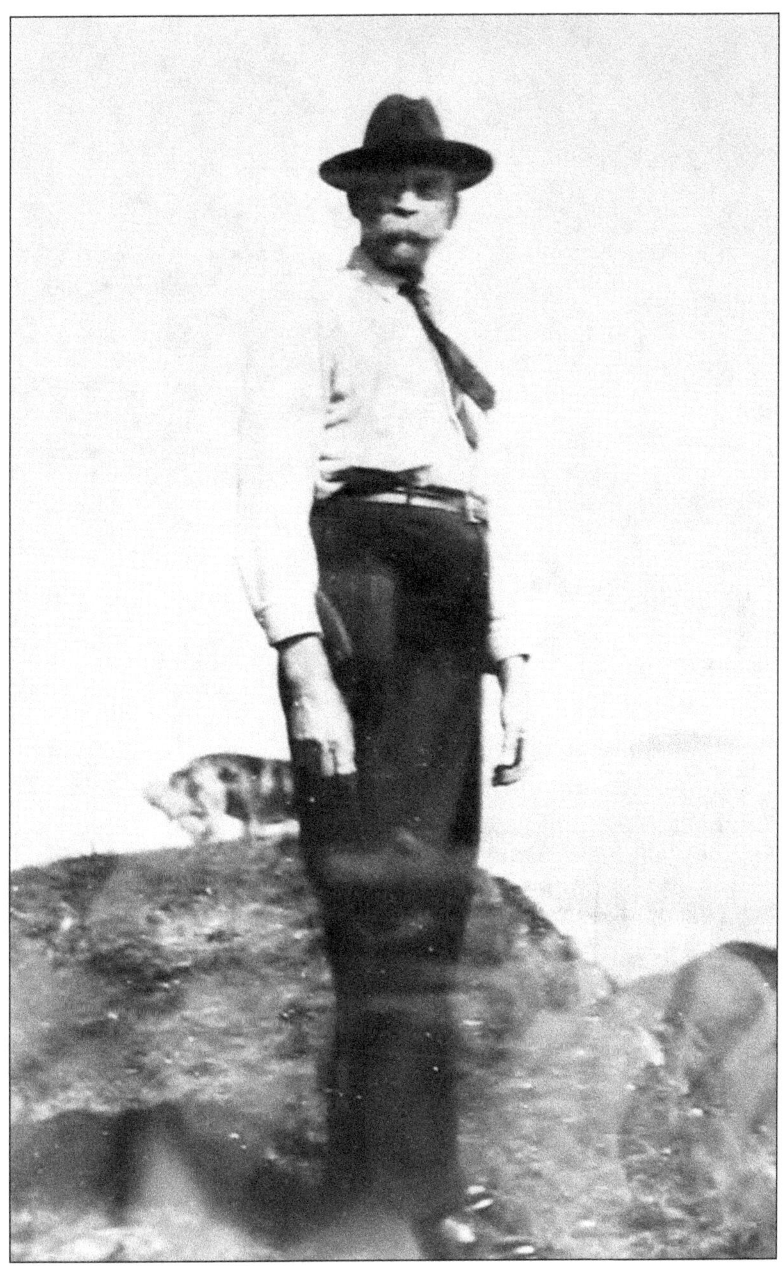

In this c. 1916 picture, the Admiral stands on Upper Flag Island, across the channel from Eagle Island. He appears relaxed while visiting his sled dogs and stands proud and thoughtful while looking back toward Eagle Island. His son once said, "We stay in Washington every winter, but we really live on Eagle Island," and across the channel from where Peary stands is that home. The Pearys lived summer after summer on Eagle Island, away from the world, arriving as early in the year as possible and staying as late in the fall as they could. The Admiral's last summer on Eagle Island was in 1919; he passed away in 1920. The Peary family continued to summer on Eagle Island until Marie and Robert Jr., in a gracious act of charity, gave the island to the State of Maine to be shared with all citizens as a state park. Peary's legacy continues and his spirit remains on, as if he had just left Eagle Island to go to Harpswell to pick up the mail.

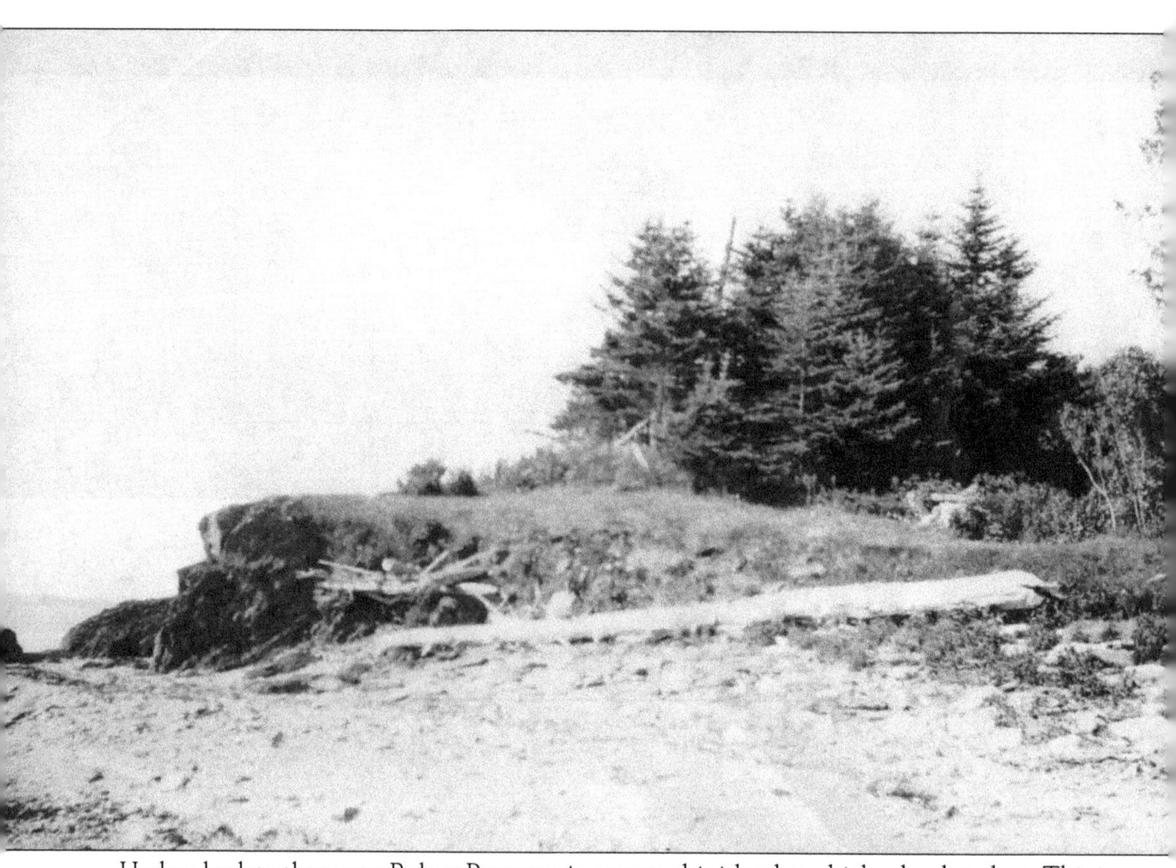

Harken back to the young Robert Peary rowing out to this island as a high school student. This is what he saw—a Maine island with a rocky shore on which he could build a home. Today, visitors to Eagle Island, a Maine Historic Site and a National Historic Landmark, can sense a little bit of why he thought the island a "magical place." Come and decide.

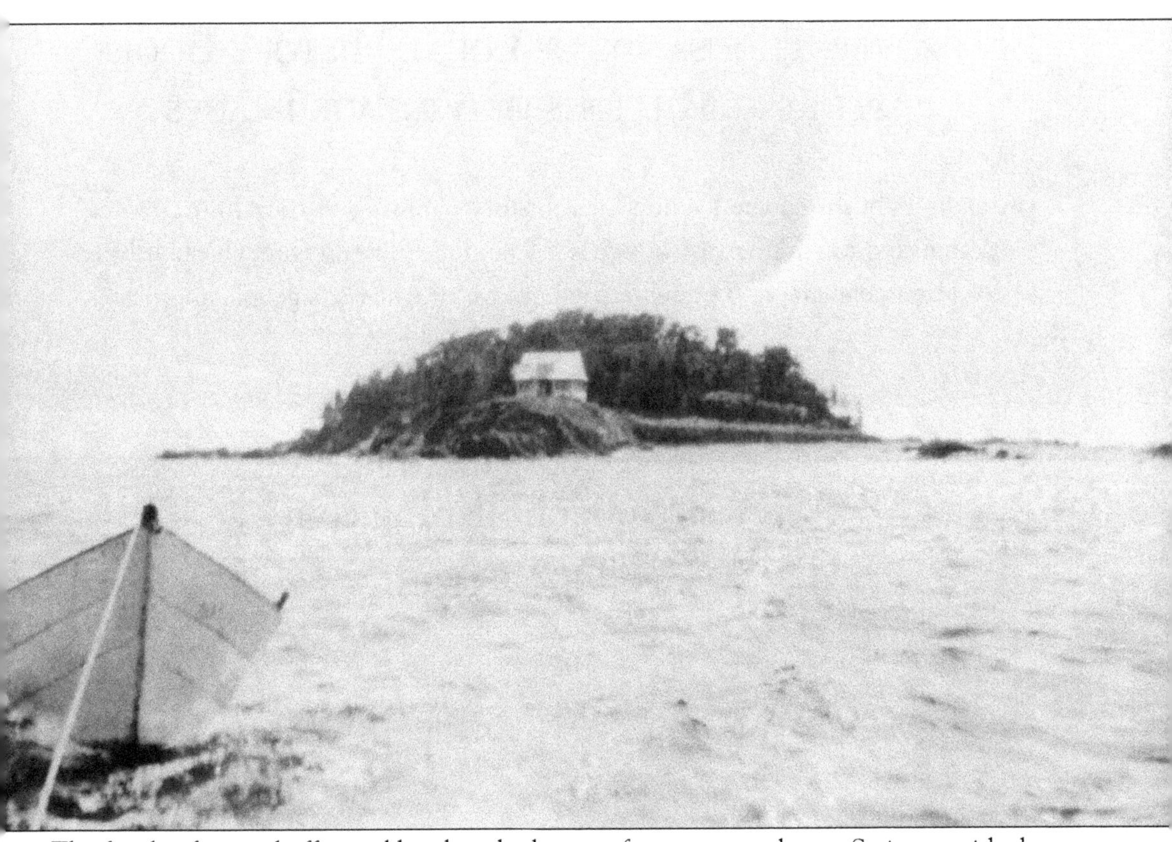

The family of a naval officer seldom has the luxury of a permanent home. So it was with the Peary family—until 1904 when the cottage here on Eagle Island was completed. Admiral Peary called Eagle Island his "Promised Land." The Peary family called it "home."

Consistent with our mission to preserve history on a local level, this book was printed in South Carolina on American-made paper and manufactured entirely in the United States. Products carrying the accredited Forest Stewardship Council (FSC) label are printed on 100 percent FSC-certified paper.

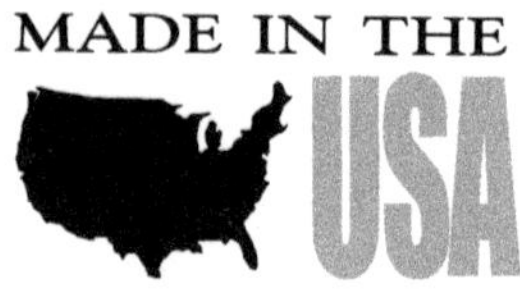

www.ingramcontent.com/pod-product-compliance
Lightning Source LLC
LaVergne TN
LVHW081540100826
845153LV00004B/278
* 9 7 8 1 5 4 0 2 1 6 4 1 0 *